IN THE ZONE

ZONE

EPIC
SURVIVAL
STORIES
FROM THE
MOUNTAINEERING
WORLD

IN THE ZONE

EPIC SURVIVAL STORIES FROM THE MOUNTAINEERING WORLD

Peter Potterfield

THE
MOUNTAINEERS

Published by
The Mountaineers
1001 SW Klickitat Way, Suite 201
Seattle, WA 98134

Cloth: first printing 1996, second printing 1996
Paper: first printing 1997, second printing 1998

Published simultaneously in Great Britain by Cordee, 3a DeMontfort Street, Leicester, England, LE1 7HD

Manufactured in the United States of America

Edited by Deborah Kaufmann
Mountain illustrations © 1996 Dee Molenaar
Cover design by Helen Cherullo
Book design by Ani Rucki
Book layout by Virtual Design, Redmond, Washington
Illustration type overlays: Gray Mouse Graphics

Cover photographs: Main image, *British Columbia Coast Range*. Photo by James Martin. Inset, *Scott Croll climbing in storm, Dragons Tail, Inyo National Forest, California*. Photo by John Dittli Photography
Frontispiece: *Ed Viesturs in House's Chimney on K2, early season conditions*. Photo by Scott Fischer

Library of Congress Cataloging-in-Publication Data
Potterfield, Peter.
    In the zone : epic survival stories from the mountaineering world / Peter Potterfield.
      p.   cm.
    Includes index.
    Cloth: ISBN 0-89886-482-8
    Paper: ISBN 0-89886-568-9
    1. Mountaineering accidents—Foraker, Mount (Alaska) 2. Mountaineering accidents—K2 (Pakistan : Mountain) 3. Mountaineering accidents—Chimney Rock (Kittitas County, Wash.) 4. Mountaineering—Foraker, Mount (Alaska)—Search and rescue operations. 5. Mountaineering—Chimney Rock (Kittitas County, Wash.)—Search and rescue operations. 6. Mountaineering—K2 (Pakistan : Mountain)—Search and rescue operations. 7. Wilderness survival—Foraker, Mount (Alaska) 8. Wilderness survival—K2 (Pakistan : Mountain) 9. Wilderness survival—Chimney Rock (Kittitas County, Wash.) 10. Mountaineers—Biography. I. Title.
GV199.42.A42F676   1996
796.5'22—dc20   96–25476
                                               CIP

CONTENTS

ACKNOWLEDGMENTS

I am grateful to Scott Fischer for sharing with me—and so with others—the details of one incredible episode in an extraordinary life, and a peek at the fiery motivation that spurs it on toward ever greater adventure.

I thank Colby Coombs for his unselfish description of a personal tragedy, and for his articulate insight into one of most amazing feats of endurance ever chronicled, so that we all might be inspired by it.

The tireless hours Scott and Colby generously spent beside my turning tape recorder have made possible this glimpse into experience and character that are beyond the pale of ordinary lives.

AUTHOR'S NOTE

As this book was going to press, the sad news arrived from Nepal that Scott Fischer had been killed in a sudden, powerful storm high on Mount Everest. It is my hope that the story published here might serve as an intimation of his enduring love for the mountains by providing Scott's own insight into how bold striving done in the face of great risk can add to a life richly lived.

FALLING

I can report that it
happened with lucidity.
Nothing blurred or
was lost to velocity.
I registered the impacts,
felt my bones break,
remained aware the
whole way down.

always thought anyone who fell off a mountain simply blacked out or died of fright or by some other means was delivered from consciously suffering such a disagreeable fate. This belief persisted through fourteen years of climbing until I fell off Chimney Rock in the Cascade mountains of Washington and proved it wrong. The fall was stone horrible, brutal and painful. In the beginning there was faint hope: could this be a terrible dream? Then there was only gravity and acceleration and the certainty of death.

I am still appalled by the violence of it, still amazed I am here to wonder at my survival. I think about the fall from time to time, less now than in the first few months after it happened. When the memory pops up I just ride it out, let it roll on where it will. I am often surprised by the small, quirky details thus revealed—such as the color of my blood splashed on the red rock, or the fact that the fall was very noisy but completely lacking a visual component. Perhaps because I never suppress it, I never dream about it. I can report that it happened with lucidity. Nothing blurred or was lost to velocity. I registered the impacts, felt my bones break, remained aware the whole way down.

The fall got me thinking. What is it that induces some people to pursue climbing despite the risks? Climbing is widely perceived to be dangerous, and perhaps it is, although I never considered it so. In all those years before my accident, nothing much had happened to me. I took a few minor falls, mostly at top-roped crags, when pushing my experience and trying moves harder than I normally would attempt made sense. I got lost a few times on snow-covered approaches in the Cascades and

Rockies, and got off route on big mountains. I had a lot of terrifying moments when I was at the limit of my ability, certain I was going to fall, but didn't. I think right there, that's why most climbers keep climbing.

Climbing for me was a weekend thing, a genuine recreation, and the time I spent in the mountains added joy and interest to my life. I knew others who were seduced by climbing, taken over by it, people who left work and family to follow it toward a new life. But for me, climbing was just fun. Sometimes it was too cold, or too hot, or too much hard work, but mostly it was a lot of fun had with interesting people in pretty places. That's what I thought it would be. Most people begin climbing in their teens, a good age, I think, because that's when one is fearless. I came to climbing later, in my early twenties, after reading Maurice Herzog's book, *Annapurna*. Herzog's well-told tale of that early French expedition to the Himalaya (those guys weren't even sure where Annapurna was, much less how to get to it) was quietly, consistently fascinating. I had to find out what climbing was about.

Even though by then I was not a kid, I took chances early on. I tried harder climbs than I should have, went up Colorado "fourteeners" in threatening weather, got sand-bagged into trying to climb frozen waterfalls in Ouray when I didn't know an ice screw from a bridge bolt. The irony is that there were no consequences to my bad judgment, only a lot of fun and interesting experiences. It wasn't until I had reached a level of skill and maturity when I no longer took real chances, when I thought my judgment and conservative approach would see me through a lifetime of climbing without serious incident, that I got creamed.

That, apparently, happens to a lot of people. Like the Zen master who focused on golf balls and then found them everywhere, once my consciousness was raised I found climbing disasters everywhere. Even among my small circle of immediate friends and climbing acquaintances, from weekend climbers such as myself to professional mountain guides and big-league, high-altitude climbers, many had stories to tell of climbs gone wrong and consequences suffered. There was no end to the oddness of them, for in climbing as in life, things go wrong in all sorts of ways.

My friend Stimson Bullitt, his son, and two companions set out for a weekend climb of Mount Rainier via Liberty Ridge in 1979. The first two days were full of fun and excitement as they ascended the graceful ridge that rises above the icy chaos of the Willis Wall, Rainier's impressive north face. When the party had reached a point above 12,000 feet, an unpredicted and unseen storm—it approached from the southwest—hammered the climbers unexpectedly.

In the heavy snow and whiteout that followed, further progress was impossible. The climbers dug platforms in the narrow ridge for their bivvy sacks and hunkered down for the night. But snow fell in unbelievable abundance, more than three feet the first night alone. The climbers were covered by snow, which wet their sleeping bags and left them on the verge of hypothermia.

When the next morning brought no respite, the men dug a snow cave in which to take shelter until the storm abated. They hacked with ice tools until they struck solid rock and were left with a very shallow cave, one so small that as they sat in it their feet protruded. The four men remained there for sixty-two hours, as the storm continued to dump snow and send avalanches over the lip of their cave and onto their sleeping bags. The food ran out, then the fuel. The men huddled together for warmth. There was nothing to eat, and nothing to drink. Their situation had become desperate.

Stimson, aged sixty, was by then too weak to climb safely, so the three younger men decided to go for help. Knowing the ridge below them was subject to lethal avalanches, the three weakened mountaineers attempted to climb up and over the top of Rainier and down the standard route on the other side. Chest-deep snow stopped them mere yards from the cave, so reluctantly they started to descend the dangerous ridge. Stimson wished them well.

But just hours after they had climbed below him, Stimson saw a series of tremendous avalanches roar down the ridge. He knew no one could survive slides of that magnitude and presumed his son had been killed. He was overcome by grief, and gave little concern to his own deadly predicament. "No notion of survival remained," Stimson said, "even one fathered by hope, as hope was gone. To last a few days was my guess."

But the next day, when a search plane flew directly toward his tiny shelter, he knew he had been saved. In a few hours an army helicopter arrived and lowered to him what looked like a short length of two-by-four at the end of a slender cable. When weighed against the alternative of dying in the cave, the frightening prospect of the rescue rig didn't seem so bad.

Without hesitation, Stimson grabbed the pencil-thin cable, straddled the board, and gave the high sign to the pilots. Immediately he was snatched off the ridge and hurtled in a heart-stopping arc out over the abyss of the Willis Wall almost 8,000 feet above the nearest ground. It was the ride of his life, the ride of anyone's life. As the helicopter crew began to winch him aboard, the seat arrangement began to spin—slowly at first, and Stimson was reminded of childhood games on playground swings. But as the rig began to spin with terrifying speed, he wondered if he could continue to hold on. Just as he feared he might be thrown clear, the helicopter crew hoisted him aboard.

Once on the ground, his only remark to the authorities was a question: "What word of my boy?" When he learned all three men had suffered frostbite but were safe, Stimson wept for the first time.

While Stimson's escalating epic took days to unfold, other incidents are brief moments of pure adrenaline and fear when the climber involved escapes unscathed save for the indelible, sobering clarity of the terrifying moment—which lingers. Fred Stanley was leading a hard pitch on Liberty Bell near Washington Pass in the North Cascades when the rope came untied from his harness. Suddenly, and without really wanting to, he was soloing a hard route. Any fall would be a fatal fall. He made it to a safe place without incident, but that moment has stayed with him, standing out among all the eventful years he has spent in the mountains.

Events such as these, unexpected and unwelcome, bully their way in to intrude on an otherwise normal day of climbing, and have the power to change the course of lives. Jim Nelson and his friend Dan Cauthorn set out to climb Slesse Mountain near the border between British Columbia and Washington State. They were young but already had considerable alpine experience, with hard climbs in the rugged Cascades behind them. Approaching the base of the long rock route, Nelson crossed a steep patch of snow above a cliff. He was blasé and confident and did not bother to get out his ax or otherwise take precautions. When his feet shot out from under him, he was already on his way over the cliff. He landed in the snow about 40 feet below.

The fall left him with a broken leg and a ruptured spleen, and he spent a miserable night with his injuries while Cauthorn raced out for help.

"I was overconfident and climbing recklessly, no question," said Nelson later. "So certain was I of my skill and ability that I would have done most of the route—a 5.8—unroped. Zooming off that snow slope really changed my attitude about climbing."

The sobering incident led Nelson down a new path. He became an expert on climbing safety. He studied rope techniques and hardware failures, perused the literature of accidents, and familiarized himself with the kinds of things that go wrong. He became, unobtrusively but relentlessy, an advocate of smart climbing. Nelson has for the past twenty years worked as a professional mountain guide, spent more days out each year in the mountains than almost anyone, and has not had a serious incident since.

Accidents are usually like that: by the time the climber realizes something is happening, it has already happened. One man on his way into a wilderness climb of Sloan Peak in the Cascades fell off a log while crossing a creek. He was killed when he fell on his ice ax, inflicting a fatal wound. There is no time to react, only to pay the piper for mistakes already made.

A rare exception to this happened in Alaska in 1990. Denali National Park rangers reported that Jim Bouchard and Gary Donofrio were climbing Mount Deception, after making the five-day trek to the peak from the Parks Highway. By April 8, they had climbed to 2,500 meters on the Southeast Spur where, around noon, they stopped for a lunch break.

With the meal over, Donofrio continued to lead out along the corniced ridge of the spur. Bouchard, who was still tied into the rope with Donofrio, was quickly putting a few last items into his pack before getting serious about the belay. That situation is so familiar to me that I think all climbers can relate to it. It is as if we think, Well, he's not going to fall right *here*, not yet, I think I'll get that apple (or take that picture, or put on my anorak) before settling in with the belay device.

Donofrio climbed up the ridge, perhaps 30 feet higher. Bouchard was ready to close up his pack when he saw a large section of the corniced ridge collapse right in front of him. Bouchard watched as his partner Donofrio disappeared in the cornice debris down what Bouchard knew was a 75-degree slope. Bouchard was about five feet on the other side of the fracture line. He stood there with his pack while the 150-foot rope coiled at his feet whipped out really fast, making a mean kind of hissing noise as it went.

Bouchard realized he had about a half second to do *something* or get plucked off the ridge like a fishing fly to join Donofrio in a fatal fall. In that millisecond, he made the right decision: he jumped off the other side of the ridge. He wasn't sure exactly what was down there, but he figured it was another snow slope. As he jumped off the ridge and started his own self-induced fall, he wondered on the way down if he would develop enough momentum to counteract the force of Donofrio, who had been falling longer and so had gained more speed.

When the rope went taut and Bouchard was jerked to a sudden stop, he saw that he had only fallen about 30 feet. Donofrio's greater momentum not only arrested Bouchard's fall in a heartbeat, but started pulling Bouchard rapidly *back up the slope*. He tried to slow his ascent by kicking his crampons into the slope and digging in with his hands. The counterbalanced rope finally achieved enough equilibrium to stop when Bouchard was about 15 feet from the ridge crest, and Donofrio was about 130 feet down the other side.

Bouchard had the rare opportunity to avoid disaster, and pulled it off. He was able to hoist Gary Donofrio back up the slope, but his partner was severely injured. They descended the mountain together until Bouchard realized his partner could go no farther. Leaving the injured man behind, he raced out to the highway for help. Donofrio was airlifted by helicopter to Anchorage.

And that is the thing about climbing: it is not all fun. When a climb goes bad, it can become the threshold to a grim, life-changing experience. Instead of a normal day climbing with friends, wisecracking, laughing, and enjoying the mountains, there is instead pain, grief, and a world of trouble. The climber can find himself looking at the color of his own broken bones, realizing he has entered a new sort of place, a bad place, one that is seldom visited by humankind.

In this uncharted region, life becomes totally different from the day-to-day existence one has grown accustomed to. The climber has to do *something*, or expire. There is no audience, no roar of the crowd, just a broken climber with a whole new reality. People who have been through this and come out the other side prove that survival is a decision as much as anything else. It comes down to will and attitude, played out at the ends of one's physical strength. Some people make it, some don't. But the ones who do have interesting stories to tell.

MOUNT FORAKER

The falling avalanche
debris continued to
pummel him with
tremendous force, so
much that in a second
he was thrown backwards
and began hurtling down
the slope upside down
and on his back.

n June 1992, Colby Coombs and his former college roommate, Ritt Kellogg, returned to their base camp near the Kahiltna Glacier landing strip in Alaska's Denali National Park. Just returned from a climb on Mount Hunter, the two friends were midway through a month-long mountaineering trip in the Alaska Range when they trudged up to their North Face tent, pitched on the far side of a snowy rise to face away from the busy airstrip. The landing area is on a relatively flat section at the 7,200-foot level of the glacier. During good weather, the glacier acts as a runway for a steady stream of wheel-ski-equipped Cessna 185s, crammed with McKinley-bound climbers, arriving from the village of Talkeetna.

Hundreds of climbers from around the world land each season on the Kahiltna to attempt Mount McKinley and its neighboring mountains. In 1992, more than 1,100 climbers made the pilgrimage. The transient population that ends up on the glacier includes serious expedition climbers and raw neophytes on guided climbs, adventurers, dopers, drinkers, and marginally socialized eccentrics looking for an extreme experience. There can be as many as a hundred people in base camp at any one time. The mix of humanity in residence around the landing zone makes for a bona fide scene, an often social, sometimes unruly polyglot mob of people preparing to move higher on Denali or other peaks in the range, or waiting to be flown out. The inbound climbers range from the old hands, studiously casual and unimpressed, to the first-timers who are excited and eager, some stunned into speechlessness by the austere grandeur of the Alaska Range. Outbound climbers are flush with success or bummed by failure, and many are merely relieved to finally be leaving after three to five weeks in that icy environment without a bath, or a spouse, or an avocado.

So busy is the Kahiltna strip that a de facto air traffic controller and base-camp manager—Annie Duquette—spends the entire season, from May to July, in a rigid Weatherhaven shelter right on the glacier. Officially her job is to manage arrivals and departures, and to report on weather conditions for the air services in Talkeetna. But her practical common sense and winning way make her resident lord of the fiefdom and ad hoc manager of the crazy Kahiltna scene.

"There are so many nutcases who go there," observed veteran climber Greg Child. "If it weren't for Annie there's no telling what would happen. I mean, some of those people would set up their tent right on the runway. She keeps the place relatively under control. But it's because she's such a good soul that people are drawn to her."

Duquette's comfortable and centrally located base camp inevitably becomes a required stop for rangers and climbers, and therefore an unofficial clearinghouse of information on who's where and what's happening. Coombs and Kellogg, hoping to put some distance between their tent and the noisy activity of the airstrip, had established their camp about 100 yards on the far side of Duquette's Weatherhaven.

At twenty-five years old, both Coombs and Kellogg were not just experienced climbers but outdoor professionals as well. Coombs led trips in Alaska for the National Outdoor Leadership School. Kellogg, who knew Alaska from his days as a climbing guide on Mount McKinley, worked in Maine as a sailing instructor for Outward Bound. Close friends and accomplished climbers, both were familiar with the Kahiltna scene. But Coombs and Kellogg were not so jaded that they were blasé about some of the macabre events that transpire around Denali.

In fact, on the very day in early June when they had arrived on the Kahiltna, the park service Lama helicopter flew over them as they pitched their tent. Slung beneath its fuselage was a grisly cargo. Four body bags dangled unceremoniously beneath the lightweight, high-altitude helicopter, containing members of the Canadian team who had tumbled to their deaths down the Messner Couloir on Denali. It was an eerie reminder of the severe demands Alaskan mountains make on climbers, and the ultimate price they can exact.

Colby Coombs and Ritt Kellogg, however, had extensive experience not just in climbing mountains but in the Alaska Range itself. Coombs had climbed McKinley years earlier, and Kellogg was schooled in the terrain and weather of the range by virtue of his guiding experience on Denali. For years, the two close friends had climbed together frequently, mostly in Colorado, but also in Utah and New Mexico. They enjoyed doing rock climbs in the warmer weather, but in winter often ventured out on ice-climbing and backcountry-skiing forays throughout the Rockies. After graduating from college, the demands of work had split them up, so the Alaska trip was pure fun for both of them, a rare chance to spend some time together after a long period of working at opposite ends of the continent. They felt not only comfortable with the challenge of the range but eager to get going on another climb.

Ritt and Colby had just returned from the Kennedy-Lowe Route on the North Face of Mount Hunter, an exciting route up a high-angle face and a wildly corniced horizontal ridge. They were back at the Kahiltna landing zone to await the arrival of another of Colby's friends before setting off on at least one last route before their holiday ended. It was a particularly ambitious one: the first ascent of an unnamed ridge south of Mount Hunter's West Ridge.

On June 13, right on schedule, they were joined by Tom Walter. Walter, at thirty-four, was the senior member of the threesome with an impressive climbing background. Besides his almost continuous climbing and backcountry trips in the Rockies, he had ventured to Asia where he had put up a new route in Pakistan, on the Ogre Stump. Like the others, Walter had done a fair amount of climbing in Alaska, including several seasons guiding in the Alaska Range. A chance meeting with Colby had brought him back.

Just before leaving to meet Ritt, Colby had run into Tom Walter at the National Outdoor Leadership School headquarters in Lander, Wyoming. They started chatting, and when he learned Colby would be climbing around Denali, Walter decided to come along. With a few weeks to spare before meeting his wife Lisa in Anchorage—they had planned an extended sea-kayaking trip together—he realized he could fly into Denali and spend his free time climbing with Colby and Ritt. In fact, it was Tom Walter who had suggested the new route on Hunter, and both the younger men agreed it was a good, hard climb, well suited to the strengths of their party.

But while flying in to the Kahiltna from Talkeetna in one of K2 Aviation's Cessnas, Tom had gotten a good look at the route they wanted to climb. What he saw gave him reason for pause: the unclimbed ridge—from which he had been forced to retreat two years earlier—was in terrible shape, possibly due to the earthquake that hit the area the previous year. The route looked unclimbable, and was certainly dangerously unstable. As it happened, Colby and Ritt had been able to look over the proposed route while descending from their recent climb, and they shared Tom's opinion. So when Tom climbed out of the Cessna on that sunny day in June, wearing his usual wry smile and loaded down with cookies and beer for his companions, it was clear that the party's first order of business was to decide on an alternative route.

That afternoon, the three friends put on skis and glided away from base camp's cluster of tents. They skied along the north side of Hunter's West Ridge looking over climbing routes that from afar had looked interesting. But on closer inspection, nothing they saw looked particularly appealing, just the usual icy chaos, wild flaring cornices, and unstable snow. "It all looked pretty hairball," remembered Coombs.

Returning to base camp, Tom set up his red tent in the snow next to Colby's yellow one. The climbers constructed an elaborate outdoor kitchen complete with benches and cooked up a big pot of spaghetti. It was a spectacular environment for an *al fresco* dinner: a small village of tents on the vast Kahiltna Glacier, surrounded by majestic peaks of the Alaska Range, with Denali towering above everything. The three climbers sat around their tents that evening, laughing and joking and finishing their feast while they decided what to climb. Colby suggested a route on Mount Foraker. Visible across the glacier from base camp, the route was known to be long and hard. To Colby and his friends it looked like fun.

The next morning, there was another elaborate base camp feast of pancakes to start the day. The climbers' attitude was feast or famine:

feast at base camp while you can, famine when you're on the mountain to save weight. Over breakfast, the men considered their options, eventually settling on Colby's suggestion: the East Face of Mount Foraker via the Pink Panther Route (so named because the party that made the original ascent had carried a stuffed pink panther for good luck). Almost the entire massive East Face of Foraker was exposed to potential avalanches from hanging glaciers and cornices, except for that one dramatic line. Still, it was a serious route that was rarely climbed. Obviously, the Pink Panther was a challenging undertaking, even for the three experienced climbers. One big factor in its favor, however, was that it seemed largely free from objective dangers such as avalanche and falling rock or ice. With their decision made, Colby, Ritt, and Tom spent the rest of the day sorting gear and hardware, packing food, and preparing for the week-long climb ahead of them.

The next evening—June days in Alaska are virtually endless, so daylight activity is possible around the clock—the climbers set out on skis down the Southeast Fork of the Kahiltna Glacier. All three were roped together to minimize danger from unseen crevasses. Colby was pulling a small sled with a week's worth of food and fuel. The other two carried loads in their packs. Annie Duquette happened to be standing in front of her base-camp shelter that evening. In the softening light of dusk, she watched the three climbers move quickly out across the glacier. "Many times I've watched people set out toward Foraker," she said. "Sometimes I get a bad feeling. Foraker is dangerous. But those three guys seemed strong and confident. They struck me as very capable. I can't say why, but for some reason I watched them ski quite a distance across the glacier."

Ritt, Tom, and Colby skied down the Southeast Fork and crossed the four-mile-wide main Kahiltna Glacier itself. By 11:00 P.M. they reached the base of the East Face of Mount Foraker, and the start of their climb. As they closely scanned their route from just below it, they saw what they expected to see: a serious mixed climb, long and technical, quintessentially Alaskan in character. That view of steep ice slopes, frozen couloirs, and ice-glazed rocks stretching up almost 9,000 feet would have intimidated some parties. But Colby and his friends

Mount Foraker and its prominent Southeast Ridge. The climbing route followed the major buttress on the right side of the Southeast Ridge. (Photo: © Bradford Washburn Collection, # 7089)

were psyched to get going, confident the route was well within their ability. It seemed to be in decent shape, and in the worst case—if the weather got really nasty—there were escape options, ways higher up to retreat off the route without going to the summit.

In fact, the climb the three friends had chosen was a significant variation of the original Pink Panther Route, one that might be called the Pink Panther Direct. The main point of difference involved a subsidiary ridge that emerges from the face below the Southeast Ridge proper. The top part of that ridge ends in a steep rock buttress, partially covered by ice and snow. The buttress was bypassed by the original party, which ascended by easier ground off to the side. Colby, Ritt, and Tom planned to work up to the Southeast Ridge in a more or less straight line, climbing that rock buttress in the process. Standing on the glacier, the three friends suspected that the rock buttress would turn out to be the crux of the route, hands down. They were right.

"It was great climbing," remembered Coombs, "super, probably the best route I've ever done. It was hard, but it just had everything."

The climbers cached their skis, the sled, and some other gear on the glacier at the base of the climb, at about 7,500 feet elevation. Anxious to get going, they were dismayed to see low clouds begin to form, then thicken around the peak. It was the first sign of bad weather in ten days, and it presented a problem. Because the route began with a long, steep S-shaped snow couloir, a potential funnel for loose snow avalanches, it was no place to be in a snowstorm. The three climbers decided to see which way the weather went before starting up.

They didn't have to wait long. Conditions grew worse quickly. Soon snow began to fall in discouraging abundance. Prudence dictated a delayed start, at least until the weather showed some signs of improvement. Ritt Kellogg and Colby Coombs climbed into the yellow Bibler Impotent they had used on Mount Hunter. Tom Walter dug a shallow snow trench, constructed a crude igloo of snow blocks over it, and took shelter in his bivvy bag. They figured they might as well get some sleep while they waited out what they hoped was a brief snowstorm.

When they awoke the next morning, they saw that about three inches of new snow had accumulated overnight. Snow was still coming down, and the marginal weather gave no encouraging sign. But when the snow let up briefly in late morning, the three friends, impatient to be off, rationalized that the weather was improving. Since it wasn't snowing, conditions at that point seemed acceptable. So at about noon—it was June 15—they began climbing. They carried with them the small tent, two ropes, two ice tools apiece, both ice and rock protection, and enough food and fuel to last for five or six days on the mountain.

The first third of the route was up the steep S-shaped couloir, which the first-ascent party had characterized as scary and intimidating. But the three experienced climbers moved steadily upward. Tom led the way up the couloir, followed by Colby and then Ritt, all tied together with

165-foot ropes. Climbing the almost 2,000 feet of snow-filled gully with ice axes and the front points of their crampons, they moved very quickly by climbing together with running belays.

Only twice on the couloir section did the threesome use traditional fixed belays, a safer but slower process in which only one climber can move at a time. By making extensive use of running belays, all three could climb simultaneously yet still be protected by an anchored rope in the event of a fall. Running belays allow experienced climbers to make quicker progress, where terrain permits. The only delays occur when the leader puts in protection (ice screws or rock pitons), the middle person clips through the "pro" as he climbs past it, and finally when the last climber on the rope takes the hardware out on his way up.

The couloir ended in a rotten, unappealing waterfall-ice pitch. Swinging his axes, Tom climbed through the nasty, unstable waterfall as Colby belayed him. They had climbed the couloir. The weather was cloudy and gray. Blustery winds whipped up snow flurries and spindrift. But it was not unseasonably cold, not by Alaska standards. All three climbers were dressed the same: polypropylene long underwear, pile shirts, and Gore-Tex jackets and windpants.

"We were cruising," remembered Coombs. "It wasn't easy climbing but we felt strong, and could cruise along. It felt great to be out there with Ritt and Tom. We were really getting into the climb."

Above the waterfall the climbers worked through a series of more challenging rock bands. Colby led up through the first of these, which was hard enough that he had to remove his mittens and climb barehanded up the rock. The climbing was tricky and thin, characterized by small holds and snow-covered rock, but the rock bands were not high. Tom and Colby swung fifth-class leads up through these series of rock bands, which were separated by relatively low-angled snow slopes. It was classic Alaska Range terrain. Above the rock bands, they topped out at the foot of a narrow ridge. There, after more than twelve hours of continuous climbing, they dug in late in the evening on the fifteenth.

They were eight full pitches above the top of the couloir when the three friends carved out a platform on a small flat area at the base of the knife-edged corniced ridge. Ritt and Colby put up their yellow tent,

Top: *Tom Walter;* Left: *Ritt Kellogg;* Right: *Colby Coombs* (Photos: Colby Coombs collection)

while Tom took shelter in his bivvy bag with another makeshift ice-block igloo overhead to keep the snow off. They started melting snow with a small hanging stove suspended from a tent pole. As always, the menu was instant soup—made extra thick by using a little less water than the directions called for—sprinkled with grated parmesan cheese. It was a far cry from the base-camp feasts, but it was lightweight fare, and easy to prepare. By eating food that called only for boiling water, they never got the pots dirty by cooking in them. It was a practical and easy way to eat, filling and relatively nourishing to boot.

After dinner, they drank mugfuls of tea and hot water to stay hydrated after the exertion of the day's hard work. The three climbers were pleased with their progress and optimistic about the climb. The first ascent party had taken three days to reach that point, at approximately 10,000 feet. Colby, Ritt, and Tom had put almost a third of the entire route behind them in just one long day of hard climbing.

On the morning of June 16, the small party was greeted with more new snow and whiteout conditions. They could see only a few feet, but that was enough to show them that about two more inches of new snow had fallen that night. The wind was not blowing hard, but still it was obvious that moving higher was impossible in the poor visibility. The climbers were forced to wait out the weather, time which they used to make instant oatmeal and hot chocolate. As the typical Alaska Range scud and wind swirled around them, they squirmed lower in their sleeping bags, waiting for a break.

Before noon, the clouds began to thin out. Within a few hours, visibility unexpectedly improved. The view opened up, and they could see down their route to the glacier below. The climbers roused themselves and decided to use the break in the weather to move higher while they could. Lacing up double plastic boots, attaching crampons, packing away their bivouac gear, and hoisting their packs, the three men pushed off up the knife-edged ridge. Colby led the way. The ridge was too narrow to walk on, so they traversed along just below the ridge crest, side-stepping on the steep snow and ice slope. It was like moving sideways along a wall of snow and ice pitched back more than 70 degrees. The climbing wasn't difficult, but it was tricky and thought provoking. The exposure was extreme. If someone were to lose his footing here, it was

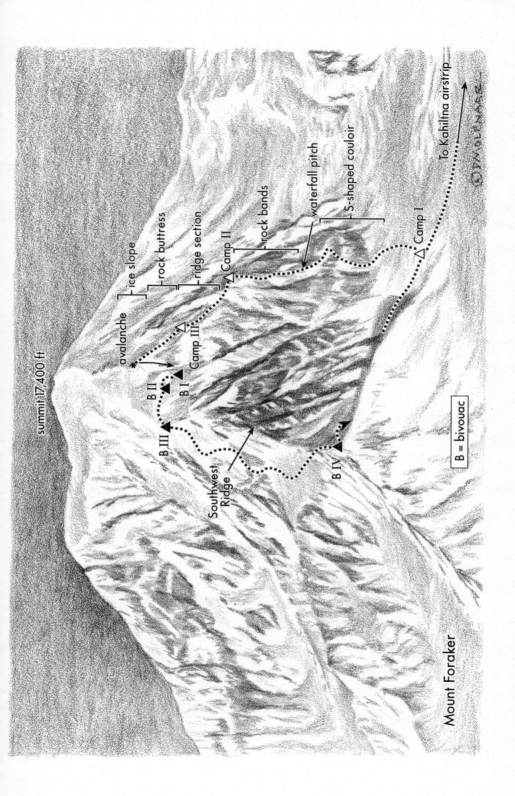

summit 17,400 ft

avalanche

ice slope

rock buttress

ridge section

Camp III

B II

B I

B III

Southwest Ridge

Camp II

rock bands

waterfall pitch

S-shaped couloir

Camp I

B IV

To Kahiltna airstrip

©TMcLENNAS

B = bivouac

Mount Foraker

a long way down. Colby put in ice screws as he led, and the party moved quickly along, well protected by the running belays.

As afternoon turned to evening, Colby, Ritt, and Tom climbed on through the diffuse daylight of the overcast Alaskan night. By early morning on June 17, the climbers had reached the top of the corniced ridge. Colby had been leading all day. Now at about 11,000 feet, they were just at the base of the unclimbed rock buttress. The three climbers still felt strong despite more than twelve hours of climbing, and they wanted to press on with the difficult climbing on the rock above. That thousand feet above them, they knew, would be the hardest and most technical section of the climb. But even though the wind and snow had let up, the party was forced to stop yet again as low clouds began to form. Conditions weren't really that hostile, but visibility grew steadily worse as the clouds clinging to the mountain thickened. To negotiate a route through the unknown problems of the rock buttress, it was imperative that they be able to *see* where they were going. Fog and low clouds almost completely obscured the route ahead, and that made venturing onto the unknown ground above unwise.

To make matters worse the weather seemed to be deteriorating, not improving. Colby was growing weary of constantly having to monitor the weather. Paying close attention was the only prudent course of action when climbing in the Alaska Range during marginal conditions, but it was tiresome. Colby longed for a stretch of good weather that would allow more carefree climbing with his friends. But he knew that wasn't going to happen. Reluctantly, they prepared a bivouac. They took turns digging a snow cave, one that was big enough for all three of them to sit in. Once inside, Colby started the stove and began melting snow for soup and hot drinks.

Although they were above 11,000 feet, huddled in a tiny cave as the clouds swirled wildly about in the blustery wind just outside, Colby, Ritt, and Tom were content to be where they were. Tom and Ritt had never met before the climb, but in those few days had become friendly. Colby had figured his two friends would get along well. In some ways they were unlikely partners. Tom was older, balding, and lanky to the point of being skinny. Ritt was quiet and thoughtful,

Camp II on Mount Foraker, showing the tent shared by Coombs and Kellogg and the snow hole/igloo used by Walter (Photo by Colby Coombs)

described by one friend as "handsome and strong and good at everything he tried." Both men loved climbing and had easygoing personalities, without the big egos a lot of climbers seem to possess. Despite their differences in age and style, Ritt and Tom were enjoying each other's company on the climb and each had come to respect the other's ability.

"It was fun," remembered Coombs. "We were having a great time, just cracking jokes in the snow cave, eating and drinking. Every now and then we'd stick our head out to see what was happening outside. Nothing had changed, so we'd go back to having a good time. It was casual, and fun. We were just jabbering away about anything, and all of it had nothing to do with the climb. We were enjoying the whole thing, maybe bumming a little bit about the weather."

The three climbers had wanted to spend some time together in the Alaska Range, to take it on its own unpredictable terms, and do a hard route in that environment. That was precisely what they were getting, even if the weather wasn't what they had hoped for. Colby Coombs and Ritt Kellogg enjoyed being together again, even in those marginal conditions. In the intervening years since college they had become close friends. They knew each other's parents and family, had shared a hundred adventures, and had missed the companionship they shared when climbing or skiing in the mountains. But as capable as the two close friends were, Tom Walter, almost eight years older, was even more accomplished in the mountains.

"Tom was definitely the most experienced of the three of us," remembered Coombs. "We were both glad that he could come along. It just turned out that he had some time before meeting his wife in Anchorage, so he joined in. Tom and I really hadn't done much climbing together. We did this one big ice climb together in Cody. It was incredible, starting out with a detached tendril of ice you could put your hands around. *That* was a hard climb, and it was a good way to get to know somebody. The two of us had such a good time we both wanted to climb together again. I had known about Tom for years and had heard about some of the things he had done. I was impressed. He's so unassuming and laid back about it, and that's what makes him so likable. He's the kind of guy who hates training, who looks kind of skinny and lazy, but he can get off the couch and crank a 5.11."

The three climbers made a strong, relaxed party for whom the subtle psychological pressures of big mountains, the fatigue and discomfort of forced bivouacs, and the sheer boredom of waiting out storms was familiar stuff. They felt at home in mountain situations that would unnerve less experienced climbers—even on Foraker, even in crummy weather. It was part of the fun. Despite the conditions outside their cramped snow cave, the three friends felt comfortably within the limits to which their combined ability and experience could take them. Retreat was considered a rational option, but that was a decision that needn't yet be made.

The most difficult section of the route, the rock buttress, still lay ahead. Beyond that was the long, straightforward ice slope leading to the crest of the Southeast Ridge proper. From that point, it would be a simple snow slog—albeit a long one—along the Southeast Ridge to the summit of Mount Foraker. If the weather got worse, the three left open the option of completing the route to the ridge crest, the hardest part of the climb and therefore the heart of the route, but descending via the Southeast Ridge instead of making the relatively easy climb to the summit.

More snow fell that day and during the night. As the morning of June 18 arrived, Coombs looked out of the snow cave to find not just more new snow accumulation, about three inches, but a virtual whiteout. The blustery winds that had dogged them the whole way blew spindrift around the cave entrance. The three climbers were forced to wait until almost noon, when the weather unexpectedly showed a pronounced improvement. The wind died down and even traces of blue sky appeared through the ragged, windblown clouds. Now was their chance, and the three friends decided to seize it. If they could get through the rock buttress they could dig in above that, and so be safely bivouacked if the weather really took a turn for the worse. Even if conditions remained poor, as they had been for days, Coombs felt confident the threesome could reach the crest of the Southeast Ridge proper.

Having made the decision to climb while they could, Coombs, Kellogg, and Walter tackled the unclimbed rock buttress. Trying to pick out the most promising line, they moved steadily upward although the climbing was every bit as challenging as they had anticipated. They found technical, snow-covered rock, and they were high enough that altitude became a factor. It was easy to see why the first ascent party had chosen to bypass this section. The buttress proved hard, a thin route that involved challenging mixed climbing on ice and rock with minimal protection.

Tom, belayed by Colby, led the first pitch. He had to climb barehanded in places to make his way up the steep rocky buttress. Holds were downsloping and often covered with snow or ice. Tom climbed quickly, always trying to follow the easiest route through. Higher up, he was able to place good anchors for a belay. Colby followed, belayed by Tom from above. As he moved higher, Colby saw that the buttress never let up. The difficulties were sustained but, so far, manageable. When he reached Tom's belay stance, Colby continued climbing while Tom belayed Ritt up to the anchors.

"It was full on, really difficult stuff," remembered Coombs. "Going up the buttress was a lot like climbing in Scotland, except we were climbing at about 12,000 feet and flirting with an Alaskan storm. We were carrying pretty big packs too, and that made it kind of interesting."

The rock was steep, and in places coated with thin, unstable layers of ice, snow, and spindrift. Coombs used his whole repertory of techniques, sometimes climbing with one bare hand on a rock hold, the other clutching his ice ax, planted in a marginal placement, while his crampons scraped on exposed rocks. Other times he cammed his ax in between rocks and ascended that way. He frequently had to remove his mittens to make fifth-class rock moves.

"We were in the zone," remembered Coombs, "just totally focused on the climbing. You've got to concentrate in a situation like that. It was hard, but it was great climbing. You just get into a state of mind where there's nothing else to think about except the next move. This was what we had come for. It was fun, really high-quality mixed climbing."

Tom and Colby swapped leads as the party of three climbed up the buttress. Ritt was happy to leave the leading to the other two—Tom, the old hand, Colby, the gung-ho, natural-born technical ice climber coming into his own. In several places the rock was so steep it was actually overhanging. In one section, the only way to climb higher was to follow a thin ribbon of hard-water ice set way back in a V-shaped notch of rock. The notch was too narrow to allow his crampons onto the ice runnel, so Colby had to lead the pitch hanging off his ice axes with his crampons scraping off either side of the rocky notch. The buttress seemed to have everything.

The three climbers made steady progress up the frozen, rocky buttress. They climbed carefully, not worrying about speed, and even though protection was at times marginal, all the belay anchors were bombproof. They felt they were climbing as safely as they could up the challenging buttress. As they climbed higher, they were relieved that they could see well enough to pick out from below the most promising line above. Visibility remained reasonable until the climbers were just

300 feet short of the top of the rock buttress. At that point, the weather broke, big time.

In a matter of minutes conditions deteriorated dramatically. A wicked wind kicked up, the strongest they had experienced so far on the climb. Low clouds and fog rolled in quickly, making it impossible to see more than a few feet above them. But the climbers were still on the steep, technically demanding buttress. There was no place to stop. They had no option but to finish the buttress, feel their way upward through the whiteout, finding the line of least resistance as best they could by feel and intuition. Through the thick cloud, Tom led up the last of the steep, icy rock until finally the buttress eased and petered out.

Despite the severe, almost desperate conditions at the top, the three friends had managed to complete the unclimbed buttress. It was an all new route, a significant contribution to an elegant line, and they felt great. They were also relieved to be done with it. "I hope we don't run into any more of *that*," Tom joked, referring to the crux pitch about 500 feet below, which Colby had led. They found themselves on much easier ground, at the bottom of a 1,400-foot ice slope that rose directly to the Southeast Ridge proper at an angle of about 60 degrees.

By then, the weather had become ugly. Conditions had been marginal during the entire climb, ever since they had left the Kahiltna Glacier, but in the past few hours had grown dramatically worse. The three men had for days moved upward through clouds, wind, and occasional snow flurries, but nothing so serious that it threatened their safety. Coombs, Kellogg, and Walter had just finished the most demanding thousand feet of the route, exhilarating climbing in ever-worsening conditions. But there at the top of the buttress, on the rock-dotted ice slope leading steeply upward, the weather situation had become serious. Visibility was by then down to almost zero, a total whiteout, and the wind grew in power with alarming suddenness. Each gust, it seemed to Colby, was stronger than the last. Snow swirled around them.

All of them recognized this as a potentially serious change in the weather. Whatever system had been toying with the three climbers for four days was coalescing into something more substantial. Since the weather was coming at them from the south, Coombs suspected it was

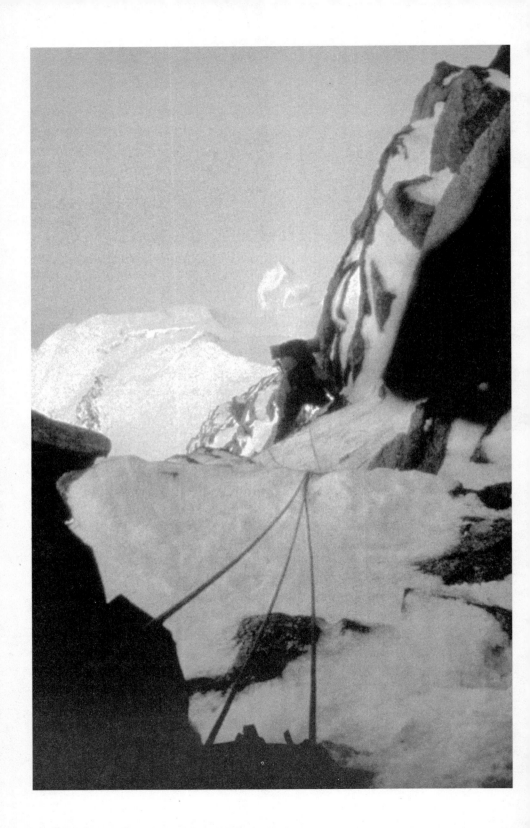

a major system out of the Gulf of Alaska. He had sufficient experience in Alaska to know that wasn't a good sign. The Gulf spawns major storms throughout the year, the kind of weather that can prove fatal to climbers caught in exposed positions high in the Alaska Range. Foraker, in particular, was not the place to be. Located on the edge of the range, the 17,400-foot mountain was exposed to the full brunt of Gulf storms, and the high wind and heavy precipitation they usually bring. The three climbers faced a bad situation that was rapidly growing worse.

All they wanted to do now was climb up the route to the relatively low-angled Southeast Ridge and bivouac against the weather. But the growing storm had arrived with such fury that they began to wonder if the safest course of action might be to stay where they were and dig in. None of them wanted to do that, not there, but they realized it might be the prudent thing.

With the wind gusting at more than 40 miles per hour and visibility almost nil, the three climbers looked around for a reasonable place to take shelter from the storm. There was none. The ice slope was far too steep to accommodate them. Had they been truly desperate, the climbers could have hacked a ledge out of the steep ice, using their ice tools, and then taken shelter in tents or bivvy bags. But the hard ice of the slope made that an unappealing and even dangerous option. It would have taken hours of hard labor—hours they could better spend climbing toward a safer bivvy site—and none of the three viewed their predicament as sufficiently dire to warrant that kind of time or work.

At the base of the slope, Colby and Tom swung their axes into the ice for anchors. All three climbers clipped into the axes and put their mittens and overmitts back on. They zipped their jackets and put their hoods up against the strengthening wind as they huddled to make the call. Colby knew the situation had grown serious, but just looking into the eyes of his companions he could tell that far from being freaked out or at the end of their strength, Ritt and Tom were relaxed and strong.

"Everybody was real mellow," remembered Coombs. "I think that all of us were a little worried about being on that slope in the storm,

Tom Walter on the unclimbed rock buttress, Pink Panther route (Photo by Colby Coombs)

41

but all of us kept that emotion in check. The thing now was to make the right decision, be smart, do what was necessary. Nobody was on the verge of losing it. The thing about both Tom and Ritt, they're the kind of guys that even if the situation had been totally desperate, they would have just gotten more mellow. They knew getting hyper wouldn't help, they hated that. Everybody was pretty calculating, pretty even. Everybody felt okay."

The climbing below had taken a lot out of them, but all three felt more than able to make whatever move was necessary. And that, undoubtedly, was going to mean climbing higher to find a suitable bivouac. They knew they needed to get out of the weather, get some rest, and gather their strength after the taxing climbing just behind them.

"The thing about climbing in Alaska," said Coombs, "is you can climb twenty-four hours a day. The only thing that's going to stop you from climbing—besides a storm—is if you're too beat. So it's easy, even tempting, to climb into the red zone, to go beyond your reserves of strength into a dangerous place where you might make a mistake. If you're smart, you watch for signs that show you're getting tired or careless. That wasn't the case with us. We felt strong. We *were* strong, and had been during the whole climb. It was no big deal. Nobody got psyched. We were rational and in control.

"You've got to remember it was a climb—a great climb, a big one by some standards—but just another climb with friends. That was going to be it. After the climb Tom was going to hook up with his wife and go kayaking, Ritt was probably going to go back to Maine and work Outward Bound courses, and I was going to guide NOLS mountaineering courses in Alaska. It was just going to be the usual, fun's over, now back to work. For the three of us there above the buttress, it was just do the climb, and split."

Since chopping a bivouac platform would have involved a lot of boring, time-consuming work, it made more sense, the three climbers decided, to apply themselves to the 1,400-foot slope above them. Though relatively steep at about 60 degrees, the ice slope leading to the ridge above was far less technically demanding than the buttress they had just climbed. For these three climbers, it presented no real difficulties. Once at the top of the ice slope, they would be on the relatively low-angled Southeast Ridge. There the small party would be able to make a secure bivvy, or, if necessary, dig in on the other side of the ridge. Since they had plenty of food and fuel, they felt confident that once situated on the ridge they could wait out the worst of the storm.

From there, if the bad weather persisted—which now seemed likely—they could retreat down the Southeast Ridge. Coombs knew they could negotiate the descent even in marginal weather. With the real difficulties—and the dramatic crux of the climb—already behind them, the three felt as if they had achieved the heart of what they had set out to accomplish. The really hard climbing was done. Now, for the close-knit band of climbers, it was a matter of dealing with the storm, finding shelter, and getting down safely. And getting out of harm's way from the worsening weather.

"The weather was so bad at that point that all of us were thinking of just blowing off the summit," remembered Coombs, "just reaching the ridge, getting some food and hot drinks and rest, and descending the Southeast Ridge. The storm had the feel of one that was going to hang around, and I think all of us at that point were pretty tired of dealing with it. The persistent bad weather was taking some of the fun out of the climb. So we had pretty much decided that we were going to get out of there. If we did go for the summit and got pinned up there with a full-on storm, we would risk running out of food. It could turn into a bad scene.

"Descending the Southeast Ridge would have been a cruise, just running protection. There *is* avalanche danger down there because of the slope. There are some hanging glaciers lower down. And one section of the descent route is just right for snow loading, probably 38 degrees right on the button. To avoid some of that objective danger we were going to take a more direct line down the ridge. In certain sections that way would be more technical than the usual route down. But we felt it would be safer because it avoids traversing under the hanging glaciers. We'd have to be careful though, because there really is no way to bypass the slopes farther down that are most prone to avalanche."

With the summit becoming a rapidly diminishing possibility in the worsening storm, the next move was clear: let's get going, let's get to the ridge, let's get out of this weather. They all understood that whatever

43

their next move, it needed to include taking shelter from what was developing into a raging Foraker storm. But although the three friends knew from prior surveillance that the climbing above was relatively "casual," their decisions weren't done with yet.

From their base camp across the Kahiltna the climbers had used binoculars to look over this slope. What they had seen was a smooth sheen of uninterrupted blue ice, with no snow or hanging glaciers or cornices above them that might tumble down in dangerous avalanches. What they hadn't seen but soon discovered was that the ice slope itself was consistently honeycombed with air pockets. Ice screws simply could not gain adequate purchase in the rotten ice to provide sufficient protection in the event of a fall. The route was basically unprotectable. But in the storm-tossed whiteout, there was no way to scout around for another, better way up to the ridge.

With the decision made to go for the ridge, the men were faced with the choice of either ascending with traditional fifth-class belays, which with three climbers would be prohibitively slow and delay their reaching shelter, or climbing unroped, which for these close friends was not considered. The party's proven success with running belays couldn't be applied here, because the ice appeared unprotectable. In the end, they decided on what seemed a rational plan that would leave that option open: they would climb roped together, without fixed protection, but look for opportunities to place ice screws or other pro that could be used for running belays.

"It didn't seem that big a deal at the time," remembered Coombs. "We had a lot of experience climbing and even teaching behind us, and we all knew that if you're going to be roped together and exposed to someone falling who might not be able to self-arrest, then you should anchor the rope somehow or just solo—climb unroped. But we made a decision based on the fact that we were caught in a storm and we needed to find shelter, the climbing above was not difficult for any of us, and we wouldn't consider climbing unroped."

The three climbers started up. As the storm raged around them, blowing snow through the soupy whiteout, the small party cramponed up the ice slope. Tom Walter led out, tied in to Colby Coombs with a full-length 9-mm climbing rope, 165 feet long. Coombs, in turn, was tied in to Ritt Kellogg with a 165-foot length of 7-mm static line, extremely strong for its diameter but without the elasticity of a traditional climbing rope. They worked up the honeycombed slope without placing protection, moving quickly. It was, by then, the wee hours of the morning of June 19. They had been moving nonstop for more than fifteen hours. Although there was plenty of daylight to the endless Alaskan day, the near whiteout made it impossible for the climbers to see each other.

The unforgiving ice slope was the kind of terrain where experience and technique mattered, where doing the right thing by rote and keeping one's cool were crucial. A single slip by any one of the three could prove fatal for the entire party: one falling climber would pull the other two off the slope as well. Colby climbed carefully but quickly. The trio of figures made good time up the slope by moving simultaneously. Climbing with crampons and ice tools, the three friends continued up the slope without stopping. The slope wasn't so steep as to require front-pointing, as the S-shaped couloir had been. Here, Colby climbed by front-pointing with one crampon and placing his other crampon into the slope flat-footed. It was very secure. He used his ice ax—sometimes the ferrule or shaft, sometimes the pick—as a third point of balance. The ice slope was frozen hard, and his ax penetrated the surface only a fraction of an inch, but that was perfectly adequate for maintaining balance. He never had to swing his ice tools. His crampons bit securely into the slope as he climbed.

With his head down—there was nothing to see anyway—Colby stared straight ahead at the red rope lying on the slope a few inches from his face. If the rope stopped momentarily—meaning that Tom was resting briefly, or pausing to place his ax or scratch his nose—Colby would stop as well. When the rope started moving again as Tom resumed climbing, then Colby would move up, also. That way, no slack developed in the rope between the two men. There was no conversation between the climbers as they worked up the slope. There was nothing to say.

For more than a thousand feet, the three friends moved up the slope in unison, encountering no unexpected difficulty. The climbing was merely a series of repetitive actions: step up, place the ax, do it again. The weather, however, remained awful. Visibility was so bad that the climbers never did see each other despite being only 150 feet apart. Even though they were tied together, each man was essentially alone, isolated in a small, white world of fog-enshrouded ice and snow. But the lack of visual contact had no adverse effect on the three climbers. Their safe, rapid progress seemed to confirm that they had made the right decision to climb without fifth-class belays. Their stamina, and experience, were showing. They were on autopilot. Before long they would reach the ridge crest, and there, a safe place to bivouac.

With more than two-thirds of the slope behind them, the three continued climbing in the same order they had begun. Since there were no fixed belays, there was no need to swap leads or change positions on the ropes. Tom continued leading, followed by Colby, then Ritt. Colby was climbing methodically, taking two steps, planting the ax, then repeating the process. He was fatigued, and his legs ached, but he was not winded. For him, the steep slope was more a kind of plodding than a technical challenge. As he moved higher, Colby's thoughts wandered. He wished the weather were better. Colby and Ritt had completed the Kennedy-Lowe Route on Hunter just the week before, but they had failed to summit because as they approached the top they were caught in an approaching storm. Rather than risk getting trapped up high by bad weather, they had descended. Now the same thing was happening again. It was a bummer, no question. Colby, like anybody else, had hoped for better weather on his vacation. It's always much more fun to go to the summit, especially in the Alaska Range, where the view from the top truly can be worth all the trouble and work it takes to get there. But here, Colby knew, you take what you get.

All along, the three climbers had had to be careful—hyper even—about the weather, constantly monitoring the marginal conditions and gauging the consequences of their actions and decisions in the face of it. For Colby, at least, and possibly for all three of them, this heightened weather consciousness, and the continual need to keep a close eye on conditions, had become wearing. The unrelenting vigilance had created a far different atmosphere than if they had been climbing in fine conditions. Climbing these beautiful Alaskan mountains with Tom and Ritt in bright, endless daylight would have been entirely different. It would have been much more fun, much more easygoing. Concern about the marginal weather added an element of seriousness to the climbing that Colby would just as soon have skipped.

"After weeks of that kind of intense weather watching," Coombs said, "you can almost feel as if you're being hunted. There's just something about the Alaska Range. The routes are steep, there is objective danger all around. You've got to pay attention all the time, and that can get old."

Colby's calves were starting to burn from the steady exertion of cramponing up the slope. He was getting tired, too, from the more than sixteen hours of continuous climbing. He climbed with his head down, which was his most comfortable position while cramponing up the slope. He knew that at their current rate it wouldn't be long before they reached the safety and relative comfort of the crest of the Southeast Ridge.

Muscles aching, Colby continued climbing up the mountain, following the rope that disappeared into the fog but which was tied to Tom somewhere up above. They had been on the slope for hours when the rope stopped momentarily. Colby didn't even bother to look up. He couldn't see Tom through the whiteout anyway. But he stopped when the rope stopped, not wanting to allow slack to develop in the rope between him and the climber above him. He was only vaguely aware of Ritt, also out of sight, climbing 150 feet below him.

Suddenly, in a microsecond, Colby knew something was wrong. For one fleeting moment as he stopped, he thought he saw something funny happening to the rope above him, as if it were going slack or inexplicably coming down. Without knowing exactly what was wrong, his first reaction was extreme alarm, *red alert*. He had time to think, What's happening, before his instinct proved well founded: suddenly his immediate environment changed from the familiar, cloud-enshrouded ice slope and the sound of his own breathing to disastrous confusion. Masses of snow smashed into him. Everything changed in a heartbeat. Subconsciously, Colby realized what was happening even if he didn't have time to formulate the word. *Avalanche.*

Avalanching snow instantly knocked the climbers off the slope. But to Colby, it seemed as though the events of the accident unfolded in sufficiently slow motion that he could perceive them if not understand why they were happening. At first impact, before Colby realized it had happened, the snow falling from above ripped him from his stance. Immediately, and with practiced skill, Colby tried to self-arrest by digging the pick of his blue-handled Chouinard ice ax into the slope. But the ice was too steep, too hard, and already he was falling downhill too fast for the maneuver to be successful. The falling avalanche debris continued to pummel him with tremendous force, so much that in a second he was thrown backwards and began hurtling down the slope upside down and on his back.

Like a flipped-over turtle, Colby felt totally helpless, though there was nothing he could have done even if he were in a more accustomed attitude. But it was the speed of his fall that registered with him most strongly, and alarmed him most. He felt himself falling faster and faster, hurtling downward utterly out of control. "I could feel the speed pick up, and I knew I was going at terminal velocity," Coombs remembered. "You're just not supposed to be moving that fast. The speed of the fall was really scary, really incredible."

The avalanche arrived with such suddenness that trying to think of what could be done in the alarm-bell reality of the fall did him no good. His attempt at self-arrest was completely instinctive. Colby already knew everything that mattered, that he was falling off a mountain out of control. The noise and confusion in those few fleeting fractions of a second eclipsed any lucid thinking through of precisely what had happened, or why. It happened too fast. Colby was essentially helpless once he was knocked off the slope. And while not sure he fully understood what had caused the avalanche and fall, Colby instinctively knew that it was bad, really bad. Tossed around by a force he had never experienced before, he knew that death was likely. "I don't know what a freight train feels like, but the avalanche was incredible, just irresistible. I had *no* say in what was happening."

The last thing he remembered as he caromed down the slope was impacting a minor bump in the surface of the ice and being launched into the air.

ometime on the morning of June 19, 1992, Colby Coombs opened his eyes. He was cold through and through, a killing cold right down to his bones. Pain, deep and unrelenting, permeated his entire body. His Gore-Tex jacket and pants were covered by a light snowfall. He recognized the clear, bright light of morning, a light unlike any other time of those endless Alaskan days. He knew he was Colby Coombs, he knew he was on a climb, but he was uncertain just then about other details. The skin of his face felt cold, and when he looked down, he saw he had lost his mittens. His hands were cold and numb.

Rousing himself, he looked around. He recognized his surroundings. *Ahh*. Quickly, it started coming back. The avalanche. He realized he was hanging from a climbing rope. He looked across a frozen slope embedded with occasional rocks. There, not ten feet away was Tom Walter, hanging from the other end of the same rope at precisely the same elevation. He remembered Ritt and looked down. The 7-mm rope tied to his friend still hung below him, but it was not loaded, not taut. Instead it hung loosely, the end of it out of his field of vision somewhere farther down the mountain. Ritt was nowhere in sight.

But the 9-mm rope to which both he and Tom were tied was fully weighted, and both climbers hung from their harnesses supported only by the thin red rope. Colby's chilled brain gradually returned to lucidity. They were on Foraker. An avalanche had knocked them off the slope. He presumed that when he was launched off the slope and became airborne, he had been knocked unconscious. Looking up, he saw that the red climbing rope that supported himself and Tom was caught on a rock protruding from the slope. The rope, Colby deduced, must have snagged on that rock as both climbers fell after having been knocked off their stances by the avalanche. He guessed that the rope's getting hung up like that had saved him from falling farther. It had probably saved his life.

Coombs' whole being was in agony. His first attempts at movement were unbearable. Every little part of his body gave off extreme pain, yet some parts were discernibly worse than others. He was hurt badly.

When he looked over and saw Tom hanging just a few feet away, he thought: Tom is dead. He couldn't be sure. Tom was facing the other way, and from where he hung on the rope, Colby could only see the back of Tom's parka. But just the manner in which his partner hung from that rope aroused in Colby an unbearable sense of dread and sorrow. As he took in the ghastly scene, hardly believing the violence that had been wreaked on his small party of laughing friends, his only thought was that it was probably even worse than it seemed. He was afraid that Ritt might be dead, too, still tied to the 7-mm rope and hanging somewhere below him. Man, this sucks, he thought. This is really bad. This can't be real.

For Colby at that moment, reality took on a new and horrifying feel. Coombs realized he had entered a situation that exceeded any previous experience he had known. This was bad beyond imagining, cold and real, totally unescapable. In a way, he couldn't believe it had happened. But in another way he knew with an awful certainty it had. The simple fact of it was so appalling as to be unbelievable. Suddenly, this mountainside, this familiar environment, became foreign to him. He had never known such grief. He had never had a climbing accident. He had never been in so much pain. He had never been so cold, so thoroughly, completely cold. He knew that what lay ahead was going to be difficult way beyond anything he could imagine, and difficult in many different ways. This, he thought, is a whole different deal. And there was no way out of it.

He tried to move a little but found he couldn't really use his left shoulder. Any movement at all elicited a sharp, disabling pain. His neck too was stiff and painful, so rigid with pain he couldn't turn his head at all. That could be bad, he noted unemotionally. The only way he could look around was to turn his whole upper body, which generated more pain from his wrecked shoulder. His left ankle throbbed and ached, and, he found, could bear no weight. He saw, too, that the crampon on his left boot had been lost in the fall. His ice ax was gone as well, along with both mittens. Fortunately, he still wore the thin glove liners he had worn beneath them. Luckier still, the persistent bad weather had brought wetter weather and warmer temperatures, which had probably saved him from severely frostbitten hands.

He couldn't believe he was alive, but at the same time he felt half dead. He was damaged and hurting. He was acutely thirsty, his mouth and throat dry and raw. He was cold, so cold. Oh man, he thought. I can't believe this. Could he move? Could he get to Tom? Could he get to Ritt? Could he get down? He was going to have to take it one step at a time.

He thought back to the avalanche, trying to understand what happened. He realized it had been instantaneous, his stopping when the rope stopped and then—without warning just suddenly getting hit. There was no tug on the rope. It wasn't as if Tom had released the avalanche and it was by then below him, it wasn't as if Tom was holding on waiting for Colby to get hit and then trying to hold him. No, he thought, Tom was definitely in it. The momentary flash of sensation he had had of the rope falling must have been real. But what had hit them? he wondered. All the way up that final section, he had seen *no* snow on that slope. We must have climbed into an unstable snow layer recently deposited on the ice slope just below the crest of the Southeast Ridge, he thought, just walked into some fresh, wind-deposited snow resting on the ice. When that blue ice gets loaded with snow, he knew, there's not much of a bond. It must have just let go, he thought, and come crashing down on the small party.

Although he couldn't know it at the time, Colby and his friends had climbed to within a few hundred feet of the crest of the ridge. They had almost made it to safety. When National Park Service rangers flew in a helicopter over the accident site later, they saw Tom's ice ax sticking out of the snow, still driven into the slope just 200 to 300 feet below the Southeast Ridge proper. The three had climbed more than a thousand feet of the ice slope before being hit with the avalanche at about 13,200 feet. The place at which the climbers had come to rest after the long fall was at approximately 12,200 feet, just above the top of the rock buttress they had climbed, and slightly to the left. They had fallen approximately a thousand feet, coming to rest only when the rope between Colby and Tom had snagged on the rock near the bottom of the ice slope.

Having lost one of his ice axes in the fall, Colby grabbed his second ice tool and began working his way over to where Tom hung from the other end of the rope. It was only ten feet away over relatively easy ground, yet the badly injured Coombs could move only slowly and gingerly toward his friend. With some of his weight still on the rope that held him from above, Colby partially pulled himself over, partially scrambled in a clumsy way over to Tom, who hung in total stillness at the other end of the rope. Once he had arrived next to his friend, Colby situated himself as best he could beside Tom, anchoring himself with his ice tool and supporting himself with his good leg.

It took just a moment for Colby to determine that his partner was dead. Tom was cold and motionless, his body stiff. There was no carotid pulse. His face was covered completely by what Colby thought was snow. But when Colby reached out to brush the snow from his friend's face, he couldn't do it. Trying again, Colby was shocked to see that it wasn't spindrift or loose snow that obscured Tom's face, but a hard mask of opaque white ice, frozen firmly in place. Colby could not remove it, and assumed the snow from the avalanche had frozen there after the accident. The mask of hard névé was eerie.

Oh, man, thought Colby, Tom is dead. Tom is really dead. What does that mean? He could begin to understand, but he didn't want to know. He found he couldn't think clearly through the fact of Tom's death, the finality of it, and what it would mean to so many people. He remembered that Tom's wife was arriving in a few days to join him. Hanging there on the slope in that mean wind, Colby could hardly stand the thought. The idea that Tom had been killed was literally overwhelming. Vaguely, like a shadow, or a great darkness, Colby could see the enormity of the tragedy. But he also knew he could not enter it, that he could not survive that. And at that point he made a conscious decision *not* to deal with the death of his friend—not now. He knew he wouldn't be able to function if he dwelt on what had happened. Instead, he knew he had to become pragmatic, to simply and carefully do now what he must.

By refusing to deal with Tom's death, or grieve over it, Colby found he could think about the reality of his own desperate situation. It was a trick, he knew, but it was a way out of the pain and grief that threatened to overwhelm and incapacitate him. He thought, I've got to think only about what I need to do now, and what I need to do to get off this mountain. If I don't get down alive, Colby thought, nobody is ever going to know what happened up here. Surprisingly, that became a strong source of motivation. Colby did not want to die.

"That might sound like an obvious thing," Coombs remembered, "but as soon as I realized Tom was dead, I knew I wanted to live—if I could. That was partly pure survival instinct, I guess, but it was also practical. I wanted to get back so I could tell others what had happened. And I'm very close with my mother, the idea of vanishing without a word was unacceptable. I wanted to get back to see her, and that became a strong driving force, maybe my strongest motivation. I didn't know if I could live or not, but I knew then I was going to do whatever I could to get off the mountain."

As Colby hung from the frozen ropes beside Tom's lifeless body, the cold wind whipped across the mountainside. The rocks and snow around him had taken on an exaggerated intensity, as if his perception had been altered. Already numb with cold, Colby knew he was going to have to numb himself somehow to the grim reality of the accident. Tom's death had triggered a strong, lucid realization: Coombs knew that if he were to live, his determined, conscious decision to eliminate emotion would have to be unshakable. In fact, he could sense it happening already, automatically, as if his mind's reaction to the accident were to shut down the feeling part of his consciousness. He would simply refuse to allow self-pity for his own situation, or grief over Tom's tragic death, to affect his judgment or prevent his own survival. So with pure force of will, as a pragmatic survival stratagem, he put off dealing with the death of Tom, and steeled himself for what he would find when he located Ritt. Emotion was an indulgence he couldn't afford, or even survive.

Colby realized that to reach safety he was going to have to ignore his pain as well. Although he knew intellectually that he couldn't actually *eliminate* the pain that wracked his whole body, he was determined not to allow it to get in his way. Colby didn't know how badly he was hurt, and surprisingly, he found that it didn't seem to matter. He had significant first-aid training, but all that went out the window. Like Tom's death, there was nothing he could do about his injuries. He wasn't bleeding, so there was nothing urgent to be done. The situation came down to the fact that if his broken body could keep going long enough to make it off the mountain, good. If it couldn't, there was nothing he could do about it.

"My body was like a machine to me," Coombs said, "and up there it was like, uh-oh, it's broken. It doesn't work. But as far as I was concerned, I was determined to get as much use out of it as I could." What mattered now was to survive, and to somehow get off the mountain. He would go as far as his broken being would take him.

Since finding Tom's body hanging from the rope, Colby had not been able to shake the sick certainty in his gut that Ritt, too, had been killed. He held out hope that his best friend was still alive—after all, he himself had survived the fall while Tom did not. Still, Colby realized not only that Ritt's chances were extremely small, but that he almost seemed to *know* that Ritt was dead. As he hung in the bitter wind next to Tom, he saw even more evidence of the terrible violence of the accident. Below Tom's body, a bloody streak stained the frozen slope, extending below him more than 30 feet, as far as he could see. If was as if Tom's body had been drained of blood.

Colby realized he couldn't stay there for long. He had to get moving. But to do that, Colby was going to need to replace the climbing gear he had lost in the fall. Slowly and painfully, grunting and breathing audibly, Colby leaned down and removed Tom's left crampon. Holding it carefully, he struggled to attach it to his own left boot. With only limited use of his left arm, he found everything was hard to do, everything. Injuries to his shoulder and neck made each movement frustratingly slow and painful. He kept at it until it the crampon was securely fastened to his boot. It seemed a decent fit. One of Tom's hands still retained its mitten and windproof nylon outershell. Colby removed the shell and placed it over his lightly gloved left hand, then removed the Dachstein mitten and put that on his right hand. That should keep my hands from freezing, he thought. He wasn't sure what exactly he needed from Tom's pack, so he removed it completely and clipped the pack to the ice-ax anchor beside him. A rack of ice screws still hung from a sling around Tom's neck. As the leader on that final ice slope, Tom had carried the hardware in the event a suitable placement was found. Now Colby realized he needed the screws to make rappels on the descent.

As he retrieved the jangling rack of ice hardware, Colby saw the screws were covered in Tom's blood.

All the while he was examining Tom for signs of life, and retrieving potentially life-saving items to use on his descent, Colby still hung from the rope looped over the rock above. He knew he was going to have to extricate himself from the rope system before he could attempt to climb lower to look for Ritt. He also knew it wouldn't be easy. The ropes were frozen, the knots impossibly tight after the high-loading forces of the fall. Colby half-stood on the slope, clipped to his ice tool for protection. He was partially hanging from the rope, partially supported by his good leg, as he worked out the best method of removing himself from the rope system that would still provide a usable section of rope to use for the upcoming descent.

He arrived at what seemed the logical solution: he would simply cut the rope just above his own harness. That would leave him with almost the full length of usable climbing rope—assuming he could dislodge it from above. He took a knife out of the front pocket of his bibs— a knife he had carried there for years in the event of emergency but had never before needed to use—and opened the blade. Reaching down, he sawed on the 9-mm rope a few inches above the knot that was tied to his harness.

What happened next came as a shock. As soon as Colby cut through the rope, Tom's body dropped away violently, rocketing out of sight down the mountain. Colby, stunned, watched the body fall until it disappeared into the abyss just off the left side of the rock buttress, taking the climbing rope as well. *What!* Colby thought. Watching Tom's body instantaneously drop away took Coombs completely by surprise. Standing on the windswept slope, he stared down the mountain where Tom had disappeared. The incident was shattering—not just because Tom had fallen like that, but because he had caused it to happen. It also brought back to Colby the reality of the situation, that he was still on steep ground on a big mountain. If he weren't careful, if he didn't pay attention, he, too, could rocket down the mountain.

"When you think about it," Coombs said, "of course it's obvious that Tom was going to fall once I cut the rope. It was a bad idea, and probably reveals something about my state of mind that I didn't realize what would happen. For some reason, I thought that my cutting the rope to free myself was not going to disrupt the situation any further. Seeing him drop away like that, just disappear, blew me away. It was very upsetting."

Colby, dumbstruck, remained where he was for a moment, clutching Tom's pack. Still shaken by what had just happened, he knew he had to do something. He knew he needed to start moving, to try to find Ritt, and to somehow begin what was clearly going to be a difficult, if not impossible, descent. But he had been hanging from the end of a rope for half a day, he was chilled and broken and tormented by the tragic circumstances he faced. His thirst and pain and fatigue had affected his thinking and judgment. What he wanted most, and realized he needed most, was water and warmth. He needed to recoup his strength while he figured out his next moves. He desperately needed to get out of that chilling wind.

Looking around he saw that only ten or fifteen feet away a small rock protruded from the slope, creating a tiny, downsloping ledge that just might be big enough for him to sit on without sliding off the mountain. Gingerly, still carrying Tom's pack as well as his own, he began traversing toward the tiny rock platform. Numb with cold and in agony from his injuries, Colby took a few tentative steps. Just getting right over *there*, he realized, was going to be hard. How on earth could he get off the mountain? He knew he had to find a way to use his damaged body, to improvise a way to climb with one useless shoulder and an ankle that could bear almost no weight. With each move his body radiated pain. God, he thought, it's only ten feet. With his ice ax placed in the slope at shoulder height, he held onto that while he shuffled his feet. Then, moving his ax farther forward, he took a step with his good leg and drew his injured left foot alongside. In that way he slowly traversed the slope. Once he had hobbled to the rock protruding from the snow, he swung the ice tool in a fast arc, setting its pick firmly into the slope. He clipped a carabiner into the head of the ax, and with a hitch tied himself into the anchor with the 7-mm rope still attached to his harness. He also clipped both his and Tom's packs to his ice-ax anchor.

Maneuvering his body onto the small downsloping ledge formed by the rock, he retrieved from Tom's pack his friend's Ensolite pad and yellow bivvy bag. Sitting on the rock, still wearing his boots and crampons, he climbed on top of the thin foam insulating pad. He tried next to crawl inside the bivvy bag. His neck and shoulder were so badly injured, it was a difficult, even comical task to get inside the protective fabric of the bag. Finally, he got his legs inside and was able to pull the windproof material up around him. Once he was more or less inside, Colby found he was unable to zip the bag closed. Still, it would have to do. Spindrift and surface snow blew all around him in the freezing wind. Sitting on the small rock embedded in the exposed slope, half in and half out of his dead partner's bivouac bag, Colby took stock of his situation.

It was the afternoon of June 18, approximately twelve hours after the avalanche. A cold wind blew unabated and showed no signs of diminishing. Colby's head pounded, and from his neck emanated a pain that seemed to signal a serious injury. Concussion? he wondered. Broken neck? His left shoulder hurt so intensely he was certain he had broken something there. The extreme discomfort in his left ankle continued even at rest, and he suspected more broken bones, possibly the ankle or the lower leg bones. His thirst raged, but he had no water and his present situation offered no hope of setting up the stove to melt snow. He wasn't even sure he had the stove with him. Looking down, he could see the slack 7-mm static line descending out of sight below him. Somewhere down there was Ritt, his best friend.

There was absolutely no sign of his friend. Sitting on his rock, Colby mustered his strength and yelled Ritt's name down into the void. No voice answered back. Colby hoped Ritt was down there somewhere, taking whatever shelter he could, just as he himself was doing. Again and again, Colby hollered Ritt's name. There was only the sound of the wind.

Perched uncomfortably on the rock, Colby tried to rest. But every few minutes he was wracked by full body shivers. He knew the uncontrolled shivering meant he was dangerously hypothermic. He knew hypothermia would dull his thinking, sap him of strength, reduce his slim chances at survival. He had to warm up. Although it had stopped snowing, the unrelenting wind blew snow and spindrift across the slope. The bivvy bag offered some protection from the wind, but since Colby was unable to close the zipper snow blew in through the opening, making his situation more uncomfortable. The downsloping rock on which he sat made a poor shelf. Colby found that he kept sliding downward, sliding off so far that he found himself hanging from his tether, which was still attached to his ice-ax anchor. He couldn't completely trust the anchor, so each time that happened he had to painfully squirm back up into a semisitting position on his rock.

For the remainder of the day, and through the diffuse light of the Alaskan night, Colby remained on his rocky perch. He took comfort in the fact that at least he was out of the chilling wind. The periods of shivering seemed to be less frequent. His miserable bivouac afforded no sleep, but it did offer the chance to remain at rest and gradually restore his body warmth. Occasionally, as he huddled on the rock, he yelled Ritt's name down the slope. There was no answer.

The hours went by. Viewed from afar, Colby was a mere tiny speck wrapped in Gore-Tex fabric on the massive flank of Foraker. Sitting there, numb, he still could barely believe what had happened. He knew his situation was desperate. Sometimes he thought about what he should do next. He knew that, between them, he and Ritt had carried the lightweight Bibler tent and the stove. He wasn't sure who had what, but he knew he needed both of those items to survive. He also knew he needed to get to Ritt to find out what had happened, to help if he could. Though troubled by the fact that his calls to his friend had gone unanswered, he still hoped that when he found Ritt, Ritt would be doing the same thing that he was doing—hanging on. Colby retreated into a zombie-like state, sitting motionless on the rock, hurting and cold, not sleeping, not really thinking, either. He craved water. He kept sliding off the rock. His refuge was tortured and uncomfortable, but it was still rest. The hours ticked by.

By morning of June 20, the wind had died down. Colby discovered that he had warmed sufficiently that he was no longer shivering uncontrollably. His bivvy bag was, by then, filled with snow, but his clothing had helped to keep him reasonably dry in the cold, desiccated air. Knowing he could get no further succor from more sleepless inactivity in his comfortless refuge, Colby stirred. Moving stiffly, registering the pain of his injuries, he began to crawl out of his makeshift shelter.

He had warmed up and gotten some rest, but by now he was almost maddened by thirst. There was nothing he could do about that now, not there. Colby had to get down to Ritt. He would deal with water later. He set about making a rappel down the rope to discover the fate of his friend. In an irrational act of neatness, Colby rolled up Tom's bivvy bag and stowed it beside his partner's pack. It was as if Tom might come back to get his gear, and Colby wanted it to be in good order.

As he prepared to get moving, Colby realized he still wore his Petzl climbing helmet. Reaching up with his good hand, he unfastened the buckle and removed it. He saw that the hard plastic shell had been shattered in the fall. Touching his head, he found that his hair was matted with dried blood. The lightweight helmet had probably saved him from a fatal head injury. But the fact that his head was bleeding despite the hard hat was evidence of a powerful impact. That blow, he figured, had not only knocked him unconscious but was probably the source of the pain in his head and neck.

Moving methodically and with care, trying to act despite his frightful pain, Colby swung Tom's ice ax, placing the pick deep in the slope next to his own ice ax. With a nylon sling he rigged an equalizing anchor so that any load was evenly borne by each of the two axes. There, that's a reasonable anchor, he thought. Colby untied from his harness the 7-mm static line that was still attached to Ritt. He tied his end of the rope into the equalized anchor. From a gear loop on his harness, he removed his Sticht plate, a simple belay device made of a single piece of machined metal alloy. Colby pulled a bight of rope through the device and clipped his main harness carabiner to the loop of rope.

Mindful of his marginal mental state, Colby looked again at his rig: the rope was tied into the axes, and he was clipped into the rope. That's right, he thought. It looked okay. Forcing himself to be careful, Colby felt ready to rappel down to Ritt using the belay device. He checked the axes again, which appeared soundly placed. Satisfied his system was safe, Colby put his weight on the rope and began descending, slowly, using his good right leg to control his body attitude. As he started the rappel, he noticed his helmet lying in the snow. It was probably useless, he thought. His neck hurt so badly, anyway, that he was reluctant to carry the extra weight. Plus, there was this: it felt to Colby as if his head had actually swollen so much the thing might not fit. He continued down without the helmet.

His plan was to descend, find out what had happened to Ritt, then climb back up—with his friend or alone, as the case might be. He needed to climb back up to retrieve the two axes that comprised his rappel anchor, and also to begin his long descent of Mount Foraker. To get off the mountain, Colby knew he needed to traverse hundreds of yards leftward, to the southeast, to reach the crest of the Southeast Ridge (at a point much lower than their original ascent route would have taken them). Descending to the place where he expected to find Ritt would take him off course, far below the most efficient escape route, hence his need to climb back up to his anchor before starting his journey down the mountain. Colby held out hope that he and Ritt would be making the descent together. He knew he would soon find out.

Rappelling with the belay device was no problem for Coombs. He often did that to save the weight of carrying both a rappel device and a belay device. His downward movement was somewhat herky-jerky, but he made ragged progress down the thin 7-mm line. As he descended, the rope passing through his hands, he was appalled to see the damage the static line had sustained in the fall. Big chunks had actually been torn out of the already thin rope, and it showed signs of wear and abrasion along almost its entire length. With a much narrower diameter than a standard climbing rope, the static line was strong and lightweight, and therefore easier to carry. But severely damaged as it was, Colby knew the margin of safety it provided was slim.

He had descended more than 100 feet below his anchor when he came over a lip and got his first look at Ritt. His friend was lying upside down, stuck at the bottom of a steep snow slope. The last 20 or 30 feet of rope were wrapped tightly around Ritt's chest and torso. Colby's heart sank. It looked bad. He continued descending until he reached the spot where his friend had come to rest, about 140 feet below Colby's rock-ledge bivouac site. Colby reached out to his friend. Ritt's body was rigid. He touched his neck, pressing hard on Ritt's cold flesh. There was no pulse. Ritt was dead. Colby wondered why he himself had escaped mortal wounds in the avalanche when Ritt and Tom did not. He could hardly believe what he was seeing. This person with whom Colby had shared so much of his young life, so much fun and adventure, laughter and easy friendship, was gone.

He was angry and sad, his self-imposed hard exterior penetrated by the awful revelation. When he turned his friend slightly for a closer look, he wasn't prepared for what he saw. Ritt had no face. The same weird death mask of hard névé that had obscured Tom's face covered Ritt's, too. Colby stared, disturbed and fascinated by the bizarre phenomenon. The frozen snow made a perfectly formed mask that completely covered Ritt's face, and only his face. Colby tried to brush it away, but the frozen death mask was so hard it was impossible to remove. The effect was a near total removal of his friend's identity. It was creepy and weird, but in a strange way peaceful, too.

"When I think back on it," Coombs said, "it was probably a good thing that their faces were obscured. Otherwise, it would have been all the more difficult for me to put my emotions aside and focus on how to survive. But it was so bizarre. I had never heard of that before and didn't know what to make of it, or how to think about it."

Being confronted with Ritt's death was almost more than Colby could bear. He had held out a forlorn hope that he would find his friend alive, even though since finding Tom's body he had tried to prepare himself for the cold reality he now faced. But even in his hardened frame of mind, Colby could feel the anxiety that had gradually—almost unnoticeably—built up as he descended the rope now grip him as Ritt's death became cold, irrefutable fact. In that instant, Colby just stopped. Forcing himself to take control of his emotions, he resisted thinking about Ritt. With pure will he simply refused to allow himself to dwell on Ritt's death and the sorrow that sad reality entailed. He refused to let himself feel *anything*, to allow that huge emotion even the smallest space in his consciousness. And in that moment, he found he could think about what mattered for his own survival. Colby needed the stove, and the tent. And, above all else, he needed water. More than twenty-four hours without a drink in the cold, dry air had weakened him. His situation was desperate. If he were going to survive, he would have to act.

Perched on the steep slope with his good leg locked, Colby reached down, unfastened the buckles, and opened the drawstring at the top of his friend's pack. But Ritt's body was so tightly wrapped in the last

20 feet of rope that Colby was unable to get inside the crammed interior of the pack to retrieve the gear he needed. Remembering what had happened higher up, when Tom's body had suddenly shot down the mountain, Colby tried to figure a way to get into the pack without dislodging Ritt's body from the mixed snow-and-rock slope where it lay. Taking extreme care, Colby slowly moved Ritt toward him a few inches so he could have better access to Ritt's pack. As he did that, Ritt's body immediately became dislodged and fell from the slope.

Not again, Colby thought, as his friend's body spun free of the tangling line and hurtled down the mountain. Colby watched in horror as Ritt's body continued to plummet, unwinding from its wrapping of rope. Suddenly, the 7-mm line loaded with the full force of the fall. The rope became as taut and straight as a steel cable, instantly yanking Colby from his stance. Since the static line had none of the elasticity of a traditional climbing rope, the force of Ritt's falling body violently wrenched Colby's being, enveloping him in a delirious, deranging wave of pain, then throwing him back against the slope. Colby was left hanging from the rope by his belay device, his injuries torqued and hammered by this new violence. But in those awful, terror-filled seconds, Colby's attention focused not on the excruciating pain that assaulted him but on the fatal fall he was sure was about to begin. Both he and Ritt were stopped only by the 7-mm rope anchored off the two axes set in the slope higher up. Both the anchor and rope were marginal. Colby felt certain that at least one would fail, and he would tumble with Ritt down the rock buttress to his death when the rope broke or the anchors pulled.

"I just thought this is it," Coombs said, "and I envisioned starting to bound down the side of the mountain with Ritt. There was nothing I could do. But, when we both stopped falling, the anchors held. I couldn't believe that. And the 7 mm didn't break. I couldn't believe that, either. We were both hanging from that tattered rope. I couldn't believe I was alive, but I was in agony."

Shaken and left dangling from his belay device, Coombs scrambled to get some kind of footing on the slope. He could hardly believe he had made another mistake in judgment. I must be bad off, he thought. What troubled him was that he couldn't figure out what he might have

done differently. The slightest touch had sent Ritt tumbling off. Miracu-
lously, the thin, beat-up static line had stayed in one piece despite the
force of two falling climbers. He looked up toward his ice-ax anchor,
but that was out of sight above. Through his agony, Colby listened to
the sound of his own ragged breathing as he clung to rocks protruding
from the snow slope. The momentum of the fall now spent, he peered
down to where Ritt's body had come to rest at the end of the static line,
about 30 feet below. Colby, although he by then had one leg lodged on
the slope, was still partially hanging from his belay device which was
now well and truly jammed in the taut static line. He knew he was in a
precarious position, vulnerable and exposed, dangling from his marginal
anchors on a compromised rope. But he was stuck. There was no way
to unload the rope and free his jammed belay plate.

Coombs knew he had to extricate himself, and quickly, before the
rope broke or the anchors pulled. Still reeling from the violence of the
fall, he could only marvel at the intensity of the pain that wracked his
body. By now, he desperately needed a drink to slake a raging two-day
thirst, a thirst exacerbated by the grief and struggle of the past few moments. He still had not retrieved the life-saving items he needed from
Ritt's pack, which remained attached to Ritt's body at the end of the
rope. There was no way to descend Foraker without the fuel, stove, and
tent. He had to figure out a way to extricate himself, descend to Ritt,
and get the things he needed.

Hanging there, Colby's experience with rope systems and climbing
techniques enabled him to formulate a resourceful escape. The slope
on which he found himself was not so steep that it prevented his standing on it with his cramponed boot. Supporting his weight on one leg,
Colby managed to take from his pack his Petzl ascender, which was
similar to a Jumar rope clamp, a cammed device which can be slid up
a rope but cannot slide down unless a lever on the clamp is released.
He attached his ascender to the rope below his jammed belay plate.
With his weight now off his harness, Coombs unclipped the locking
carabiner on his harness entirely, leaving the jammed belay plate on
the rope. He then clipped his harness into the ascender and descended
to where Ritt's body hung by down-climbing the rope, using the ascender to regulate his descent and prevent his falling.

Arriving finally where Ritt had come to rest, Colby wasted no time. He was able now to get into his friend's pack. He found a half-full water bottle and immediately pulled it free. The water inside was unfrozen, and Colby unscrewed the lid and chugged the contents in several gulps. The water was restorative, temporarily relieving his nagging thirst. But Colby knew he was seriously dehydrated and needed much more. That would have to wait. Once again beside his friend's body, he had to deal all over again with the fact that Ritt was dead. He had to struggle once more to keep his emotions at bay. But that was becoming easier, as if he were getting more practiced at it, or his mind automatically had just shut down that part of his thinking.

Working methodically, like a robot on autopilot, Colby retrieved the tent, the stove, the fuel. He found some food and took that, too, stowing all the gear in his own pack. Ritt's ax must have been lost in the fall, so Colby removed the second ice tool from Ritt's pack. The slope was too hard for the shaft to penetrate, so Colby swung the tool into the slope, firmly setting the pick into the ice. He anchored Ritt's body to the mountain by tying the 7-mm rope from Ritt's harness to the ice tool he had just set in the slope. After he had secured Ritt, he cut the rope above the ice-tool anchor. With the other climbing rope already lost with Tom's body, Colby knew he would have to descend Foraker with only that fragment of trashed static line.

With Ritt anchored to the slope, Colby used his ascender to climb back up the rope, which was still tied off to the axes up by his bivouac site. Once he had climbed above the jammed belay play, he stopped to retrieve it, knowing he'd need that to make more rappels on the descent. He was more focused now on his survival, better able to ignore the pain as he climbed, better able to push his emotions aside. Arriving back at his bivouac site, Colby began to think in earnest about his descent strategy.

He knew he would have to traverse southeast, climb sideways until he could gain the crest of the Southeast Ridge. But he was operating on pure adrenaline now, and knew that fatigue and hunger eventually would catch up to him. He knew it was imperative that he find a place to make some sort of tolerable camp, a place with fewer discomforts than his miserable bivouac. He needed to get rehydrated, and to get some kind of rest.

The long day and night he had spent on his rock after finding Tom had given Colby a chance to carefully look over the terrain around the accident site. Though the avalanche had carried them off their intended climbing route, Colby had a good idea of the lay of the land. He had seen what appeared to be a small flat area maybe 200 or 300 yards away, just on the other side of a broad, shallow gully. To get there he would have to traverse a large, funnel-shaped basin southeast of his bivouac rock, and go up and over a rise where a small glacier was nestled beneath a headwall. It was that small section of glacier that appeared to offer his best hope for a relatively flat bivvy site. But could he get there? Colby was about to find out if he was able to climb.

Thirty-six hours has passed since the avalanche. In his pack, Colby had a sleeping bag, an Ensolite pad, and the stove, tent, and fuel. He had food in the form of instant soups and instant oatmeal. He had the rack of hardware, mostly ice screws but also a few pitons and other pieces of rock protection. Having neatly stowed Tom's gear by his pack, Colby took a final look around his bivouac. There was only his useless helmet. He left it, and set off.

His very first steps revived concern that his damaged ankle would all but preclude actual climbing. With his crampons placed into the slope, his ankle was forced in a steeply uphill position, causing pain so acute he couldn't bear weight. He wondered if he would have to crawl down the massive flank of Mount Foraker. He took another step, trying to keep his ankle and lower leg rigid. That was a little better. As he experimented with other techniques, he found that he could front-point with a tolerable level of pain and discomfort. For some reason his ankle could bear weight when it was held absolutely straight, without pointing outward or inward or up or down. He took another sideways step. It was slow, really slow, but at least he was moving. He looked over to the flat spot. It wasn't that far, maybe twice the distance of a football field. He took another step. Colby tried not to think about how many days it would take at this snail's pace to get down to the glacier. He just took another step.

With food and fluids his main concern, he moved away from the scene of the accident, away from the bodies of his partners. With his right hand, he could hold an ice ax in the usual way. With his left hand, he found that by adjusting his grip so that he held the other ice tool by its head, his injured shoulder could bear some of his weight and assist in keeping his balance. In that manner, he traversed across the ice slope, moving steadily but slowly, front-pointing sideways and slightly upward. He was on a course that would eventually take him to the crest of the ridge. But he wasn't trying to go that far. He only needed to cross the basin toward the small, flat glacier he had seen from his earlier bivouac. There he could regroup. He knew he had to take care of his body or it wouldn't get him off the mountain. He had to reach a safe place, where he could rest and get something to drink, and something to eat. He had to reach that place as soon as he could.

After the traumatic events of the past two days, Colby found that to be once again climbing was somewhat comforting, and familiar. Climbing was what he knew; he could do that all day. But in another sense, this short traverse was a completely new experience, fraught with uncertainty, like learning to walk again. His inelegant climbing technique, dictated by his injuries, was all new to him. It was cumbersome, unpracticed, and inefficient. He found he could do nothing by rote, but had to concentrate on every step, every placement of his axes. His years of climbing experience were of little use to him as he struggled across the basin. And the necessity to remain focused, to take extra care, added to his already crushing fatigue. He found himself losing his fine focus, and his mind wandered dangerously.

More than halfway across the slope, Colby suddenly stumbled clumsily. His ankle roared with pain as it twisted, his shoulder throbbed as he caught himself with his ax. But he regained his balance. The misstep was like a slap in the face. It brought Colby back to mental alertness, refocused his attention on his makeshift climbing technique. He began to realize exactly what he was in for, and he wondered if he were up to it. Could he, in his diminished state, hold his concentration on the long descent? He could tell, by now, it was going to take days of slow, painful work.

Still at more than 12,000 feet on Foraker, Colby knew even a healthy climber would take a day or two to descend. He wondered if he could hang in long enough to make his way down using the cumbersome and exhausting technique he had been forced to adopt. He wondered if he would be able to handle the unknown technical problems he might encounter on the descent. But most alarming to him were his lapses in attention. One wrong step could be fatal, and he knew he couldn't allow himself to stumble again. Unlike the hundreds of other descents he had made, where he could rely on his experience and judgment, where he could operate on a kind of autopilot, he knew that here was something all new. He thought: This is going to be hard.

In the evening of June 20, after nearly a day of painful, hobbled climbing, he arrived beneath the small headwall. He saw immediately that he had lucked out. The glacier fragment was slightly downsloping, but otherwise made a perfect campsite. Man, he thought, this is great. Without much effort at all he was able to clear a flat spot for the tent with his ice ax. The Bibler he had taken from Ritt's pack was extremely easy to set up. Colby just removed it from its bag, shook it out, and crawled inside, popping the poles into place from the interior. The Bibler stove was made to hang from where the tent's center poles crossed in an X. Colby quickly put together the apparatus, attached its fuel canister, and scooped a potful of snow from outside the tent. He took a plastic lighter from the pocket of his climbing bib and held the flame to the stove as he opened the valve. The stove sputtered and hissed, then began its usual low roar. Relishing the prospect of food and drink and rest, Colby pulled his sleeping bag and insulated pad from his pack. He spread the pad on the floor of the tent, and sat up with the sleeping bag pulled up around him. In the yellow glow of the confining tent interior, Colby listened as the stove melted the snow. For a little while, at least, he was out of harm's way. He had not only begun his epic journey of 10,000 steps, he had finished the first stage.

When the water in the pot was boiling, Colby poured some of it into his ten-ounce insulated mug. Taking a few sips, he savored the warm liquid but found it almost too hot to drink. It cooled quickly, though, and he soon had drunk it all. He poured another mug full and drank that, too. He added more snow to the pot and kept the stove going. Ensconced in his sleeping bag, he could feel his body begin to warm up with the hot fluids. He knew he was dehydrated after days without a drink of any sort, except the contents of Ritt's water bottle. He drank mug after mug of hot liquid, more than a half gallon in all. He refilled his water bottle to drink later.

After several drinks, Colby pulled a packet of Nile Spice Soup from his pack, a double portion, and poured the dried powder into his mug. He added boiling water, but not quite the specified amount, creating a thick, stew-like soup. From a Ziplock bag he grabbed a handful of grated cheese, sprinkled that on the hot soup, and stirred the mixture. He consumed his hot meal, eating slowly, savoring it, and made another mug of hot water. He drank that, and decided he was still hungry enough to make another cup of soup.

As he ate, he could tell by the light filtering through the yellow fabric that it was evening. Here was a much more comfortable place to spend the night—level, sheltered, warm, and with none of the torment he had experienced in last night's rocky bivouac. It was, he knew, a miracle that he had found this, the only flat place around where he could have camped. It had saved his life. There would be no sliding off his perch tonight. His body radiated deep, debilitating pain, but it had gotten him this far. He marveled at how much damage the human body could take and still keep functioning. He felt lucky that whatever his injuries were, they seemed manageable. He could still function, a remarkable enough fact. He wondered how he could have survived the fall when Tom and Ritt did not. Luck, he guessed, but he didn't feel lucky. In the reasonable comfort of his camp, however, it seemed that after the horrible events of the past two days, the odds finally were turning in his favor.

"I felt like a such gimp, but it was like, I don't care," Coombs remembered. "I had gotten that far, I was going to go as far as I could. That night in the tent I felt like things were beginning to go my way. I felt like getting off Foraker was going to be the hardest thing I'd ever done, but for the first time I believed that if I gave it everything I had I might get down."

In the warm haven of his tent, Colby took refuge not just in his improved circumstances, but in the comfort of his "personalized" faith. His unique and highly unconventional relationship with God, which he had enjoyed ever since he had spent a year traveling around the world after college, definitely helped sustain him.

"I believe in God," Coombs said, "and that night I really felt his presence. I felt that I had gotten into this situation on my own and I was going to get out of it on my own, but there was the sense that God was watching over me. My feeling was that if I tried as hard as I could, he would be there if I needed help. People probably say, 'Yeah, right, of course you felt God's presence—because you're all busted up and in an altered state of consciousness, so of course you'd feel God's presence.' But I'm telling you, I felt God's presence because I felt his presence." Colby asked God to keep his body going long enough to get down off Mount Foraker.

"That's nothing new. I pray all the time anyway, for the slightest thing. Even if I'm just out climbing for the day, I'll pray, 'Please let me make this move because my last piece of pro is way down there.' So I'll pray to make that move. I pray all the time. It's just part of me. I'm not a fundamentalist, I don't even go to church much. I've got a lot of bad habits. But I definitely believe in God, and I don't think God holds any of that against me."

Colby finally turned off the stove. His desperate need for food and fluids had been satisfied. Now he hoped to get some rest. He hurt all over, hurt worse than he ever had before, so he wasn't sure if he would be able to sleep despite his fatigue. But at least he was warm, and at rest. He was no longer thirsty or hungry. Gingerly, he lowered himself into a reclining position. Halfway down, his neck suddenly exploded in excruciating pain. Colby instantly reached to support his head with his hands. Gently lowering himself against the insulating pad, he lay still, gasping, waiting for the agony in his neck to subside. The pain gradually retreated to the more or less tolerable background level he had suffered ever since the avalanche. Wow, that's bad, he thought.

Colby tried to relax, to let his weary body rest. This, he thought, is hard. He lay there, looking up at the walls of the tent, thinking once again that he needed to get down, to get some medical help as fast as possible. He realized that he was a long way from being safe. He was in a bad way. He might not make it. Just lying there hurting was almost more than he could bear.

For hours he lay wrapped in his sleeping bag, resting but unable to sleep. The pain in his neck was relentless. Colby didn't know it yet, but he was lucky to be moving at all. In the fall he had broken his neck in two places, with displaced, unstable fractures of his C-5 and C-6 vertebrae. Somehow his spinal cord had remained intact. His body hurt all over, particularly his ankle and left shoulder, but at rest, the agony of the neck pain made his other discomfort seem minor. The need for sleep gnawed at him, but sleep would not come. He took comfort in knowing that at least his fatigued and aching body was getting some respite from the exhausting work of climbing.

Colby lay awake in the tent as the hours passed. In the middle of the night, he tried to sit up to have a drink from his water bottle. He discovered he couldn't do it, not even close. Each time he tried to lift his shoulders off the insulating pad, the pain in his neck caused him instantly to stop struggling and lay back down in defeat. He realized he would have to learn to sit up all over again, just as he had to learn how to climb all over again. Experimenting with different techniques, he found that if he grabbed his hair with his hands—taking some weight off his neck—and heaved with his whole body, he could rise up a few inches before falling back down. He worked at that, heaving and heaving again, finally perfecting the maneuver so that on his fifth or sixth heave he could rock himself into a sitting position. Successful at last, he sat upright, thinking, This is ridiculous. I can't even get out of bed, how am I going to get off the mountain?

Eventually, Colby took a long drink from the water bottle and carefully lay back down. Having given up on sleep, he still wanted to get as much rest as possible. The continuous daylight of the Alaskan summer would have allowed him to climb around the clock. Had he been healthy, he probably would have done just that to speed his descent. But in his present state he knew he needed to prudently husband his strength. He needed to rest—even if it were only this painful, sleepless rest as he lay in his tent.

He tried not to think of what lay before him, what the next day would bring. He already knew what he had to do. A day, maybe more, of traversing would take him to the crest of the Southeast Ridge. From there, he would have to find a way down the ridge—a route that he could negotiate in his present condition. He didn't know the route, didn't know what he would find. He would just have to see. At the moment, it seemed a good idea to remain where he was, conserve his energy, and prepare his broken body as best he could before setting out again. Reasonably comfortable and secure, time didn't matter to him. He didn't care how long he remained in the restorative comfort of his camp. If he could have slept, he might have stayed for days.

But in the bright light of dawn, Colby figured he had gotten whatever benefit he could from his sleepless haven. It was time to get moving. Once again going through his painful sitting-up routine, which would have been comical were it not born of desperation, he heaved himself upright. Pain permeated his broken body in a way that still surprised him. Reaching outside the tent, he scooped a potful of snow and lighted the stove. Though sleep had remained elusive, Colby knew that his bivouac had been life-saving. He was well hydrated, well fed and, at least to some extent, rested. He felt able to continue down. For how long he didn't know, but he would go as far as he could.

When the water boiled, he made more hot drinks and a mug of instant oatmeal. The simple camp chores of putting away the sleeping bag and tent took longer than normal; it was an hour before he was ready to venture forth. Alone, totally on his own, he was surprised that he felt psyched to get going, even optimistic. He felt as though he was as good as he could have been, given the tragic events and dire situation in which he found himself.

He thought about what he would need to get off Mount Foraker. He knew he couldn't carry a lot of gear because his shoulder and neck hurt so much, yet he still agonized over what to take and what to leave behind. What if he found himself in a situation where he needed just the right piece of gear? What if the descent took longer than he imagined, and he was stopped short because he didn't take enough food?

He was determined not to make a dumb mistake by leaving something important behind, yet he knew carrying equipment he didn't need would wear him down. In the end, he decided on two more days' worth of food and fuel. Because he wasn't exactly sure what he would encounter on the way down, he took the entire rack of bloody ice screws. With them he hoped to be able to rappel past technical sections of the descent route, difficulties that he couldn't down-climb due to his injuries and hobbled climbing technique.

He set out on the morning of June 21, the third day of the post-accident ordeal. From his campsite, he needed to reach the crest of the ridge. From where he stood, the route was all sideways, and it seemed to go on forever. As he looked it over, he was discouraged by the distance that lay before him. There was nothing for it but to continue. Using the stiff-ankled, front-pointing traverse style he had perfected the day before, he began the long march. At first he seemed to be doing about as well as he could. His leg and shoulder shot streamers of pain through his consciousness with every step, but he was actually getting used to that and was better able to ignore it. His concentration seemed to hold. But after a mere hour of climbing, he already could feel fatigue begin to build. This was going to take a long time, he thought, and remembering the stumble from the day before, he tried to force himself to remain sharply focused. He found that if he let his mind wander for even a split second—to think about what had happened—it distracted him enough that he would place his foot down slightly the wrong way and then be punished with consuming pain. It was swift negative reinforcement, and it taught him to pay attention.

The terrain was a mixture of snow and ice canted back at about 50 degrees, which actually suited his unconventional means of locomotion. Since he could climb only by keeping his ankle straight, he traversed by facing the slope, kicking in with his cramponed boots. For balance, he held an ice tool in each hand, placing them in the slope with each step. He moved sideways a few inches at a time. Sometimes his front points penetrated only an inch or so into the hard ice. In other places, where the ice gave way to softer snow, he could kick his foot in and bury the whole toe of his boot. That was easiest, and most secure. Each time he encountered the relatively soft snow, it was as if he had been given a small gift, a break that might make the difference between success and failure.

His progress was discouragingly slow. Traversing was hard, plodding work. The need to be continually focused, to think about every awkward, painful step, was mentally draining. On and on he climbed, planting his front points into the snow, using his axes for balance. He didn't trust himself to take a break, fearing it might be tempting to remain where he was, too tough to force himself to get going again. He did occasionally stop in his tracks and rest, breathing heavily with the exertion, but he never took off his pack, never sat down. Moving at a snail's pace, he knew steady progress was the only way he could make significant headway.

Slight of build, but strong, Colby had always tried to be a fast climber. But not today. Today he climbed slowly, so slowly, a function of his gimpy climbing technique and his need to take care with each step. At least he felt as though he were climbing safely. The pain kept him sharp, and his focus had not wavered much. He was getting into a ragged groove, concentrating on the icy slope, the placement of his feet. The tragic circumstances of the accident were less intrusive on his thoughts this day than they had been. He concentrated on his boots, the ice axes, the surface of the slope. But since he had with him only two days' worth of food and fuel, the slowness of his pace concerned him. That anxiety fueled his drive to continue on, helped to keep other distracting worries at bay.

The traverse seemed endless. Colby kept climbing leftward, kicking with his right boot, gently stepping with his left, carefully placing his axes, then doing it all over again. He thought, Don't slip, think about what you're doing. Late in the afternoon, when he was more than halfway through the seemingly endless traverse toward the ridge crest, a slight miscalculation of angle as he placed his left foot suddenly forced his full weight onto the smashed joint. The thunderbolt of pain caused him to inhale sharply in reflex and lean against his axes in palpable agony. He stayed like that, crumpled against the slope, for a minute or two, waiting for the searing pain to subside enough to continue moving.

That leg must be toast, he thought, but I don't care—I don't care if after all this they chop my foot off. It doesn't matter. I'm going to keep using it until it gives out. He took a sip from his water bottle and climbed on, putting the pain from his neck and his shoulder and his ankle in a place in his mind where it didn't matter. It was another trick, he knew, but it was effective. He was prepared to sacrifice the foot. What *did* matter, he knew, was for that leg to continue to work, at least for another few days.

By late afternoon, he had traversed the snowy, rocky slope to the point where it joined the shoulder of the Southeast Ridge of Foraker at about 11,000 feet. He was almost a half mile southeast and 2,000 feet below the point where he and Ritt and Tom had expected to crest the ridge at the top of the long ice slope. He had arrived. Colby was beat, physically drained by the effort it took to get there. But it was a milestone of sorts, a way to measure his progress. Finally he was into the descent proper. From here, it was literally all downhill. He needed to descend about 4,000 feet of ridge, a piece of work that would be very different, and much more difficult that the long traverse just completed. If he could manage that, then he would have to figure a way to somehow get back across the Kahiltna to base camp. From his vantage point on the ridge, he could actually look down and see the airstrip and tents of the base camp far below him.

He was spent, completely exhausted by the nonstop physical exertion and mental fatigue from hours of constant vigilance. And suddenly, there was nowhere to go. Looking around, he realized that for the first time in that long day of climbing, he faced a technical problem where his trusty, hobbling traversing technique would do him no good at all. Below him, blocking his progress down the ridge, was a headwall. A relatively minor feature in the massive scale of Mount Foraker, it was for him a formidable obstacle all the same: a frozen wall forming a giant step of glacier ice about 60 feet high. Had he been healthy, he probably could have found a way around the headwall on one side or the other. But not today. He was too tired, and he knew his ankle wouldn't tolerate the awkward footing required to descend the steep terrain. He would have to rig a rappel and descend that way.

Taking an ice screw from the sling around his neck, he placed it into the ice and turned it with his hand until the threaded hollow screw began to penetrate the ice. He was using Russian titanium ice screws, which are light and extremely sharp. When it was buried a few inches, Colby used his ax as a lever to rotate the screw right up to the hilt into the hard glacier ice, causing it to extrude a solid core of ice out of its open top end as it worked its way into the glacier. He clipped a carabiner to the screw. Uncoiling the 7-mm static line, he threaded the rope through the carabiner. With a piece of the rope still anchoring Ritt to the mountain, the static line Colby used was now probably only 140 feet long. He pulled the rope through the 'biner to its midpoint, then threw the rope off the headwall, checking to be sure that both ends fell to the glacier ice below. He pulled a bight of doubled rope through his Sticht plate and leaned back against the rope, testing the anchor. It appeared sound. Colby stepped over the precipice and began a slow, controlled descent, using his good right leg to keep him off the face of the headwall. He eventually landed on a small platform of glacier ice, a flat spot just below the headwall. It was a lucky break, the first relatively level terrain he had encountered all day on the long traverse. His energy gone, he knew he could safely go no further today. This would be home for the night.

Colby once again set up the tent and got the stove going. He was wasted. A deep fatigue penetrated his bones. But the opportunity to set up another reasonably secure, comfortable camp, to replenish his body with food and fluids, was more than mere physical respite. It was a psychologically restorative act, a remnant of climbing normalcy in the midst of his life-and-death ordeal. As his dinner of soup cooked, he wondered how long he could keep up this sustained level of effort in his diminished circumstance. He felt lucky to have found another comfortable camp. He knew that real rest and even a temporary period of relative security was crucial to his ability to carry on.

Despite the twenty-four-hour daylight and the opportunity it offered for long climbing days, his fatigue and injuries had forced Colby into a more normal day-and-night schedule. He had seen that his reserves of energy and concentration could see him through twelve hours or so of continuous descent, but no more, at least not safely. The desperate necessity to concentrate was wearing, and the constant agony of his fractures insidiously debilitating. The result was a finite number of climbing hours that he could tolerate at a stretch. He had hoped to put more terrain behind him, but this would have to do. And it was okay, it was progress. He would regroup and venture out once again tomorrow.

He consumed mug after mug of hot water, and prepared another double dose of soup and cheese. Even at that, he knew there was no way he was replacing the calories his intense efforts had burned off. But his hunger and thirst were completely satisfied, a fact that contributed to a sense of at least marginal well-being. As bad off as he was, at least he wasn't wet, cold, hungry, or thirsty. He was already so close to the physical breaking point that additional hardship like that might have done him in. He could be safe and comfortable in his camp. His unswerving drive to retrieve the tent, stove, and other life-saving gear from Ritt's pack had proven the difference between a fighting chance and no chance at all.

After dinner, Colby again risked lying down in his sleeping bag. He did so with some trepidation, knowing it was perhaps an irreversible act. He honestly wasn't sure he would have the strength at that point to sit back up, given the difficulty of the absurd contortions he had to go through to accomplish that simple maneuver. He didn't care. Maybe in a few hours his strength would return. In the meantime he would just remain on his back, at full rest, not stirring so much as a muscle. Lying there he slowly realized that despite his exhaustion, sleep once again would not come. This frustrating, relentless lack of sleep was catching up to him. It was the one real physical need he had not been able to meet. The thought of another sleepless night tormented him, but he knew that short of painkillers or a miraculous rescue, this was a reality he had to face. He was going to have to function as best he could in a sleep-deprived state.

The discomfort of unrelenting pain from his shattered body was aggravated by the necessity to rest with his left boot on. One of the great, simple pleasures of a high mountain camp is to remove one's heavy plastic mountaineering boots and snug down in the relative comfort of a sleeping bag. But Colby was denied that comfort. He had not dared to remove his boot since the bivvy below the rock buttress. He knew that keeping his boot on and laced up was a potentially life-saving precaution. If he removed the boot, he was almost certain that his ruined ankle would swell so much that he would be unable to put the boot back

Self-portrait, taken by Colby Coombs during the third bivouac of his descent of the Southeast Ridge

on. That would create a fatal situation, as without the boot he couldn't climb at all. He would be stuck. But more and more he worried about what was happening to his ankle and foot inside the boot. Were bones protruding from the skin? Was he bleeding? Was there sufficient circulation to his toes? Could he be getting frostbite? He couldn't check on any of that, and feared the price of his descent might be his foot. The prospect of losing the foot was becoming more real to him, yet there was nothing he could do about it. No sense taking chances. He was keeping the boot on.

Lying in the tent, Colby reflected on the events of the day. He had made real progress. The intense physical pain of climbing had not

77

compromised his determination to keep moving—and to keep focused. The long, seemingly endless traverse was actually over. His route to safety was down, down, down. The novelty of climbing with a broken leg had become less strange to him, and so less fatiguing to execute. His mental lapses of the first day had not recurred, and Colby attributed that to a more practiced concentration and his ability to put the tragic events of the accident out of his mind. The commitment to keep moving, and the mental stamina to resist the temptation to take rest breaks, well—that was climbing, that was old hat sort of stuff, the kind of wilderness skills he had honed to a high degree in his short adult life of adventure.

The weather had cleared sufficiently that he could actually see other peaks of the Alaska Range around him. In the distance, he could make out parts of the West Buttress route on Denali. From his bivouac, in fact, Colby could, at times, see all the way to base camp, more than six miles away. He could actually see Cessna 185s landing on the glacier airstrip. The flow of traffic in and out of the glacier seemed fairly regular. He knew that climbers were coming and going, laughing and joking. Things were normal down there, there was no tragedy, no life-or-death struggle. As he wistfully looked out over the scene he knew so well, Colby could feel the inner strength he had mustered to get himself off the mountain—to get down at any cost—waver slightly.

Maybe, he thought, I could just hang out here and wait. He thought that if he waved the bright yellow Bibler tent, someone might see it. Frustratingly, he realized that if he had a radio he could call for help. In the improved weather rangers probably could have plucked him off easily with the Lama helicopter. But Ritt and Tom had shared Colby's ideal that wilderness climbing was all about self-reliance, and the party had made the decision not to carry a radio. It was a decision he had cause to regret. The mere thought of no longer having to deal with his desperate, hobbling travel, the do-or-die struggle with his life in the balance, was seductive. Colby allowed himself to savor the thought of being rescued. But he soon realized it was pure fantasy. From base camp, he was an insignificant speck on the massive flank of Foraker. If he survived this ordeal, it would be under his own steam. He knew it was up to him.

"I realized I was on my own," Coombs remembered. "It was up to me to get my own butt off the mountain." As the fantasy of an easy rescue faded, Colby grew even more determined to get down. No matter what, even if it came down to crawling on his hands and knees, he was going to make it. After days of struggle, he had come to view himself differently. He felt that he already was in a strange in-between state, half dead and half alive. All emotion had been banished from his consciousness. He was focused, committed to success, oblivious to the torture of his injuries. For Colby, the situation was completely matter-of-fact, viewed with no trace of self-pity. He would either get down or he would die. The clarity of his perception generated no fear or even sadness. He would keep trying.

"At that point, with some progress already behind me, I could tell my attitude had changed a little. I was a veteran by then. My resolve had grown stronger, and the situation more simple. I was going to keep going until I died. I'd either make it or not," Coombs remembered. "I viewed the situation realistically. No one knew what had happened to our party, no one knew where I was. In some ways, the outcome was up to me. All it would take was one little slip, and that would be it—I'd die, too, and no one would ever know what had happened. But if I *didn't* make a mistake, if I could keep going, I just might reach base camp. That part was up to me. Other things were out of my control. I might get avalanched again. I might suddenly die from my injuries. There was nothing I could do about that. I was just going to keep going."

He spent another fitful night. The food and drink kept his body functioning physically, but he felt as though he was getting a little weird mentally from the lack of sleep. Several times during the night he faded away, perhaps dozing off. But he got no real sleep. Most of this period of repose was spent simply lying on his back, staring up at the tent, surrounded by the down sleeping bag and the enveloping texture of his pain. He was, by then, accustomed to it. He never tried to sit up—it required too much work. He lay quietly, his aching muscles at rest, his mind numb to the unrelenting desperateness of the situation. It had become his reality. He faded in and out.

When morning came, Colby faced the monumental task of sitting up. With a sigh, he grabbed his hair and began his ridiculous routine. It had become familiar. He heaved and heaved, grunting and groaning. After about seven or eight heaves, he eventually achieved a sitting position. Man, he thought, that's just crazy. He looked out of the tent and saw to his dismay that overnight the weather had turned bad. Snow was falling. Visibility had dropped to maybe 100 feet. Colby knew that might be a serious problem. He didn't know the route, he couldn't continue descending unless he could see where he was going. Almost out of food and fuel, he couldn't hunker down and wait out the weather. A long storm, even a fairly mild one, might do him in. But there was nothing he could do about that. He scooped up a potful of snow and started the stove.

With the boiling water, Colby made the last of his oatmeal. He realized the double meals at his last two bivouacs had depleted his food supply. He was out of food. That meant he had to make real progress, to cover significant distance today regardless of the weather. As he drank the last of the hot water he again checked the weather. It was packing in, but didn't seem to be working into a full-on storm. The snow had let up. By noon conditions had relented to the point that Colby felt climbing was possible. It was time to get moving. It was the morning of June 22, the fourth day since the avalanche.

As he packed his gear, Colby realized he was weaker than he had been the day before. The pain and sleepless nights were gradually taking a toll. Today, he would have to be careful. He put on his crampons and looked over the route below him. Yesterday had been all sideways traversing, well suited to the stiff-legged style he had been forced to adopt. But last night's rappel to descend past the headwall had been the harbinger of things to come. He could see that below him the ridge was a tangle of broken glacier ice, heavily crevassed. The climbing was obviously going to be more involved, more technical. He could tell there was going to be much time-consuming routefinding as he tried to wind his way through the crevasses and headwalls that made up the broken, glaciated terrain below. In a healthy state, the climbing would have been casual, no challenge at all. But now, Colby knew he would have to be smart. He couldn't waste time and energy on dead-end routes, he couldn't waste his limited supply of hardware trying to bypass the technical sections. This was going to be completely different. He started cramponing down the slope, his ankle in agony as the steeper ground forced his foot into awkward angles.

He had gone less than 500 feet when he was stopped by another headwall. Once again he took an ice screw from the blood-stained rack. He placed the screw, threaded the rope, and made a short, 40-foot rappel. At the bottom he pulled the rope through, abandoned the screw above, and began once again winding his way through seracs and crevasses. In another couple of hundred feet, he came to another headwall. This one he found he could outflank, saving his ice screws for use later on.

All that day, he descended in this manner, looking for a way around crevasses and headwalls, down-climbing when he could, roping down when he had no choice. To his dismay he found there were lots of little headwalls he simply couldn't get around. His solution was always the same. Take a screw from the rack, put in the screw, make the rappel, pull the rope down, and leave the screw. He rigged the rappels carefully, concentrating on the safety of his rope systems. He knew that one little slip could bring his retreat to a fatal halt. Even though the rappels were short, a fall from any of them could have inflicted injuries that, even if they didn't kill him outright, could exact the same result by leaving him stranded. Where he could, he outflanked the obstacles. But the steeper ground was hard on his ankle. The pain was almost unbearable. He tried to ignore it. He made progress, but he was running out of hardware.

Cramponing down the slope below one of the headwalls, he reached a rocky cliff that led steeply down to a more gently angled glacier slope. There was no way around the rocks, and there was no way his useless ankle would permit him to down-climb the snow-covered cliff. It was going to take another rappel, and a long one, almost the entire length of the doubled rope. But after rigging the anchor, he found that even on rappel the descent might prove his undoing. He still had to use his feet to control his rappel, and the uneven rocky band forced his leg into awkward, intensely painful angles. He couldn't figure out a way to use his feet without twisting his wrecked ankle, sending heartrending bolts of deep pain through his body.

"Roping down off the headwalls was relatively easy," Coombs remembered, "because I could use my right foot to keep myself off the ice. But the rock was much harder. I had to figure out a way to use my bad ankle. The rocks dictated where I had to put my feet, and the slightest little twist on the ankle and the pain just skyrocketed. I knew I had broken the joint badly, and didn't know how much longer it would support my weight. I was afraid of damaging it to the point where I could no longer climb."

At the bottom of the rock band, Colby had to take a short breather. He hobbled around on his fractured lower leg, wondering how much farther it would take him. But his progress down the ridge had gone surprisingly quickly, and he found himself on the lower section of the ridge. The weather seemed colder. While he put on his mittens, he noticed that clouds had started building above.

Before him was a long, relatively low-angled traverse section that would be easier to negotiate than the broken ground above. But the easy slope had several dangerous features. Immediately below the low-angled slope was a 1,000-foot-high cliff. To get down, he would have to traverse just above that cliff across the entire slope. He would have to somehow stay critically focused for every step, as any slight stumble could throw him off his feet and send him sliding over the drop-off to certain death.

As he began the delicate traverse, an even more dangerous situation became apparent to him. Just above him were all those hanging glaciers and seracs through which he had just climbed. At any moment any one of them might send down a barrage of ice that could instantly crush him. He knew that an entire party of Japanese climbers had been wiped out that way at this very place, eight climbers killed in one small avalanche. The glaciers up higher just calve off and dump tons of ice downslope. It was very much like playing Russian roulette. There was no way to know when the glaciers were going to move a mere inch or so, and that was all it would take to send tons of debris down on whatever or whoever is below.

He had no choice but to continue, to take his chances with the objective danger. Colby set off as smartly as he dared, hoping speed would limit his exposure to the lethal icefall above. But speed was impossible on his broken limb. Hobbling as fast as his ankle would allow, he was careful not to be reckless. If he so much as caught his crampon points on his pant leg, he might tumble over the cliff directly below him. He had to move as fast as he could while still maintaining a degree of safety. This was the worst so far. Through a growing fatigue, Colby tried to focus his concentration. He sweated profusely with the effort.

But as he traversed across the slope he became even more unnerved when he encountered a deep, polished groove. Looking ahead, he saw dozens of avalanche chutes, evidence that falling debris from above had been channeled time and again into the same fall lines. The falling ice had carved deep bowling alleys into the icy slope every few hundred feet. Each of these chutes was bordered by a low ridge of old debris on either side. As he made his way across the slope, Colby had to climb up and over each ridge, then down into the bowling alley, across the dangerous hard ice of the avalanche path, and then up and over the other ridge. Once out of that bowling alley, he could traverse only a few hundred feet before encountering another ridge, and another bowling alley. It was slow, exhausting work, and dangerous. Colby, dismayed by the awful terrain, climbed doggedly on, moving as fast as his fatigue and pain allowed. Every few seconds he cast a wary eye toward the hanging glaciers above, hoping to get advance warning in the event anything might be breaking loose or on its way down.

The slope was unrelenting, but Colby climbed stubbornly on. By noon, he had completed most of the long traverse without incident. His luck had held. He neither saw nor heard any avalanches. But time was passing. As the day waned, Colby hoped cooling temperatures would further freeze into place any loose debris, and thereby lessen the risk of avalanches falling on him from above. He could see only a few more bowling alleys ahead of him before he could get off the long traverse. As he climbed down into one of the debris chutes, he gingerly placed the cramponed boot of his broken left ankle gently but firmly onto the hard-ice surface. He brought his good leg down quickly, and just as he prepared to take another step, the crampon on his right leg broke contact with the ice. Colby started to fall.

Just as it had during the accident, the early-warning system of his trained climber's mind sent red-alert signals racing through his consciousness. As Colby started to slide, he knew that right below him was the 1,000-foot drop-off. If he went over that, he would fall all the way to the big glacier below and a certain death. He was headed directly for the abyss, and the speed of his fall began to increase as he slid down the smooth ice of the avalanche-polished bowling alley.

Instinctively, Colby drove the pick of his ice ax into the slope, forcing it deeper by rolling on top of it with all his weight. Suddenly, the ax dug deeply enough that it lodged in the ice slope. Abruptly, his slide was arrested. With a jolt, as the pick of the ax gained purchase in the ice, he stopped dead. But the force of his self-arrest wracked his body, the brunt of the sudden impact borne by his injured shoulder. His mind exploded in a burst of pain. He felt ripped in half, completely traumatized. He would find out later that the self-arrest had torn apart the two halves of his fractured scapula, displacing it by inches. The pain was so spectacular, so beyond what he had ever experienced, Colby feared he might pass out. He lay there on the icy slope, his weight on his ice ax, gasping for air, blinded by pain.

He realized that he had almost made the fatal mistake he had been determined to avoid. To die now, so close to the end of the technical problems, would be such a cruel joke. Slowly, Colby regained his composure. He rose carefully to his feet, literally trembling with adrenaline and relief. He climbed over the small ridge of debris, out of the bowling alley, and resumed his hobbling traverse. What passes for twilight in Alaska in June was already upon him. He was shaken, and, by now, approaching exhaustion. But he was driven onward, focusing on each step. He wanted desperately to get off the slope, to find another place to rest and regroup. He climbed on, alert and focused. The slip was a wake-up call, a grim reminder that he walked a tightrope, his margin for error practically nonexistent.

As evening turned to nightfall, Colby climbed on in the never-ending daylight. When he reached the end of the long traverse, he was confronted with the most serious obstacle he had faced all day. A headwall nearly 70 feet high blocked his route off the slope to more moderate ground below. He could find no way around it, and even if he had found a way to outflank the big wall he didn't think in his fatigued state that he would be able to down-climb. He would have to rappel here as well. But as he prepared to rope down, he discovered that he had only one ice screw left. With no hardware, roping down past steep difficulties would no longer be possible. Not knowing what he would face below, he knew it was only prudent to retain at least a few screws with which he could negotiate any nasty surprises to come. His margin of safety had been shaved even more.

Placing the screw, Colby rigged the rope. It was long enough to reach the bottom of the headwall, but barely. He descended the static line as he had all through the broken headwall section above, slowly and carefully. Once on the slope below, he started to retrieve the rope by pulling on one end. It moved a few feet, then jammed. Uh oh, Colby thought. He pulled as hard as he could, but the rope wouldn't budge. He yanked on the other end of the rope, hoping to pull it through the other way. That didn't work either. Somehow the rope had become jammed around the ice screw. It was stuck.

Colby knew there was no way, absolutely none, that he could climb back up the headwall to free the static line. If he tried to Jumar up the rope, it might suddenly dislodge and send him cratering to the bottom. Climbing the vertical ice with his crampons and ice axes was clearly out of the question in his damaged condition. He stood at the base of the slope, looking up at the jammed static line, knowing that he would have to abandon the rope. He would have to descend the rest of the way with no rope at all. He could make no more rappels. Any technical difficulties encountered would have to be down-climbed. It was a discouraging thought, and Colby wondered, Is this the fatal incident, will this be the detail that kills me? In his struggle to descend, Colby had walked a fine line, where any mistake might be his last. It was live or die, every day, every step, and the high stakes of his game were wearing him down.

Exhausted and worried, Colby knew that if he tried to go any farther that day he might make another mistake, a deadly one. It was time to get some rest, to regroup. He wondered: How long can I keep going like this? His last rappel had left him on a reasonably level place on a subsidiary ridge coming off the Southeast Ridge. It would make as good a campsite as any. As Colby got out the tent, he knew that this would be a different sort of bivouac. He could get some rest and something hot to drink, but there would be nothing for him to eat. The food was gone. The ice screws were gone. The rope was gone. It seemed to Colby that his difficult task was getting harder, and more problematic. Any real difficulty now might stop him.

He started the stove and put the pot of snow on to melt. Colby felt his stamina waning, but even though he had never been on the route before he knew he was getting closer to the bottom of the ridge. Despite all the rappels he had been forced to make through the headwalls, all the time-consuming routefinding through the maze of crevasses, despite even the terrifying slip in the bowling alley, he had made good time that day. He had descended most of the big Southeast Ridge of Foraker, and—by sheer luck—survived the avalanche danger of the lower section. He was almost off the ridge. As he drank a mug of hot water—it was all he had—he could feel his resolve to succeed strengthen. If he could get off the ridge, if he could get across the Kahiltna without falling in a crevasse, he would be at the end of his seemingly ceaseless ordeal.

It was time to risk lying down. He carefully held his head on the top of his neck as he lowered himself to the insulated pad. His absurd difficulties in lying down or sitting up had become an everyday part of his life. So had climbing with a broken ankle. So far he had found a way to function despite his problems. Just a few more days, maybe less, and he would be safe. As he lay in his sleeping bag, looking up at the yellow interior of the tent, he knew he would get no sleep tonight. That, too, was part of his life now. How long had he been without real sleep? Four days? Five? It hardly mattered. He was going to keep moving as long as he could.

Still on his day-and-night schedule, Colby roused himself at the first bright light of morning. With no oatmeal to make it worth the trouble, Colby dispensed with starting the stove. He quickly packed his gear, hoping to get a long day of travel in before his growing hunger slowed him down. With no rope and no hardware, no food either, his pack was lighter now. He felt as though he were entering a new stage in his loathsome journey.

Scouting for a route, Colby took a direct line down a low-angled slope that he hoped would lead to the glacier itself. He saw no seriously broken sections of crevasses or headwalls which might stop him—a good thing, since he had no gear to circumvent such obstacles. It seemed the best route. Slowly, deliberately, and with an intense concentration, he cramponed down the slope. He tried to keep his broken ankle rigid, but the downsloping pitch to the route inevitably wrenched it with every step. His pain was a familiar companion, if a hated one. He kept going, using his ice ax for balance. He felt lucky to have found a slope free from technical problems, one he could negotiate without real difficulty.

Halfway down the last section, he suddenly heard a loud but muffled *whump!* He froze. With alarm he watched as the whole slope settled visibly, tons of snow consolidating before his eyes. Radiating cracks appeared everywhere around him. The unexpected phenomenon scared Colby to his bones. Colby had seen big slab avalanches. He realized the entire slope was unstable and might slide at any moment. If that happened, he could easily be buried forever under tons of snow and ice debris.

Colby stood there, frozen, absolutely still. Would the whole slope move? He waited, but nothing happened. He reasoned that his traversing across the slope had fractured the crust and set it off, so he dared not continue in that direction. The hard truth came to him: to continue down his chosen line almost certainly would set off an avalanche. He was going to have to climb all the way back up the slope and find a different, and, he hoped, safer way to descend. It was a crushing blow. He had made good progress all morning, but now he was going to lose it all. Colby knew he would burn up a lot of energy climbing back up that slope to where he had started. As he began plodding up the slope—one of the few uphill sections he had negotiated since the accident—he realized that the rising slope forced his foot and ankle into an extremely painful position. Each step sent sharp stabs of pain through his lower leg as he hobbled upward. But there was nothing Colby could do for it. He was not tempted to just continue downhill and take his chances with avalanche. He was amazed the slope didn't go, and he knew it had been a lucky break, a reprieve. He was determined not to make a dumb mistake now. He had made it this far. He was determined not to let his desire to get off the mountain force him into a stupid mistake that would kill him. He would be careful. He would go back up and find a safer way down. Breathing hard with the effort, his face twisted from the pain of moving uphill, he slowly retraced his steps. Man, Colby thought, if it's not one thing, it's another. Would it ever let up?

Once back at the top of the slope, he selected a downhill line that seemed to cross a more evenly sloped and therefore more stable section. As he descended, the mere thought of nearly having triggered an avalanche gnawed at him. Yet he hated spending his precious reserves of strength covering the same ground. If only that hadn't happened, he thought. The unstable slope had cost him almost half a day. Already it was near evening. He could feel his strength beginning to ebb. It was as if his ordeal kept getting more difficult, kept testing him anew. Each time he thought he was nearing the end, he was met with some new, fiendishly unexpected difficulty. He continued climbing downward, forcing himself to concentrate.

Taking the new line down, he descended below the point where the slope had settled. His new route showed no ominous signs of fracture. He had made the right decision. As he worked his way downhill, moving gingerly on his bad ankle, he realized that he had arrived almost at the point where the Kahiltna Glacier meets the Southeast Ridge of Foraker. He threaded his way down a few final snow slopes, and found himself on the relatively flat ice of the big glacier itself.

He was off the mountain, but now wary of a new danger: crevasses. On active glaciers, climbers always move in groups of two or three or more, roped together so that if one climber falls into an unseen crevasse, his partners can stop his fall. But Colby had no choice except to negotiate the big glacier on his own. Covered by a layer of snow, there was no way to be certain exactly where the crevasses lay. Colby could only make an educated guess based on his knowledge of glaciers. Using his practiced eye, he took what appeared to him to be a safe route. In just an hour he reached the point where he and Tom and Ritt had stashed their skis. It was the evening of June 23.

Colby could muster no jubilation. He was beat. Seeing the skis and other gear stashed where he and his friends had left them brought back the harsh reality of the accident and its tragic outcome. His reaction to arriving at the cache was complex, but above all he felt a sense of relief at getting off the ridge, at getting this far. He had made it off the mountain, something that a few days ago had seemed to be an unattainable feat. It had been close, so close. One less ice screw, one slip, one unstable slope, and he, too, would have perished on Foraker. But he was not yet out of danger.

He had, however, reached the last stage of his epic escape. He had only to cross the Kahiltna to base camp. But hidden out there under a covering of snow were a hundred huge crevasses, any one of which could simply swallow him up without a trace. He considered making another bivouac that night at the old camp, and regrouping as best he could without food or sleep. Five days of the hardest physical work he ever had done, and the most anguished prolonged psychological stress he ever had endured, had left him a kind of hollow shell, an automaton forging relentlessly on. But he was not so far gone that he couldn't see that he was nearing the end of his epic ordeal. The prospect of reaching his destination spurred him on. There really was no choice.

Ahead of him lay five miles of relatively flat but heavily crevassed glacier. Crossing the Kahiltna on his own, he knew, was extremely dangerous. The worst thing he could think of was to die now, now that he was within sight of safety. He could actually hear the Cessnas flying in to the Kahiltna strip. A week ago, he had made the journey across the glacier in two or three hours. He figured it would take twice that long now. Despite his fatigue, despite the long day of concentrating on safely finding a way off the ridge, he was sure he could bring his maximum effort to bear. He might not make it, and he knew that, but it wouldn't be for want of trying or for making a dumb mistake.

He looked over the gear that he and Tom and Ritt had left almost a week earlier. It was just skis and the sled the three friends had used to haul their food and fuel across the glacier. But for some reason, maybe just a climber's instinct, Colby didn't want to abandon Ritt's and Tom's beat-up old stuff. But he couldn't carry it all. It was Ritt's stuff that haunted him most. The two of them had spent so much time together, had looked after each other and their stuff on trips and climbs of all sorts. In the end he decided that he would carry his friend Ritt's heavy and hard-to-carry mountaineering skis back. He knew it was a dumb thing to do, but he didn't want to leave them.

He prepared the small plastic sled, which was a cheap one, like the kind you get for kids at the supermarket. Colby attached the sled to his harness with a couple of lengths of water-ski rope that were already affixed to the sled. He would use that to carry all the gear. Taking off his own pack, he tied that in the sled, and tried to attach Ritt's skis in such a way that they were as balanced as possible. It was almost midnight when he stepped into his own skis. He was ready. The cold mental fortitude that had enabled him to endure the hardship of his descent took control of him now. He almost expected something new and cruelly difficult to present itself, and he felt ready for it. He must not let down his guard now, not yet.

Even though his injuries made his skiing style as unconventional as his climbing technique had been, he knew the skis would help keep him out of crevasses by spreading out his weight. With skis on he could cross snow bridges that would have collapsed under the weight of a man walking.

In the pale light of the midnight sun, Colby began his trek back to base camp, a tiny, solitary being in the vast grandeur of the Alaska Range. He moved slowly. The sled proved a heavy and awkward burden. Top-heavy with the skis, it often turned over. Each time, Colby had to stop, go back, wrestle the sled upright, then straighten out the harness lines and resume pulling. He moved on, dragging his injured leg while using his good leg and the ski pole in his good right arm to generate forward momentum. He moved slowly. He could see in the glacier slight indentations, subtle indications of the great yawning chasms beginning to melt out as the Alaskan summer progressed toward its zenith. He hoped that the snow covering the crevasses was still thick enough to bear his weight. He jammed and poked with his ski pole as he went along, hoping to discover weak snow bridges before they collapsed beneath him.

As he made his weary way across the huge glacier, Colby noticed an unusual layer of lowering clouds begin to form over the Kahiltna.

They probably heralded a major shift in the weather, and Colby was glad he had not waited at the cache.

Colby kept a wary eye out for crevasses. But just as he crossed a marginal-looking snow bridge, the clumsy sled tilted and threatened to fall in a crevasse. Colby hurried back to right the sled and get off the bridge of snow before it collapsed under his weight. Colby's anxiety level was rising. Man, this is dangerous, he thought. But not a hundred yards farther, the sled once again turned over and actually began sliding down into a crevasse, threatening to pull Colby in with it. He managed to once again retrieve the sled and wrestle it right side up, but he was panting like a wrestler. Colby was reaching the end of his endurance. He knew he was dangerously tired. The next time the sled almost fell in a crevasse, Colby simply dragged it along on its side until he got back on more stable ground.

He skied on. There were more snow bridges to cross, and each time it seemed the stupid sled turned over and almost fell in. Colby was getting freaked. He thought, I can't let anything happen now. As he approached the base-camp area, he could make out the cluster of tents. By now he had reached a part of the glacier he knew fairly well, and he felt safer. As he skied on, he could see individual tents. He had not seen or heard any airplanes, however, and began to realize that in the time it had taken him to cross the glacier, the weather had changed dramatically.

The clouds he had seen forming earlier had coalesced into a solid black-gray ceiling that hovered over the glacier. Visibility was beginning to drop radically. Colby was puzzled by the ominous clouds dropping down—slowly but seemingly inexorably—all around him. He had never seen anything like it in Alaska. He skied on into the weird weather.

Colby couldn't know it, but Mount Spurr, a volcano near Anchorage, had erupted. The belching volcano had sent a plume of ash downwind toward Denali. What he was seeing was not weather, but the massive ash cloud descending on the Kahiltna. To Colby, the dark clouds were just more bad weather and a vindication of his decision to press on that night.

Under the lowering clouds, Colby moved slowly across the glacier. As he approached the first outlying tents, he thought, If anybody's watching they must think I'm a really bad skier. Colby skied right up the runway, just a hundred feet from the line of tents. He saw a couple of guys, who obviously had recently come off Denali, setting up their tent. They were the first people Colby had seen since the accident. He felt uneasy, and uncertain how or if he should approach them. He felt as though he were a man with a terrible secret. Colby wondered if it showed. He felt shy, and strange. He felt like a dead man back in the land of the living.

Colby was dragging his injured foot behind him as if he were a character in a bad horror movie. It made his progress jerky and inelegant. One side of his head was caked in blood. He was holding his left arm at a strange angle, clutched up like a raven's claw, only because that was most comfortable position for his fractured scapula. He knew that his unkempt appearance would have attracted attention anywhere but here on the Kahiltna. Here in the early hours of the morning his broken exterior could still pass for normal. He skied past the guys setting up their tent. They said nothing to Colby, and he said nothing to them.

"I felt so ragged," Coombs remembered. "I felt like I was on my last legs. I wondered if I would ever be the same. But I didn't care. I really didn't care. I was just so relieved to be in a place where my life wasn't on the line."

Colby skied up the little rise toward Tom's red tent, which had been left standing when they left for Foraker. But the little hill, which had seemed a mere screen for the noise of the airstrip, was, in his present state, a formidable obstacle. Colby was so tired he had to stop and rest three times, huffing and puffing like a marathon runner, to get over the little hill. The threatening black clouds had come down so low that visibility on the glacier was dropping to a few hundred feet. There was absolutely no activity at the usually busy airstrip. The strange weather seemed almost appropriate for the anticlimactic end to Colby's epic journey. It was 5:00 A.M. on June 24, five days after the avalanche. For the first time since the tragedy, Colby could relax.

"I was just so psyched to be finally out of harm's way," Coombs remembered. "At last, I was safe, actually, physically safe—no ice slopes, no headwalls, no rock buttresses, not even any crevasses. I was so relieved to be out of danger."

Colby, utterly exhausted, skied up to the little tent and dropped his poles. He could think only about food and sleep. He had been going for almost twenty-four hours and was completely exhausted. But at the edge of his consciousness emerged a dark thought: he knew that Tom's wife, Lisa, whom Colby had never met, would soon arrive in Alaska for their kayak trip. Colby knew he needed to get word to Tom's family, and Ritt's, about the accident. He thought about going over to Annie Duquette's Weatherhaven and reporting the accident. But Colby didn't know her very well. And it was, after all, five o'clock in the morning. To Colby, it seemed rude to barge in and awaken her. Tomorrow morning will be soon enough for all that, he thought. I've got to get some rest, get something to eat.

He stepped out of his skis and turned his attention to food. Before they had left for Foraker, the three climbers had made a big pot of spaghetti, but they had not consumed it all. Still in the aluminum pot, it was buried in the snow next to the tent. Colby dug up the old spaghetti. He was so hungry he didn't bother to start the stove. He knocked some of the snow off the cold aluminum pot, and sat there under the ominous black ash clouds and ate it cold. He ate hungrily, and fast. To Colby, the congealed spaghetti was delicious, one of the best meals he had ever eaten.

He climbed in the tent and painfully lowered himself into a reclining position, still wearing his left boot. His relief at being safe made it easier for him to finally rest. Still, Colby spent the early morning hours in a state more like coma than sleep. He drifted in and out of consciousness, aware only that he had arrived, that there was to be no more desperate struggle. But now that he had achieved his impossible goal, there lurked at the edge of his consciousness the reality of what had happened on Foraker, and the terrible consequences of that once the word was out. For those last few hours, Colby took sanctuary in that final lull before the emotional storm. For now it was his secret, his alone, and as he had on the slopes of Foraker, he could, for a few more hours, put it out of his mind.

When he roused himself late in the morning on June 24, he did so knowing it was time to get on with the what might be the hardest part of his ordeal. He managed to sit up and get dressed. Using a ski pole

as a walking stick, he hobbled the 100 yards or so to the base-camp
manager's Weatherhaven shelter. He was nervous and scared, filled
with dread. How would Lisa take the terrible news? How would Tom's
parents, and Ritt's parents? As he approached the door—the relatively
substantial nature of Annie Duquette's rigid shelter is perhaps best
summed up by the fact it had the only real door within 50 miles—Colby
could hear voices inside. Annie was famous for being friendly and open,
and it seemed to Colby there were always climbers in there bothering
her and taking advantage of her hospitality, hoping for a hand out from
her well-stocked supplies. Colby knocked.

Annie Duquette opened the door, smiling. Seeing him, the expres-
sion on her face changed. She looked Colby in the eyes, and in that instant she knew that something terrible had happened on Foraker.

"What happened to you?" she said. Colby could make no reply.
Then, in a lower voice, she said, "Where are the other two?"

Colby felt emotion well inside him. He almost burst into tears. He
was so choked up he could hardly speak. Finally, he squeaked out the
words, "They're not coming back."

Annie Duquette led Colby inside and made him sit down on a cot.
She sat down beside him and hugged him. Colby had made it. Annie
got up and walked toward the radio to put out the call.

EPILOGUE

"I could tell by the look in Colby's eyes that something terrible had happened," remembered Annie Duquette. "But after what he had been
through, just the fact that he was standing there was an incredible
thing." After getting Colby Coombs onto a spare cot in her base-camp
hut, she radioed the National Park Service headquarters in Talkeetna
of an "incident on Mount Foraker." She intentionally kept her call low-
key, because it went out over a CB band that could be picked by almost anyone.

Already 1992 had been one of the most deadly climbing seasons
in memory in the Alaska Range. Persistent bad weather and multiple

accidents had resulted in an all-time high of eleven fatalities on McKinley alone. "It had been a bad year," said Annie, "and here was this new tragedy."

Colby began to tell Annie Duquette about the avalanche, and what had happened to Tom and Ritt. He told her little of his five-day ordeal in descending the mountain, only that it had been hard and slow. She became concerned about Coombs' injuries, and realized she had to figure out a way to get him medical attention as soon as possible. There was little that could be done for him there on the Kahiltna Glacier, however, so she just tried to make him as comfortable as possible. "Just stay here," Annie told Colby, "I'll take care of you until we can get you out."

Later that day, Denali National Park mountaineering ranger Jim Phillips, having come down from the 14,000-foot level on McKinley, stopped by Duquette's Weatherhaven.

"Colby looked pretty good considering what he had gone through," remembered Phillips. "He was pretty beat up, and he clearly had fractures to his shoulder and lower leg—both were blue and swollen. He was talking and coherent, but obviously upset because his partners had been killed. He told me about the avalanche, and how he had gotten himself down."

Phillips had extensive first-aid training, but he was no doctor. He performed a medical survey of Coombs, and together they decided that whatever injuries he had sustained had likely stabilized during the five days since the avalanche. While his lower-leg fracture and broken shoulder were obvious, neither Coombs nor Phillips was aware at that point of the dangerous condition of Coombs' fractured and unstable vertebrae. Phillips concurred with Duquette that Coombs should stay with her in the Weatherhaven until he could be evacuated.

"When I think back on it," said Coombs, "I probably should have assumed I had a neck fracture and put on a neck collar or something. But both Jim Phillips and I figured that since I had been able to climb down from Foraker and get back to base camp that I would be all right until I could get to Anchorage."

But there would be no quick trip off the glacier for Colby Coombs. The usual steady stream of Cessnas from Talkeetna had been brought to a screeching halt by the thick, low cloud of volcanic ash that continued to issue from Mount Spurr. The airplanes could not fly as the abrasive ash would damage the engines. The ash had another effect as well: the dark covering of ash on the surface of the glacier airstrip had absorbed sunlight, and made the runway sloppy and soft. Colby was stuck.

"Annie had a cot in her Weatherhaven," Coombs said, "and from that point on she dressed me in her warm clothes, fed me, and asked me to stay put until the airplanes were flying again. Annie didn't want me to go anywhere."

Colby stayed close to the hut, occasionally limping around outside when the weather was nice. One day, he ventured farther. Hobbling back up the hill to his old camp where Tom's tent still stood, Colby sat down in the snow and cried. He cried over the deaths of Tom and Ritt, and the pain that would bring their families, and he cried over his own loss of his friends. It was the first time he had allowed himself to feel emotion. He was at last beginning to confront the terrible reality of what had happened on the mountain.

"Colby and I became close in those days," remembered Duquette. "It's hard to say how two people bond, but it was instant. He was great company, and so strong—he never felt sorry for himself or told me about the hardships he had suffered on his descent from Foraker. I had no clue about the extent of the ordeal he had gone through. He's stoic and strong. I knew that he was hurting bad, but none of us realized how badly he was injured until the hospital called later to tell us. I tried to do what I could, but he's a self-sufficient person and wanted to take care of himself.

"I fed him, made sure he was okay. But mostly I'd sit and listen. I think it was important for Colby to talk about the accident, and about Tom and Ritt. He wasn't worried about the delay. I really think that he would just as soon have stayed there on the glacier. After all that he had been through, it seemed to me that the hardest part for Colby was going to be the aftermath of the accident, and dealing with his own feelings and the grief of the families involved."

"I was fine waiting on the glacier," said Coombs. "I really didn't care that I couldn't fly out. I knew that meeting the families was going to be difficult, and I hadn't really sorted out my own feelings about what had happened to Ritt and Tom. Those few days on the glacier gave me some time to come to terms with what had happened on Foraker."

Although there were other climbers waiting to be flown back to Talkeetna, Colby was Annie's first priority. Finally, on the evening of June 27, three days after Colby had knocked on Duquette's door at base camp, the first Cessna was able to land. Annie Duquette helped Colby hobble down from her Weatherhaven to the landing strip. Carefully, Duquette and the pilot packed Coombs on board the small airplane.

"I had come to respect Colby in those days," remembered Annie Duquette, "and what he had gone through. I think very few people would have been able to do what he did. So a part of me was sad to see him go. But it was so critical that he get medical attention we all felt lucky the flight was able finally to get in."

With Colby on board, the K2 Aviation Cessna tried to take off. The pilot went down to the end of the glacier runway and revved its engine in preparation for takeoff. But the airstrip was still too soft from the volcanic ash. The light airplane could not generate enough speed to take off from the sloppy snow. Duquette and the pilot had to unload Coombs and walk him slowly back up to the base-camp manager's hut. The pilot, too, had to spend the night on the glacier.

There was growing concern that Colby's medical situation was becoming more urgent. By early the next morning, however, the diminishing volcanic fallout had allowed the airstrip to freeze. Before dawn the glacier was sufficiently hard that the wheel-ski-equipped, single-engine airplane could move down the runway fast enough to get airborne. Colby flew out of the mountains.

When Lisa Johnson arrived at the airport in Anchorage on June 25, the day Coombs had knocked on Annie Duquette's door, her husband, Tom Walter, wasn't there to meet her. But she recognized people she had known when Tom had served as coordinator of mountaineering programs at the National Outdoor Leadership School in Lander, Wyoming, waiting at the gate. She also recognized old friends of hers from Anchorage, people she had known when she lived with Tom in Alaska. Lisa knew right away that something had happened.

Tom Walter and Colby Coombs had met through the National Outdoor Leadership School, or NOLS, as the school is known. That connection was to prove extremely helpful to both Coombs and the families of the climbers who were killed in the avalanche. As soon as he was informed of the accident, Clark Lacy of the outdoor school's Alaska office in Palmer had made sure that Lisa was met by friends so that she would hear the sad news of the accident from people she knew.

Clark Lacy was also at the airstrip in Talkeetna on June 28 when the Cessna carrying Coombs from the Kahiltna Glacier touched down. So was Brian Okonek, owner of the Mount McKinley guide service, Alaska Denali Guiding. Colby was driven from the airstrip to Brian's house, where Diane Okonek had prepared what Colby remembered as "an awesome breakfast." After his first shower in weeks, and his first home-cooked meal since arriving in Alaska, there was only one thing Colby needed to do.

"All I wanted to do," remembered Coombs, "was to talk to Brian. And he was about the only person I wanted to talk to at that time. By then I was kind of haunted by the avalanche and what had happened. Brian knows more about climbing in the Alaska Range than anyone. I respected him so much as a mountaineer, I wanted to tell him the whole sequence of events; I wanted to hear his take on what had happened to us. All morning long I talked to Brian, just spilled everything.

"He was probably being protective of my state of mind, but he said, 'I don't know what you could have done differently.' I was really glad he never said, 'Why didn't you guys stay put, or why didn't you put in running protection.' I felt a lot better after talking about the accident with Brian."

Colby next was driven to the hospital in Palmer, where X rays revealed the fractures in his neck, leg, and clavicle. Doctors suspected a potentially serious situation in regard to the neck fracture but lacked the sophisticated equipment to confirm it. Colby was immobilized and immediately taken to Anchorage Humana (now Alaska Regional) where CAT scans revealed the dangerous, unstable fractures in his vertebrae. His doctors told Colby he had been very lucky.

During his ten days in the hospital, Colby received a steady stream of visitors. His mother, who had been in Paris, had immediately rushed to de Gaulle Airport when she learned of the accident. When she asked for a ticket to Anchorage, the airline ticket agent had never heard of the place. But she arrived anyway, providing a tremendous boost to Colby. His desire to see his mother again was one of the driving forces that kept him going during his long ordeal. Colby's sister, from Seattle, also arrived to cheer her little brother's recovery.

"Having that kind of support," remembered Coombs, "was very comforting. But I was hurting for the Kelloggs and the Walters. I could not even imagine how hard the news of the accident must have been for them, because it was impossibly hard for me. I knew the Kelloggs, and wasn't surprised to hear that they were not going to come out to Alaska. They are reserved, but very caring people—that was their way of dealing with the tragic loss of Ritt. The Walters had a different way of dealing with it. They're Californians, very open, and they wanted to come to Alaska, see the mountain, and hear every detail of what had happened."

Tom Walter's wife, Lisa, her mother and both of Tom's parents spent hours in the hospital room with Colby. Sitting there in his room, they asked Colby a thousand questions. They wanted to know as much as they could about what had happened on Mount Foraker. They wanted to know what Tom was wearing, the last thing he said, how he looked. Colby told them everything.

"As far as I was concerned," said Coombs, "I was theirs, I was theirs as long as they wanted me. I shared with them everything I could possibly think of. It was hard for me, really hard at times, but that didn't matter. I was just theirs. I remember that when they would leave for the day, I'd be exhausted and immediately fall into a deep sleep."

Both Lisa and Tom had lived in Anchorage for several years, and so had friends in the area. Lisa had the comfort of those close friendships during a difficult time. Over the objections of his doctors, Colby attended a memorial service for Tom in Anchorage, using a wheelchair to get around.

"My doctor hit the roof," remembered Colby. "He said a car could bump into us on the way to the service and wreck my neck. I went, anyway. It was important, both to me and to the Walters."

Peter Kellogg, Ritt's father, set up a $300,000 endowment fund in his son's memory at Colorado College, where both Ritt and Colby had gone to school. The college used the fund to set up a wilderness expedition program, where students who wish to venture into wilderness areas all over the world can apply for funding. Colby Coombs and another of Ritt's friends, Mike Alkaitis, decide the merit of the applications. More than fifteen expeditions have so far been backed by the Ritt Kellogg Memorial Fund.

Ritt's father also helped the Okoneks and other Talkeetnans build a memorial to fallen climbers in Talkeetna. In the village cemetery adjacent to the airstrip, the local climbing community built a substantial log structure, reflecting the American-frontier architecture of the tiny village. Peter Kellogg helped acquire the plaque set into the rustic shelter, containing the names of all those who have died climbing in the Alaska Range.

The bodies of Ritt Kellogg and Tom Walter were never recovered. Official Denali National Park practice dictates that rangers investigate all fatal accidents in the park. Several days after Colby Coombs arrived at base camp to end his five-day ordeal, mountaineering ranger Jim Phillips and a pilot flew over the site of the accident in the park service's high-altitude Lama helicopter. Described as "nothing but a huge engine with a gas tank," the Lama is one of the few machines that can fly high enough to be useful around Denali.

"During our aerial survey, we flew up and down the East Face and across the Southeast Ridge," remembered Jim Phillips. "We saw an ice ax still stuck in the snow a few hundred feet from the crest of the ridge. That meant that the climbers had gotten very close to the ridge crest before they were avalanched. We saw what looked like some equipment—a bivvy bag, maybe even a parka. It was difficult to be certain exactly what we were looking at, because all the objects were just tiny specks of color on the side of the mountain. But we couldn't for certain identify the location of either body, although we looked for quite some time. Since we couldn't find them, no attempt at recovery was made."

"Jim Phillips videotaped some of the overflight," said Coombs. "I've looked at the tape many times, and it's hard to tell what's what. I did see Tom's bivvy bag billowing in the rotor wash. And there's a tiny patch of red, which could be Ritt's parka, sticking out of the snow just below my first bivvy site. I think that the axes I used to anchor Ritt must have melted out, and he fell farther. I felt bad that we couldn't get Tom and Ritt off the mountain. Just looking at the videotape of the accident site was a sad and spooky experience for me."

For Coombs, the avalanche on Mount Foraker is something that has become part of his life, a episode he continues to live with. But it hasn't changed his love of mountains. In fact, within a year of the accident on Mount Foraker, he returned to climb Mount McKinley for a second time. He has climbed it many times since, as he currently works for Brian Okonek as a climbing guide on Mount McKinley. He also founded the Alaska Mountaineering School in Talkeetna. But the avalanche has changed Coombs forever in some fundamental ways.

"In a certain sense, I've always been all right about it," said Coombs of the accident. "I definitely don't hold anything against the mountains. For me, climbing is a way to simplify life, to learn to rely on oneself. I know there are dangers, and so did Tom and Ritt.

"Following the surgeries, I spent three months in a wheelchair. That gave me a lot of time to think about it. Maybe I tend to suppress what happened, as a matter of self-preservation, but I still think about it all the time. How could you not think about something like that? But I don't dwell on the avalanche, and as time goes by it gets easier to think about it. For a while I thought about the tragedy every day, thinking about what it would be like if Ritt were still alive, because we had spent so much time together, climbing mountains together, doing crazy, fun stuff. That's the sad part, the real grief. Part of me died on Mount Foraker, too, because there is no one left to share those experiences with.

"I often wonder how we could have avoided the accident. In retrospect, we should have done something different, just stayed put, hacked a ledge out of that boilerplate ice slope. Maybe if visibility had been better, we could have seen the snow higher up on the slope, and recognized the danger of wind slab. It's so hard to say. Everything went as planned—we just didn't foresee the avalanche hazard when we should have. Nobody foresaw it. It was just one of those things. And we paid the ultimate price."

Coombs' unprecedented survival against overwhelming odds says something about the human spirit, and the deep reserves of will and strength a human being can call upon in extreme situations. To even jaded veterans of the Alaska Range, his feat of survival stands out among the most fantastic ever recorded in modern mountaineering.

"Colby's experience was extraordinary," Phillips said. "What's truly amazing is that he survived the fall during the avalanche. That's a long way to fall, and to live through that is unbelievable. And then, with his injuries, he was still able to climb down the mountain by himself. It was a superhuman effort. I don't know many people who could pull that off."

"It's really unbelievable," said mountaineering ranger Daryl Miller. "I'm amazed that he was able to down-climb almost the entire mountain with a broken ankle, a broken shoulder, and a broken neck. But most incredible of all is that he survived the objective dangers of the route—the hanging glaciers on the Southeast Ridge make that place extremely dangerous. He was able to cross that whole area without anything falling on him. And then to cross the entire Kahiltna Glacier without falling into a crevasse. It's an amazing story.

"You could say he didn't have a choice—or rather, his choice was to either get back on his own or die out there. But what people don't realize is not just that Coombs had that desire to keep going, and the guts to pull it off, but he was able to draw on a depth of skill that other people don't have. It's not just that he *wanted* desperately to get down alive, he knew *how* to do it. He had the bag of tricks."

Annie Duquette said that Coombs' incredible survival was all the more surprising to her because on the surface he seems almost too nice, too sensitive to live through something like that. "Colby is hard to describe. At heart he's a real marshmallow," she said, "a soft-hearted, really nice guy, totally unassuming. Yet he pulls this off. He has this will that won't quit. It's all will and attitude."

"That humble, unassuming guy," said Daryl Miller, "that's what you perceive when you first meet him and take him at face value. He's really humble, really nice. You never get to really know him until you spend some time on the mountain with him. It's remarkable to see him climbing. He's a gifted mountaineer and ice climber. But the point is, you don't really find out about him until things get hard—until he's at altitude, or climbing in bad weather high on the mountain. That's when other people can't function, yet Coombs is still going strong. What you think is hard, and what he thinks is hard can be pretty far apart. That's when you understand he has not only the drive and the skills, but a reserve of strength way beyond what most people can call upon."

Before she went home to California, Lisa Johnson traveled to Talkeetna, and signed on for a flight into the Kahiltna. When she arrived, it was already July, near the end of the short three-month climbing season. Lisa got a close look at the site of the accident on the flight in. She needed to come, but she didn't spend much time on the glacier. Before she left, she went to Annie Duquette's Weatherhaven.

"Annie," she said, "you've got to do something for me. Before you leave for the year, make sure the last thing you do is say good-bye to Tom for me."

K2

One moment Fischer was
on the slope watching Ed
dig, the next he was
tumbling and rolling,
swept down the mountain
like a candy wrapper in
the breeze. THIS IS IT,
Fischer thought.

Scott Fischer checked the 1,500-foot spools of yellow-and-black 8-mm climbing rope and boxes of high-altitude rations stacked by the front door of his Seattle home. As he sweated the logistic details of his upcoming expedition, his son ambled up. Andy was proud of his dad as only a five-year-old could be. It's not every kid who can claim a famous mountain climber for a father—or has to live with the long absences that vocation entails. Their leave-taking was an emotional one.

"I love you, Andy, and I'm going to miss you," Fischer said, finally, as he leaned down to hug his son.

"You're the greatest, Dad. I love you too."

The child's eyes were damp with tears when he handed over what he and his friends at preschool had made: a string of brightly colored pieces of cloth which resembled the Buddhist prayer flags that fly from temples and homes in the Himalaya. Andy and his classmates had made the ribbons for good luck to safeguard Scott on this, perhaps the most perilous of all his journeys to the world's high mountains.

For this time Scott Fischer was not going to his beloved Nepal, but to Pakistan's Karakoram—and K2. Second in height only to Everest, K2 has earned over the years a reputation as a killer. Even Andy had an inkling that this was a more serious venture than the dozens of other months-long trips on which he had seen his dad leave. As he prepared for his departure to Pakistan, Fischer in some ways was just another climber leaving his loved ones for the mountains, an old story. The difference was that for Fischer, leaving his home like this was a way of life, and had been all his adult years.

In fact, Fischer had been home for only one of Andy's five birthdays. Since the early 1980s, he had spent much of each year climbing in Asia, Alaska, or Africa. Tall and athletic in build, competitive and confident in demeanor, Fischer lived for climbing, and was driven by it. He *liked* climbing, everything about it: the travel, the people, the challenge. Nothing excited the blond thirty-seven-year-old more than the prospect of climbing a major mountain.

But by the summer of 1992, Fischer had two kids, a dog, a house, and a yard that needed tending. And climbing was not only what he did for fun, it was what he did for a living. As the owner of Mountain Madness, a guided-climbing and adventure-travel company, leaving his wife Jean and his kids, Andy and two-year-old Katie Rose, for three months at a stretch was not at all unusual. But it *was* getting harder.

Fischer relished his roles of father and family man. But he understood that to be successful in the mountains, he had to be completely committed to climbing. So he had hardened himself to the frequent good-byes. Standing once again at his front door, he saw real pain on the faces of his children. He could see that his departures were getting harder for Andy and Katie Rose, and that's what made it harder for him. But Fischer knew that if he were not willing to endure the conflicted emotions of leaving his family, he wouldn't bring to K2 the will it takes to get to the top. He knew he had to be cold-blooded.

"I can get myself into a frame of mind where I don't miss anybody," he said, "where I'm totally into the mountain. I get psyched for the climbing. That's the lifestyle, that's my self-image—that's what I do. Unless you're willing to go there, stick around, and do what it takes, you might as well not bother."

The brutal demands of world-class climbing, much like those of international professional sports such as tennis, can tear apart families. At Fischer's level, the pressure constantly is there to climb frequently, to climb difficult objectives, and to be successful. But so far he had balanced the conflicting realities of family and career with the help and encouragement of an understanding partner.

"Scott climbs mountains because he's really good at it," said Fischer's wife Jean Price, an airline pilot. The two of them had met on a mountaineering course, when Jean was a student and Scott the instructor. She knew what she was getting into when she married him. "Like anyone with a great skill—a writer or painter—he's driven to do what he's good at. He loves it.

"The thing people don't realize about Scott is that he is a fantastic father, the best. The patience and love he shows for those kids would blow his image as a hard man. When he climbed within a few hundred feet of Everest, he later told me: 'I could have summitted, I'm sure of it. But I wasn't sure I could have made it back, so I didn't continue.' That's Scott. He loves his climbing, but he loves his kids too. I'd be lying if I said it was easy being married to a guy who does the sorts of things he does. But for me, Scott's such a special person that it's worth it. As a family we've learned to cope with the long trips."

The K2 climb, like all the others, began not with rope and ice tools but with departure gates and baggage checks. This time Fischer simply caught a ride to the airport to downplay the drama of departure. He was much like any other dad leaving on a business trip. And business it was. Each time he left for a climb, Fischer expected to be successful. He almost always was—except on Mount Everest. More than once before 1992 he had been within a few thousand feet of the top of the world's highest mountain, and each time he was turned back by weather or other factors beyond his control.

The near misses on the highest mountain of all more than frustrated him, they incited him to a quiet rage. Fischer was convinced he was as strong and as fast as anybody when it came to high-altitude climbing. That innate self-confidence, which is as much a part of his being as his blue eyes, is taken by some to be arrogance. But it comes naturally, and Fischer is unapologetic. He knows that big-league mountaineering is essentially an extreme testing of one's self-reliance, that a belief in oneself is a prerequisite for success. Getting to the top—and coming back alive—was what Fischer was all about. The bitter defeats on Everest tortured him, ate away at him little by little, and fueled in him a redline desire to climb K2.

On June 8, 1992, Fischer arrived in Islamabad, Pakistan, where he joined up with Ed Viesturs, another American lion of high-altitude climbing. A veterinarian by training, Viesturs had been seduced by climbing while in college. He spent years guiding on Mount Rainier before venturing to the big mountains of Asia. The two guides had been aware of each other for almost a decade, but they had met for the first time the previous year in a hotel lobby in Kathmandu. Viesturs was flush from success on Mount Everest, and Fischer had just returned from guiding clients up 7,000-meter Baruntse.

Over a beer in Kathmandu that day in 1991, the two climbers found they got along surprisingly well. Knowing that together they made an exceptionally strong and experienced team, the two of them discussed climbing an ambitious route. Scott already was holding a hard-to-get permit to climb K2 via its North Ridge the following summer. Both realized a technical route on the most difficult mountain in the world was well suited to their combined abilities. After a couple more beers, the two guides agreed to join efforts on K2 the following year. In a way it was an uneasy alliance. Fischer and Viesturs were direct competitors—rivals, even—in the rarefied world of big-mountain guiding. But they sensed a natural compatibility. That fateful meeting in Kathmandu was the beginning of a partnership that would be sorely tested and finally forged to a hard patina on the high, icy slopes of K2.

But by the time of their June 1992 rendezvous in Pakistan, Fischer and Viesturs both felt fortunate just to be going to K2 at all. Their carefully planned strategy for funding a North Ridge expedition had unraveled early in the year, and it appeared for a while as if there would be, for them, no attempt at all on K2 that year. Climbing the highest mountains on the planet had in the past ten years become an expensive proposition, and one fraught with the sometimes unpredictable whims of bureaucratic paper shufflers. The difficulties came down to obtaining two obvious items: permits and money. Without the permit, there would be no climbing, but without enough money to get to the mountain, the permit would not matter. While climbing in Pakistan was still considerably less expensive than climbing in Nepal, where permit fees can run as high as $60,000, it was still expensive. In 1992, a climbing permit on K2 cost $3,500 (in 1996 it cost ten times that much). Besides the permit itself, there were costs for travel, and for food and equipment and the porters to carry it to the mountain.

When their original plans for a North Ridge climb came to grief for lack of money, Fischer and Viesturs were still committed to climbing, somehow, the world's second highest mountain. They both wanted the experience, and the recognition, for having done the baddest of the big ones. On a mountain climber's resume, nothing beats the summit of K2—"as long," said Fischer, "as you come back down."

That spring, an alternate opportunity to climb K2 suddenly presented itself. Valdimir Balyberdin, the first Russian to climb Everest, wanted to climb K2 as well. He had obtained a permit to climb the mountain—an historic feat in itself as no Russian had ever before been allowed to climb in Pakistan—but the Russian climber lacked the cold cash to finance the trip. The solution for Balyberdin was to indulge in a bit of bald capitalism: he let it be known that for about $6,000, climbers could buy their way onto his permit and his expedition to attempt the Abruzzi Ridge.

To Fischer and Viesturs, joining Balyberdin's so-called Russian-American K2 Expedition offered a pragmatic solution. The fact that they were not acquainted with most of the other climbers on the expedition—nor with their levels of skill and experience—was an acceptable downside. They knew that they could take care of themselves at altitude and that they were similarly driven to reach the top. They would simply climb the world's second highest peak together under the aegis of Balyberdin's cobbled-together expedition. So, along with ten other Americans and one English climber, they accepted the Russian's offer.

"Some of the members of that expedition had Himalayan experience, some did not," said Fischer. "But it was a way to get to the mountain when our own climb didn't work out."

The entire team was supposed to join Fischer and Viesturs in Islamabad on June 8. But when the Americans arrived on schedule, they learned the Russians, who were traveling overland via the Kunjerab

K2, the "savage mountain," from the Godwin Austen Glacier at Concordia (Photo by Scott Fischer)

Pass, were delayed more than a week. Scott Fischer, however, couldn't wait for the Russian and Ukrainian members of the team. Mountain Madness had organized a trek to K2 base camp to coincide with the climbers' long approach march to the mountain. Fischer had an obligation to shepherd his trekking clients to Askole on time, and from there make the long walk up the Baltoro and Godwin Austen glaciers to K2 base camp.

Leaving word for the Russians that they had departed, Fischer and Viesturs traveled with the trekking clients to Skardu, then by truck to Askole and the beginning of the ten-day march up the Baltoro Glacier to K2. Near the end of the long march, the small group arrived at Concordia, the famous confluence of the Baltoro and Godwin Austen glaciers. Here Scott Fischer got his first look at the perfect pyramid of K2, highest in all the range and an awesome sight even to the jaded Himalayan veteran. The unusual name is a vestige of colonial British surveyors, who called the mountain K2 because it was the second peak surveyed in the Karakoram Range. For centuries before that, however, the native peoples of the region called it *Chogori*—the Big Mountain.

A different and perhaps more descriptive moniker, the "savage mountain," was attached to the peak by a 1953 American expedition that had attempted the same route Fischer hoped to climb. The climbers were repulsed by bad weather, and a member of their party died high on the mountain. Since that famous early attempt on K2, the 28,250-foot mountain has continued to live up to its reputation as the most difficult and dangerous of the world's highest peaks. By 1992, at least thirty-three climbers had died there, many of them trying to get *down*.

"One of the neat things about K2," said Fischer, "is that the hard climbing is up high." That fact contributes to the mountain's multifaceted array of lethal dangers. Bad weather, high-altitude health problems, or sheer exhaustion can trap climbers high on the mountain—and kill them before they can get down. K2's reputation as the hardest and hairiest of them all is part of what draws climbers like Fischer to it. Despite dozens of attempts, Fischer and Viesturs' intended route had not been climbed in five years.

On June 21, with the help of a few Balti porters, Scott and his trekking party reached K2 base camp along with Ed Viesturs and Thor Kieser, a Colorado climber who also had joined the Russian's K2 climb. It was still early in the season, and the Americans were well ahead of other expeditions. K2 base camp was virtually deserted except for a team of four Swiss guides and a French woman named Chantal Mauduit. The four guides and the French climber had planned an alpine-style ascent of the dangerous mountain, using no permanent camps or fixed ropes. It seemed to Fischer a bold plan, but he knew K2 had a proven history of changing the best-laid designs.

For Fischer, being once again back among the world's highest mountains was pure pleasure, a genuine epiphany, as if he were coming home. This time the sensation was made all the better because the Karakoram was new turf for Fischer, who knew Nepal's Himalaya well but had never climbed in Pakistan. Fischer loved just being there. Climbing for him was not merely the business of getting to the top, it was also the environment, the people, the setting, and the knowledge that at last the battle was about to be joined. For climbers, K2 is hallowed ground. The mountain has been the scene of uplifting triumph and great tragedy. At the beginning of his own K2 adventure, Fischer knew no better than any other what might happen that summer on the world's toughest mountain. But he embraced the challenge with obvious relish.

"When I first get to a new mountain," Fischer said, "I like to get a sense of place, hang out, take pictures, soak it all in. Taking the time to do that gives you a chance to come to terms with the mountain, and can teach you a lot about the lay of the land. In a way, you make friends with the place. You learn where the best spot for a base camp tent might be, where the avalanches come down, where the good views are, that kind of stuff. It's the only time you have to savor the place before the work begins."

On the surface it seems out of character that Fischer, who exudes the ultimate hard-man exterior, would be hanging out at K2 base camp communing with nature, and he would never use those words. But that's what he was doing, and it confirms what seems obvious, that Fischer clearly is deeply moved by great mountains. He admits he gets buzzed by their mere proximity. At K2 base camp Fischer experienced the genuine peace of a human being doing what he loves, unafraid of the gnarly hardships that lie ahead.

His situation at the 16,000-foot base camp was uncommonly comfortable. Fischer had arranged with porters and a camp staff to keep his trekking clients happy and comfortable, and so he basked in the luxury of having a cook, a dining tent and other expensive amenities. He enjoyed two pleasant days entertaining his clients and basking in the glow of K2. The Russians had still not arrived when Fischer left base camp to hike back with the trekkers to Concordia. From there, the trekking clients were to be left in the care of Fischer's Pakistani employees for their journey back to Askole. As a businessman, he was pleased that the long trek had come off without a hitch, with the exception that Fischer had to intercede when one of his female clients became the object of a Pakistani soldier's over-amorous attentions at Concordia. But back to Askole with the trekkers went the elaborate comforts such as the cook and the chairs and the dining tent. Fischer, a veteran of the mountains, liked to travel and camp in style. The Russians, however, were strictly low budget, and Fischer knew he was in for a summer of plain food and limited luxuries; he was resigned to that, and growing eager to find out what K2 was all about.

Fischer was back in base camp by June 28, and he and Viesturs wasted no time in getting to know the mountain. The pair first learned the route through the icefall, a broken section of the Godwin Austen Glacier where it tumbles steeply downhill in a chaos of blocks and seracs. "The icefall is maybe a quarter or even an eighth the scale of the Khumbu Icefall on Everest," said Fischer, "but it's still a place where you want to pay attention. If you slip, you're not going to fall to China, but it could be a bummer."

Above the icefall the climbers turned their attention to the Abruzzi Ridge itself, their route to the summit. A successful climb would make them the first Americans ever to climb the Abruzzi, which, despite numerous attempts had not been climbed in more than five years. Fischer's mountaineering gear was still with the Russians ("wherever they were"), but he didn't want to wait. So he climbed wearing his trekking shoes with Ed Viesturs' extra pair of crampons affixed none too securely. Ed had brought his full kit of personal mountaineering gear with him, and an envious Scott was trying not to think too seriously about what might happen if his own gear went far astray.

The weather turned marginal, but the way was not technical. Into the teeth of a gusty wind, Fischer and Viesturs kicked steps up steep snow and clambered up ice-covered rock. Roped together, they ascended 35-to-40-degree snow slopes interspersed with short rock gullies and sections of ice, toward the site of Camp I at 20,000 feet on the Abruzzi. "It was basically one step at a time," remembered Fischer. "No big deal, but pretty cool, though. It *was* K2."

On these lower slopes, the climbers dressed lightly in pile jump suits and Gore-Tex bibs. Their efforts in the thin air began to gradually acclimate them to the lack of oxygen at that altitude, making it possible for them to work in the rarefied atmosphere. Fischer knew acclimatization would prove crucial to their success, and welcomed the opportunity to begin acclimating early.

As he joined in putting up the route to Camp I, Fischer reveled in the climbing. He felt at home on the big mountain; he was impressed but not intimidated by its scale. Like a golfer at the Masters, or a tennis player in the finals at Wimbledon, he was comfortable at that level of challenge. High-altitude climbing was what he was good at. From childhood, Fischer had been drawn to mountains, first climbing in the Rockies as a teenager, then moving on to more remote mountains in Alaska. Now, with the skill and judgment of a lifetime of climbing, he picked his route up the steep snow and rock on the flank of K2. The neighboring peaks of the Karakoram, Chogolisa and Broad Peak, began to show themselves as he climbed higher. The view was magnificent, a remote, unparalleled universe of ice and rock. This is what he had come for. Still more than 7,000 feet from his goal, Fischer could feel the strength of the commitment he had made to himself to reach the top of the awesome peak, still so high above him that a roaring jet stream blew streamers of snow into a clear blue sky.

By June 23, Fischer and Viesturs had climbed to the site of Camp I, the first of four high camps that were to be established on the mountain. Thor Kieser and the Swiss guides, who had been climbing while Scott had escorted the trekkers back to Concordia, had put in most of the route to Camp I. Above the first camp, Fischer and Viesturs climbed on to new ground as they worked their way up toward the location for the second high camp.

As they pushed the route higher, both climbers felt the spooky, foreboding quality that pervades K2—the almost palpable infamy of this mountain on which so many have died. No other peak in the world is given as much frank respect by even the world's most jaded climbers. Not far from base camp is the funky but touching Gilkey Memorial, an inscribed tin plate set in a rock cairn constructed in 1953 by the American teammates of Art Gilkey, who died during that famous attempt to climb K2. Since then, as more climbers have died on the mountain, more plates and metal plaques with new names have been added to the memorial. The thirty-three names scratched into those still shiny pieces of metal were a grim and irrefutable reminder of the high cost K2 can exact: all those human lives lost for the sake of trying to climb the mountain—or trying to get down.

t 21,000 feet, Fischer realized he had pushed the altitude limits of his trekking gear as far as he dared. He and Viesturs started down. As they descended through the icefall and down to base camp, they were taken aback by what they saw: not just one but *three* expeditions sprawled out along the Godwin Austen Glacier, and more than 190 porters. All the high-altitude climbing gear, food, and other supplies had been carried up the Baltoro Glacier from Askole on the backs of the Balti porters. The Russians had arrived at last. With great relief, Fischer saw his climbing gear had come along as well. There on the glacier, Scott met the leader of his expedition for the first time.

Vladimir Balyberdin was a bear of man, tall and robust. At forty-one, he was the oldest member of the Russian-American K2 Expedition. The members of his "pickup" climbing team included four Russians and Ukrainians, one English climber, and twelve Americans. The expedition's Russian climbers were the first Russians ever to attempt a route on K2—or any other route in Pakistan for that matter. The changing world order had made it possible for Balyberdin to attempt the second highest mountain on the planet. He had already climbed the first- and third-highest.

"Vladimir was a pretty sharp guy," said Fischer. "You have to hand it to him for putting that thing together, for figuring out a way to climb K2. He's an experienced, incredibly talented climber. Teamwork may not be his thing, but he was totally driven to reach the top."

At base camp, in addition to the Russian-American expedition and the small Swiss expedition, there was also the newly arrived International K2 Expedition. Members of this large and well-funded group included climbers from New Zealand, Mexico, and Sweden.

As Scott looked over the burgeoning population on the glacier, the novel factor for him was that he wasn't responsible for anything or anybody. For Fischer, the natural-born guide, teacher, and leader, it was a completely new experience.

"I had never met any of these people, even those in our own group," Fischer remembered, "and really I had just met Ed a couple of times

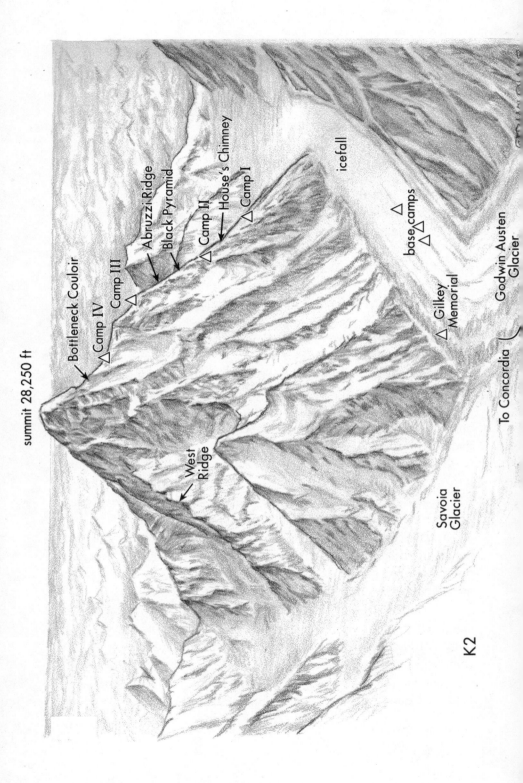

summit 28,250 ft

Bottleneck Couloir

Camp IV

Camp III

Abruzzi Ridge

Black Pyramid

Camp II

House's Chimney

Camp I

icefall

base camps

Gilkey Memorial

Godwin Austen Glacier

Savoia Glacier

West Ridge

To Concordia

K2

before this climb. Usually, I'm in some kind of leadership role and climbing with people I know pretty well. This was markedly different and a little bit bizarre. I didn't know these people. Some of them had no Himalayan experience at all. One guy left after two days at base camp. That's cool, you understand, it's just . . . different."

There were other differences in style. To Scott, the Russians—who were not well-financed—seemed to bargain too hard with the Balti porters.

"They would haggle over a quarter a day for the porters," remembered Fischer, "I suppose because they didn't have any extra money. But it led to bad feelings. At one point we heard all this noise and saw that an actual rumble with rocks and sticks had broken out between some of the Russians and the porters. It was very bizarre. My own style is to be buds—I've made lifelong friends with the Sherpas I've worked with. It's important for me to be fair with the locals. This was a whole different scene, so I stayed out of it."

Fischer set up his own tent somewhat away from the madding crowd. Being from Seattle and having a serious coffee jones, he had brought along almost 50 pounds of coffee. Inevitably, before he even realized it, the Baltoro Cafe was born.

"It was kind of fun," said Fischer. "It started out just being Ed and me, then all the cool people around K2 started coming around for coffee, next we knew there were people from base camps all around the Baltoro. Once at eight o'clock we heard some guy, this total stranger, wander up and say, 'Hey, what time does the cafe open?'"

Despite the fact that Scott knew no one but Ed from his own expedition, there were familiar faces all around him as the climbing season got under way on K2. New Zealand climbers Rob Hall and Gary Ball were both part of the International Expedition. "The Hall and Ball Show" had been on Everest with Scott on two previous expeditions, and the three were friends from climbs they had done together in the Russian Pamirs years earlier. Like Fischer, the New Zealanders had also been unsuccessful in several attempts on Everest. But, just weeks before, Hall had finally reached the summit of Mount Everest.

Ricardo Torres, a Mexican climber and leader of the International K2 Expedition, also had been on Everest with Scott. He had become the first Mexican to climb the world's highest mountain, a feat for which Torres had been named man of the year in Mexico. When they met at K2, Scott could tell that Torres still seemed to harbor an old grudge against him. It was Torres' compatriot, Adrian Benitez, an affable and gentle person, who became popular with members of the other expeditions.

For Fischer, there was a dark side to the unexpected rendezvous with comrades from his previous climbs on Mount Everest. For all of Fischer's success in the mountains, Everest haunted him. Not once, but twice, he had climbed within a few hundred feet of its summit. At K2 he found himself surrounded by some of the people who had been with him on those climbs, and their presence brought back the unpleasant memories with unexpected impact.

In 1987 Fischer had organized an expedition to climb the technically difficult North Face of Everest from China. Recalling his first leadership role on a big, complicated climb, Fischer self-deprecatingly called his leadership dynamic a "nightmare." Nonetheless, the small, strong team he had put together got within a few thousand feet of the top. Fischer himself had put in Camp IV, but was unable to return to the high camp to make a summit bid. "Black Tuesday" in October 1987 is famous for the stock market crash in the United States, but in the Himalaya it was famous for a freak early-season storm that dumped up to eight feet of snow along the length of the range. Fischer and his team were stopped cold, but other expeditions fared much worse as climbers died that day all over the Himalaya.

"With what I know now," said a rueful Fischer, "I would have stayed at the high camp and just gone for the summit from there, instead of descending. It taught me a lot. But we gave it a good try, and if it hadn't been for the big storm we would have made it."

Two years later, Fischer was named climbing leader for another Everest expedition, which attempted Everest by the South Col route. Fischer not only put in the highest camp, Camp IV, but he remained in residence at the South Col for almost six days as he made repeated summit attempts. It was a dangerous, extended stay in the "death zone," the region above 26,000 feet in which the body deteriorates rapidly from lack of oxygen. But not wanting to give up, Fischer remained, waiting

Scott Fischer at Everest Base Camp, April 1996 (Photo by Jane Bromet)

for a break in the weather. It never came. He made several attempts anyway, and each time he was rebuffed by bad weather or had to retreat to his high camp with partners who were unable to go on. On Fischer's last try for the top, he came upon a body lying in the snow and realized he had found the remains of a Yugoslav climber who had apparently succumbed after a summit attempt and was unaccounted for. Fischer's grisly find, which he later reported to the dead climber's comrades, at least put an end to the mystery. In the end, Fischer finally gave up and descended after what may have been a record stay at the South Col.

A troubling incident on that climb had added insult to Fischer's disappointment. As climbing leader, Fischer had put together the summit teams. Mexican climber Ricardo Torres had not been selected for the first try, and stated publicly that he considered the decision to be a racist one. Fischer vehemently denied that, and still does. Ironically, the second summit team—of which Torres was a member—found good weather and successfully climbed to the summit. Later, when Fischer went to congratulate Torres at base camp, Torres refused to shake Scott's hand. Three years later on K2, Fischer could tell that bad feelings remained.

But Fischer's bad luck on Everest wasn't through yet. In 1991, Fischer was back in the Khumbu region of Nepal as a member of the American Everest-Lhotse Expedition, the first expedition ever to attempt to summit two 8,000-meter peaks in one try. Fischer agreed to climb Lhotse, a near neighbor of Everest, with the understanding that he would be given an opportunity to climb Everest afterward.

"We totally smoked Lhotse," remembered Fischer, who became the first American to climb that peak, the world's fourth highest. He was pleased with the quick ascent of the mountain, but as he was descending from its summit, he saw with disbelief that the expedition's camps high on Everest were systematically being dismantled. Good weather had allowed all the expedition's Everest climbers to summit. With the peak bagged, expedition leaders decided it was time to go home. When Fischer descended Lhotse and finally reached base camp, the expedition members all gathered to welcome him back safely, presenting him with a cake festooned with decorations commemorating the first American ascent of Lhotse. Fischer was not mollified, however, and responded with an obscene question about the Mount Everest camps. He had hated being denied another shot at the mountain.

For Fischer, who had already made dozens of difficult climbs—including a first ascent on Mont Blanc, the Breech Icicle on Mount Kenya, and the highest summits in North America, South America, Europe, and Africa—failing to reach the summit on the highest of all peaks was bitter medicine. Fischer knew the summit of Everest was an accepted, if bogus, benchmark for his chosen field, and to miss not once but twice rankled the self-confident climber deeply. To be turned back due to external forces outside his control irritated him all the more. He told no one, but his experience on Everest drove him especially hard to reach the summit of K2. Except for Everest, he had not failed often in his chosen objectives. He was not going to let it happen again.

At the level at which Fischer climbed, success was seldom assured, and a comparison of efforts is not just odious but rarely meaningful. A lucky spell of fine weather and good climbing conditions can make it possible for a marginal attempt to succeed while a stronger, bolder effort might be turned back by a dozen factors. New Zealand climber Gary Ball was back on K2 for his third try on the Abruzzi Ridge. He had yet to reach the summit of the savage mountain. But Scott respected both him and Rob Hall. As the climbing began in earnest, Fischer felt that he and Ed and the New Zealand climbers would end up near the summit together before the season was finished.

That June of 1992, it was already clear to the other expedition members that Fischer and Viesturs were climbing more strongly than anyone at base camp.

"We were almost two weeks ahead of everyone else in acclimatization," remembered Fischer, "and had already been to 21,000 feet. It matters. So at that point it's us, we're the ones putting up the rope. And something else was happening. As Ed and I climbed higher, we became closer and more confident of each other."

During the interlude at base camp, the weather had turned bad. The climbers had yet to see a protracted period of good weather. Conditions in the Karakoram that year seemed permanently variable and unstable. But despite marginal conditions, back up the mountain they went. After a brief rest at Camp I on the way up, Fischer and Viesturs tackled the difficulties above.

More than 1,500 feet above Camp I, the pair encountered House's Chimney, a long, steep, technically difficult gully. It bears the name of William House, who was part of an American team's attempt to climb the peak for the first time in 1938. A famous landmark, the chimney was draped with tattered ropes from previous attempts on the summit. Viesturs led up through the ice-coated rock gully, and the pair had surmounted the first famous bit of hard climbing on the Abruzzi.

Fischer and Viesturs carved out a place for Camp II above the top of House's Chimney, at approximately 22,000 feet. Many parties on K2 establish Camp II below the chimney. Fischer had been told by the New Zealand climbers that higher was better. Gary Ball and Rob Hall had been on the mountain for two years running, and had failed two years running. They suggested to Scott that putting in Camp II below the chimney was faulty strategy. It was too low, they advised, to allow climbers to move high enough on the mountain to provide a viable shot at the summit. Fischer had heeded their advice.

The small Swiss expedition that had planned an alpine-style ascent of the Abruzzi Ridge had put their Camp II below the chimney. As the members of the small team climbed higher, they realized that an alpine-style approach was not going to work. They decided to abandon their attempt above Camp II because of deep snow on a feature known as the Black Pyramid. None of the climbers on K2 that year were surprised at the decision. Abandoning the climb is not a rare event on K2, particularly by an expedition with so few members. Any team would have to be unusually strong and fast to attempt the mountain without fixed camps. One of the expedition's members, however, the French woman, wasn't ready to quit. Chantal Mauduit decided to stay. Few women have climbed K2, and she wanted the summit bad enough to remain.

"She went for it," said Fischer. "I had to give her credit for that." Mauduit began climbing with members of the Russian-American team.

Once above House's Chimney, with Camp II securely established, Scott and Ed pushed the route higher. As they climbed, Fischer and Viesturs had fixed 8-mm rope from a spot near base camp, through Camp I, and on up to the second high camp. The fixed ropes were a practical as well as a safety consideration. In the event of storm, climbers could descend the fixed ropes even in fierce winds or low visibility. And as successive camps were established higher on the mountain, the ropes would serve as a kind of lifeline for the climbers carrying loads up and down the steep Abruzzi Ridge.

"What a lot of people don't realize," said Fischer, "is that basically the mountain only has to be climbed once. We're fixing ropes— so nobody has to actually climb it again, because now you're just juggin' ropes. Once there's a rope there, even House's Chimney isn't hard, because you're using a Jumar, so you've always got a handhold. That's worth a lot up that high. And it's not just our expedition that uses the ropes, but everybody on the mountain who gets that high will use the ropes. That's why some climbers who otherwise might not be able to get up an 8,000-meter peak can improve their chances by being on K2 with the right people."

From Camp II, Scott and Ed had stupendous views of Masherbrum and Chogolisa. The latter, Fischer observed, turned out to be a reliable indicator of weather. Most moisture in the Karakoram comes from the Bay of Bengal, to the south of Pakistan. If Chogolisa, just south of K2, is under weather or obscured by clouds, that indicates bad weather approaching K2 from the bay. If Chogolisa is clear, that shows the winds are coming from the opposite direction, from China, and that indicates cold, dry air, and clear—if windy—weather.

Above Camp II, Scott and Ed climbed up toward the Black Pyramid at 23,000 feet. The landmark feature was guarded by deep snow and offered exhilarating rock climbing at high altitude. The climbing was in fact becoming more technical the higher the climbers went. At the base of the Black Pyramid the climbers found old garbage and other artifacts from previous expeditions.

Part of the legend of K2 lies in its unrivaled history of epics. All over the mountain are places or artifacts marking the spot of some incredible tale. Between base camp and the start of the Abruzzi Ridge, the New Zealand climbers stumbled upon a grisly discovery: the skeletal remains of a human foot, still encased in a sock and boot. The climbers deduced it had belonged to the American playboy and aspiring climber, Dudley Wolfe. Wolfe was lost high on the mountain during a 1939 attempt, along with three Sherpas who had climbed back up the mountain in a vain attempt to rescue him. They all disappeared and were never seen nor heard from again. The foot found by the Kiwis had to be Wolfe's because none of the Sherpas had such big feet and none of the other climbers who have disappeared on K2 since wore hobnailed boots.

"It was still Ed and Thor and me doing the leading and fixing of ropes," said Fischer. "But by now, a lot of people are moving up and down the mountain, moving supplies. Weather seemed to follow a pattern: three days of decent weather, then five days of crummy weather. We never saw the ten days of good weather from those big high-pressure systems you get in Nepal. On K2 it was more changeable and unsettled."

Above the Black Pyramid, a change in the weather put a stop to the expedition's progress. With the establishment of Camp III delayed by heavy snow and fog, Fischer and Viesturs returned to base camp to rest in the comparative low altitude—only 16,000 feet. They resolved never to stay too long at base camp, just a few days, in order to preserve their level of acclimatization. But it was on their way back up the mountain to put in the third camp, on July 12, when the unexpected happened. For Fischer, it was to change everything.

The veteran Seattle guides climbed above base to the icefall, as they had a half-dozen times before. A particularly dangerous part of the route, the icefall resembled a bowl full of ice cubes, except the ice cubes were the size of automobiles. Located at the foot of the Abruzzi Ridge, the icefall collected all the ice moving down the glacier. Blocks of blue-green glacial ice balanced precariously on one another, or lay in a confused jumble where they had fallen. So unstable was the icefall that the route through it changed from day to day. The chaos of icy debris dwarfed Fischer as he carefully picked his way past towering seracs and crevasses up to a hundred feet deep. Fischer used footholds and handholds as he moved along in the surreal landscape, climbing cautiously but quickly.

"I was moving along at a good clip, watching for places to put my feet. That's a good place to jump, that's a good place to jump and—." Suddenly, as he prepared to make an awkward step, an ice block shifted under his foot, sending him off balance and into a gaping, 40-foot-deep crevasse. In the treacherous, moving terrain of the icefall, he could not regain his footing. Down he hurtled toward the dark-blue grotto of the crevasse.

"Falling!" he yelled to Ed as he plunged downward. Roped to his partner—he was glad he and Viesturs were roped up, and gladder still the rope was tight—Fischer fell into the crevasse. He did not fall far, perhaps ten feet. But as he instinctively put his arm out to break the fall, the force of the impact tore his shoulder from its socket. A burst of excruciating pain exploded from the ravaged shoulder. Fischer fought for consciousness. The incapacitating pain, sharp, deep and burning, had Fischer writhing at the end of the rope, dangling above the void.

"Scott! Scott! What happened? Are you all right?" Viesturs, who could no longer see Fischer, held tightly to the rope, wanting to ensure that his companion would fall no further into the crevasse.

"I've trashed my shoulder, Ed," Scott yelled back. "I think I can stay put, but I can't get out."

Unable to extricate himself from the jaws of the crevasse, Fischer escaped only when Viesturs came to literally haul him out by rope and harness. With Fischer's shoulder horribly bulging and deformed, the two guides rigged a makeshift splint from an Ensolite sleeping pad. Fischer, unable to carry it, left his pack in the icefall before he and Ed started off toward base camp. After two or three hours of careful and, for Fischer, painful down-climbing, he faced the reality that he could go no farther.

"I just can't do it, Ed. You'll have to go get help. I'll wait here." He sat down to wait on the moraine, an outcropping of dirt and rock bordering the glacier, while his partner—who feared Fischer might pass out from the pain—hurried to get help from base camp. Those hours of solitude on the moraine were an agony of physical and mental anguish for Fischer. Even then, the knowledge of impending failure was worse for the man than his physical torment. Fischer realized that his climb might be over. As he waited alone on the moraine for help, he refused to admit he would be turned away on K2. He kept saying to himself, *It's not over. I'm still going. I think I'm tough enough to keep going.*

Before darkness fell, Yuri Stefanski, the expedition physician, arrived with a half-dozen or so members of the team. The Russian doctor, after a brief examination, gave Fischer an injectable painkiller. Standing directly over him, the doctor then grabbed the wrist of Scott's injured arm and gave a mighty heave. Some of the Americans were aghast that the physician would reef on Fischer with such a vengeance without

127

making a closer examination first. But with an audible crack and another explosion of pain, Fischer felt his arm pop back into its socket.

"Is it in, is it in?" Fischer asked.

"Yes, it's in. But for you," the doctor pronounced in thickly accented English, "the climb is over. Go home."

Delirious with pain and Demerol, Fischer looked up at the others. Hurting and disappointed, he half sat up and said to those standing around him, "Five days. Give me five days at base and I'll be climbing again."

Almost two weeks later, however, it appeared to everyone that the Russian physician had been correct. Crippled and in pain, Fischer lived the life of a recluse at base camp. He watched in despair as the mountain was climbed without him. By now the other climbers were well acclimated. Activity reached a crescendo as loads were carried higher and new camps established. Fischer retreated often to the sanctuary of his own tent to deal with his disappointment.

"It's hard to be up when you're hurting and not having fun," said Fischer. "So instead of being a downer on other people, I was antisocial. People thought I was bumming out, but I was just keeping to myself. I didn't want to inflict my own problems on the others, so it was just my way of dealing with it."

Reading was one way he could keep from dwelling on his bad luck. In the confines of his tent, Fischer spent endless hours that way. He read everything he could find in base camp, sometimes two books a day. He tried to take some pleasure in running the Baltoro Cafe, but the fun had gone out of it.

He couldn't believe the others were about to climb the mountain without him. When word came by radio that Camp III had finally been established, he could take no joy in the news. It was the first camp not established with Fischer's involvement, and the news depressed him. He kept to himself. Except for brief mealtime excursions to the mess tent, where he tried to muster a friendly attitude, Fischer spent most of the day in his own tent.

Even the sight of the strikingly beautiful Broad Peak just across the valley—its long, abrupt main ridge of unimagined scale topped by three graceful summits draped in a mantle of ice and streamers of cloud—failed to lift his spirits. He found that nothing could, not with climbers leaving base camp daily with loads for the higher camps. Soon, Scott knew, those same climbers, even his partner Ed, would be pushing for the summit—without him.

And so Fischer languished in his tent at base camp, his kid's multicolored prayer flags—strung on the guy lines—flapping noisily in the dusty Baltoro wind. Lying in his sleeping bag, staring up at the little checked pattern made by the ripstop nylon fabric of his yellow and blue base-camp tent, it was impossible not to think about his diminished chances of climbing K2, not to fear yet another bitter defeat like those on Everest. But he was not ready to give up. *Oh, man, I gotta do this thing, whatever happens, I have to do it, do every step, do whatever it takes.* It became a mantra for him during those bleak days at base camp. *Whatever it takes.*

After thirteen days at base camp, his shoulder was still so painful that useful motion was practically impossible. But Fischer made a decision. What sense is there in waiting longer? he reasoned. What's the difference between thirteen days and twenty-one days? To him, there was no magic number. He had made a commitment to himself to climb K2, and he wasn't ready to give up. Maybe I should just try, he thought. Maybe he could climb with his arm strapped to his side. Maybe he could use the fixed ropes to reach the higher camps, and perhaps by then he would be strong enough to climb on his own. *Am I tough enough to take on K2 in this state?* Secretly, he knew that he was. *It's up to me.*

Most people in his situation probably would have bagged it and gone home. But Fischer possessed an almost irrational drive to get to the top of the mountains he climbed, which is why he was successful. He decided to try. Emerging from his tent, he made plans to accompany other expedition members carrying loads up to the higher camps early the next day. But when dawn broke in a fury of wind and snow, the worst weather of the climb so far, none of the others wanted to climb higher. No one would leave base camp in those conditions.

Fischer was firm in his decision, however, so into the fog and blowing snow he went, a solitary figure clad in baby-blue Gore-Tex, barely visible in the storm, climbing slowly upward. He climbed past the spot where he fell into the crevasse, past the start of the fixed ropes. The climbing was exhausting and painful; he was out of shape, and his extended stay at base camp had reduced his level of acclimatization.

Breathing thin air is a fact of life on K2, as if one were on a strange planet whose very atmosphere is different. The only way to get physically accustomed to the lack of oxygen is to climb high, then descend for a rest, and climb high again. Gradually the body adjusts. But Fischer had been stuck at the 16,000-foot base camp for weeks. He was no longer accustomed to the thinner air at 20,000 feet. Having only one usable arm with which to climb added to the difficulties, and to his fatigue. He struggled alone to Camp I, where he collapsed into the tent. The 4,000-foot climb had taken all day. By the time he crawled inside his sleeping bag, it was almost dark.

He awoke to more bad weather, more dreary storm clouds. No one else on the mountain was moving, but for Scott there was no alternative. He had made up his mind. After laboriously dressing in his pile suit and windproof outer layer, he put on boots and crampons, and began to climb slowly upward. Sucking air in the now unaccustomed high altitude, he struggled up the fixed ropes, taking a step, then a breath, sliding the Jumar up the rope, then taking another step. His damaged arm was strapped to his side with a Rube Goldberg apparatus of climbing slings and duct tape. Far below, at base camp, Ed Viesturs watched through binoculars as the tiny form climbed slowly, so slowly, through cloud and wind. Weeks ago, full of vigor and optimism, Fischer had established Camp II at 22,000 feet. Now he climbed to it without joy, exhausted and alone.

For two solitary nights he waited at Camp II, huddled in the small tent high above the Baltoro as the winds of the Karakoram whipped around the tiny dug-in tent platform. He waited for his body to recover from the effort of the past two days so that he could muster the strength for the climb to Camp III, which he had never seen. He lay in his sleeping bag, suffering both intense pain and mental anguish, his shoulder swollen and misshapen and racked by muscle spasms. Over the radio came calls from base camp—expedition members checked in by radio twice a day, morning and evening. The voices of his companions crackled through over the static, the voices of reality: "Come on, Scott, what are you doing up there *alone?* You're hurt. It's the worst weather of the trip. This is crazy. Come down." Scott replied, "It's still snowing, but I'm going to stay for at least another day. Out."

For Fischer, it was no more useless waiting at Camp II than it would have been at base camp. And besides, he had a specific purpose. He was trying to find something out: whether he was going up—or going home. But even then, he knew the answer. Slowly, the hard reality he faced alone on K2 led to a soul-wrenching realization. It was beginning to dawn even on Fischer that although he had given his all, he couldn't climb the hardest mountain in the world with only one working arm. By the third day at Camp II, he simply faced the fact that he hurt too much, that he could not do it. That day, instead of climbing to Camp III, he packed all his personal gear into his rucksack for what he knew was the last time. He started down the fixed ropes to base camp. Fischer had given up.

The black taste of his failure and bad luck was exacerbated on his desultory descent by his meeting up with Vladimir and Gennadi Kopieka, climbing strongly, on their way up—they hoped—to the summit of K2. As Fischer continued down the fixed ropes after that chance encounter, he had to fight back tears of disappointment. He hated quitting.

Once down at base, Fischer began making plans to leave the expedition. Bad weather higher up forced most of the climbers down to base as well. Only Vladimir and Gennadi remained at the higher camps. Ed and Scott were talking quietly at base camp on August 1 when the incredible news came down from Camp IV: Balyberdin had climbed the mountain.

It had taken Vladimir and Gennadi two days and three nights to get from Camp III to Camp IV. The pair had spent eighteen hours climbing to the summit from the high camp. Gennadi had managed to get back to Camp IV that night, but Balyberdin bivouacked below the summit. Incredibly, the Russian climber suffered no lasting ill effects from his night out. The Russian and the Ukrainian had climbed K2 without supplementary oxygen, and they had survived.

"You've got to respect Valdimir for doing that," said Fischer, "but a lot of us felt he went way out on a limb. That's Vladimir. He had put the whole thing together and he had gotten to the top. He was the hero."

"The Russian style was very different from ours," commented Viesturs. "They pushed the limits beyond what most Americans consider safe. But they made it, so what can you say?"

The climbers at base camp were glad to hear of Vladimir's success. But reactions were decidedly mixed. Climbing at that level is an intense, individual thing, so much so that sometimes it is not easy for climbers to take pleasure in another's success. Envy is a natural enough human reaction, but it applies even more so to the big egos and nonconformist natures of big-time mountaineers. Climbing is an essentially solitary, even selfish pursuit—the rewards are entirely personal. There is no roar of the crowd—that comes later. Even in the paramilitary climbing expeditions of the 1950s and 1960s, when it was widely assumed that if one climber reached the summit, the effort was successful, there were still bad feelings and disappointed individuals who lost out on their own chances for glory. And among the members of this cobbled-together K2 team there were strong climbers who still harbored personal ambitions for the summit, ambitions that were not assuaged by the Russians' accomplishment. Fischer was one of them, Viesturs another.

The news of the Russian's success galvanized Fischer; his cathartic personal defeat at Camp II, his giving up, his plans to leave for home, all were forgotten. Summit fever set in: if Vladimir can do it, he thought, I can do it, bad arm or no.

"Man, was I ready to go," remembered Fischer. An important factor was that he had come to climb K2 with Ed, and he was going to follow up on that if it were humanly possible. He rationalized that the past few days had seen dramatic improvement to his shoulder injury. He secretly worried about his fitness level, particularly after the difficult time he had had a few days earlier in getting to Camp II. But his persistence was winning. That trip up the mountain had probably restored some of his fitness. When he told his partner he was ready to climb, Viesturs laughed. He was skeptical of Fischer's sudden recovery, but he knew the power that drove him. Ed looked at his revived ropemate and said, "All right, Scott. Let's go."

The two men gathered their gear and started breaking trail up toward the icefall and Camp I. Fischer suddenly felt stronger. He knew his perceived strength was mostly mental, but he didn't care. He felt rejuvenated, his drive had returned. His wrecked shoulder, which had given him so much discomfort only a few days before, hampered him much less now as he climbed with Viesturs. Having been more or less immobilized for nearly three weeks, the shoulder was improved to the point where at least a partial range of motion was restored. It still hurt, but Fischer could stand the pain. He was able to manage the fixed ropes with greater ease as he climbed up toward Camp I. The Americans climbed swiftly, up through swirling clouds, reaching Camp II in time to congratulate the fast-descending Balyberdin, who looked haggard and exhausted following his twenty-eight-hour summit ordeal.

"Vladimir wasn't quite as chipper as he had been the last time I saw him," remembered Fischer. "But he had earned the grudging respect of everyone on the mountain. His summit day had been a near thing, but he had pulled it off."

The two Seattle mountain guides climbed toward Camp III. As Fischer moved higher, he was "sucking air." The long hiatus at base camp had robbed him of his hard-won acclimatization, and his one brief foray up the mountain had not restored it. He had to work hard to keep up with Viesturs, who had maintained his fitness level without a break and was moving faster than anyone else on the mountain. Fischer climbed, too, with increasing pain in his shoulder. He tried to ignore the fatigue and discomfort, and focused on the repetitive task of ascending the fixed ropes, knowing he was getting closer to the summit of K2.

Fischer and Viesturs had brought new tents to Camp III, at about 24,000 feet. From there, the two men faced a climb without the psychological safety factor of fixed ropes to the site of Camp IV, at 26,000 feet. From that final high camp, they would be in a reasonable position to push for the summit at 28,250 feet. At both the higher camps, they were deep within the "death zone," exposed to the insidious effects of altitude and the lethal dangers of the sudden, powerful storms characteristic of the upper mountain. Fischer remained confident that the two of them could handle whatever problems arose. He realized that despite his troubles, despite the lingering doubt that secretly lurked within him about his shoulder, he still had a shot at climbing K2. The mere thought was a magic elixir. *I'm back in it.* Fischer's despair of the past few weeks was replaced now by a hard, steely determination.

Fischer and Viesturs waited in their sleeping bags at Camp III for a break in the weather that would permit them to move to the higher and final camp. They were melting snow on the stove when the radio—stuffed into Fischer's sleeping bag to keep the batteries from freezing—started its familiar squawk. Through the hiss and static came an urgent call from high on the mountain. It was the voice of Thor Kieser. He and two others, he said, having spent several days in a storm at Camp IV before and after their summit attempt, were now in desperate straits. The day before, Kieser, Chantal Mauduit, and the Ukrainian Aleksei Nikiforov, had left Camp IV and climbed toward the summit. Chantal had started last, but had climbed quickly, and passed both men at a steep ice gully known as the Bottleneck Couloir. She had reached the summit, only the fourth woman in history to do so. Aleksei made the summit as well, but some hours after Chantal. Thor Kieser was forced by the worsening weather to turn back just a few hundred feet short of the top. Now, Thor reported by radio, he was particularly worried about Chantal Mauduit, who had returned to the high camp exhausted, snow-blind and, he feared, suffering from frostbite.

Fischer exchanged looks with his partner. They knew that after three or even four days above 26,000 feet, the climbers above must be near the end of their resources. They were going to need help. Between the two of them, there was no debate. It was obvious they were now the strongest climbers in a position to help. They knew, too, that launching a rescue would put an end to their own try for the summit.

Fischer was already lacing up his boots. "Let's go." There was nothing to do but make an all-out effort to find the climbers, even in the worsening weather, even if it meant their own chances for reaching the summit were eliminated. Fischer couldn't believe it, but he also knew there was nothing else he could do.

Dressed in down suits, with double plastic boots protecting their feet from the cold, Fischer and Viesturs started climbing toward Camp IV. Wind, snow, and cloud obscured their vision. Neither climber knew the route, as neither had been to the highest camp before. They were traveling blind over some of the most dangerous terrain on earth. They looked like apparitions as they kicked steps up the steep snow slope though cloud and snow so thick they could hardly see one another.

Despite his renewed vitality and commitment, Fischer's shoulder at times radiated a killing pain. He had to be careful how he used his arm, a nagging impediment that cramped his usually smooth style. He could hold an ice ax, but only if he didn't raise his arm too high. As they pushed their way upward toward the stranded climbers, visibility neared zero. To make matters more desperate, no ropes had been fixed above Camp III. So extreme are the combined effects of altitude and hard climbing that few of even the strongest high-altitude mountaineers are able to reach Camp IV on K2, much less carry the 1,500 or 2,000 feet of rope required to fix a safety line between the highest camps.

The result is that those who do reach Camp IV risk being trapped on the upper mountain by bad weather. In poor visibility the route from the highest camp to the relative safety of Camp III—and the start of the fixed ropes—is almost impossible to find. That crucial 2,000 feet is where many of K2's victims die. It is made more dangerous by the fact that the climbing is technical—requiring skill and expert routefinding to negotiate safely.

In 1986 alone, thirteen climbers were killed on K2. Five climbers perished on the Abruzzi route after they were pinned down by storm for four days and were unable to descend from Camp IV to Camp III. While the trapped climbers waited for a break in the weather, they all died. Britons Al Rouse and Julie Tullis perished at Camp IV from exhaustion and perhaps altitude sickness and other effects of the rarefied air. Austrians Alfred Imitzer and Hannes Wieser and Polish climber Dobroslawa Wolf died below Camp IV trying to descend in the storm.

Now Fischer and Viesturs, poised for their long-awaited summit attempt, struggled upward toward three climbers who were in exactly the same predicament: caught at Camp IV or somewhere below, trying to descend in the storm. *We've got to find them,* thought Fischer.

But as they climbed up toward the higher camp, Fischer and Viesturs entered an opaque cloud, a white world of fog, snow, and impenetrable mist. By now they could see nothing. Fischer knew they had to retreat, or risk getting lost themselves. Fischer stopped to shout into the ear of his partner, "Ed, we've got to go down." Viesturs only nodded. He knew there was no alternative. The condition and whereabouts of the lost climbers—Chantal Mauduit, Thor Kieser, and Aleksei Nikiforov, were unknown.

F ischer awoke in the tiny tent at Camp III, snow pressing in on both sides. It had been a fitful, worry-filled night. He started the stove as Viesturs unfastened the tent flap to peer out at the morning. "More snow," he said, but added that visibility had improved slightly. Today, they might be able to resume looking for the missing climbers. As he looked farther up the slope, Viesturs was shocked by what he saw: a lone figure, covered with snow, stumbling down the mountain. Could that pitiful stick figure be Aleksei? While Fischer made hot drinks to revive the stricken climber, Viesturs climbed out of the tent to help the Ukrainian who, as Viesturs watched, staggered 10 or 20 feet, then fell down in the snow, sitting there until he had the energy to stand up and cover another few yards.

By the time Viesturs helped guide the Ukrainian into camp, he seemed near death. "Way to go," said Viesturs, hoping to buoy his spirits. "You made it. How are the others?" Aleksei was clearly exhausted. His breathing was labored, coming in loud, heavy gasps, his face haggard and pale. He had been climbing alone for twenty-six hours, trying to escape the storm at Camp IV, trying to find his way to the lower camp. He had made it, but he arrived with bad news. The other two climbers, he reported, were still trying to get down. They were stranded, caught somewhere in between Camps III and IV. The Americans became alarmed. If Aleksei looked this wasted, in what shape would the others be in? If they were exposed, in the open, high on the mountain, their situation could be desperate. Fischer and Viesturs knew they had to try once again to reach Thor and Chantal, although Fischer feared it might already be too late.

The Seattle guides quickly laced up their boots, attached crampons, and began climbing. Struggling to break trail in snow up to mid-thigh, they climbed slowly through wind and swirling fog. Just putting one foot in front of the other was exhausting, but they kept moving and by midmorning had reached a steep snow slope less than 1,000 feet below Camp IV. As they groped their way higher—this was all new ground to them—Fischer realized that the angle of the slope combined with the layer of new, heavy snow made it prone to avalanche. Clearly, the slope could slide at any moment.

The two men recognized in the same moment that they were in mortal danger; not only was their rescue mission jeopardized, but their own lives as well. There was no way for the pair to anchor themselves to the unstable snow slope. They froze in their tracks. "Ed," Fischer shouted to his partner, "Let's get out of here!"

"Scott! Let's hang here a second to figure this out!" As they discussed how best to make a safe retreat off the slope, Fischer watched Ed, who was below him, begin to dig a hole in the snow with his ice ax, hoping that he could get deep enough that any avalanching snow would pass over him. Just then, what they feared most came crashing down.

"I never saw it," said Fischer. "It just hit me."

The avalanche struck with indescribable force. One moment Fischer was on the slope watching Ed dig, the next he was tumbling and rolling, swept down the mountain like a candy wrapper in the breeze. *This is it*, Fischer thought. After twenty years of climbing, he knew at that moment he would die in an avalanche high on K2. Viesturs, crouching in his hole, felt the avalanche roar over him, saw the world go black as the snow blocked the light. But jubilantly he realized that the pit he had dug had actually saved him, and maybe Scott as well. In that moment, Viesturs thought, hey, that's great—it's passed me and I'm still here!

But Fischer continued to hurtle down the mountain in the avalanche, passing Ed. When the rope between the two climbers went taut, the force of Fischer's momentum snatched Viesturs out of his hole like a puppet on a string. Both climbers tumbled down the slope another one or two hundred feet. But the drag on the rope caused by Ed's being pulled out of his pit slowed their fall. As they both fell farther down the mountain in the avalanche debris, their speed was reduced to the point that Viesturs was able to drive the pick of his ice ax into an icy patch on the slope, anchoring them while the avalanche swept by. Their fall was arrested.

When the roar of the avalanche ceased, two figures still clung to the steep slope. Incredibly they were alive, but they were exhausted, covered with snow and gasping for air. They had stopped just short of a cliff band and a fatal 4,000-foot fall down the mountain.

"Scott! Scott! Are you okay?" Viesturs' shout was muffled by the thick mist that hung close to the slope. "Yeah, yeah," came Fischer's weak reply. "I guess I'm all right. But my balls hurt like hell. I think my shoulder's out too."

Kneeling on hands and knees, snow and ice stuck to their faces and clothes, the two climbers were gasping like draft horses. They began to take stock of their situation. Fischer's testicles had been squeezed mightily by his harness as the fall was slowed, and he feared he had once again ripped his shoulder from its socket. Slowly, with a combination of great care and a terrible fear, he tested his arm, afraid he would find his shoulder once again dislocated. He discovered that although he hurt, his shoulder worked, and he concluded that he had only torqued the injured joint painfully. Neither climber was badly injured. And for the moment, the avalanche had made the slope safe. But Viesturs remained worried, and highly motivated to get moving.

"Let's go, let's go, let's go," he said. Getting off the slope was all he could think about. Cautiously, the pair traversed off the steepest part of the slope and continued slowly upward in now suddenly improving weather, still hoping to find the lost climbers. The raging snow and wind had suddenly turned into a sunny day, with blue sky appearing in through thinning clouds.

Suddenly, Fischer caught sight of a bright yellow object lying in the snow. He looked again—yes, unmistakably a down suit. They climbed higher until the object took on the form of the French climber Chantal Mauduit, snow-blind and exhausted, lying on the slope below Camp IV.

Thor Kieser was tied to the French climber with a short length of rope. The pair had been feeling their way down the mountain, exposed to storm and blowing snow, for two days. Valiantly, Thor had belayed the blind French climber down 50 feet or so with a length of rope, where she waited until he joined her. Then they repeated the process. In that way they had descended from the higher camp. They had made it this far, but now both were weak and dehydrated, unsteady on their feet but still able to move on their own. When Thor first saw Fischer and Viesturs, he smiled broadly through his exhaustion. Sitting in the snow, wasted, he said, "Man, am I glad to see you guys."

As Viesturs began treating Chantal's snow-blindness with analgesic eye drops, she looked up and said to Ed, "I climbed K2." Done in by the summit effort and the ensuing days of storm, she was relieved now to be safe at last. The price of success on K2 can be high. This time, Chantal had escaped with her life, but Fischer could not help but think it had been a near thing.

Scott Fischer and Ed Viesturs tied the two exhausted climbers to their own rope and began the descent in search of the top of the fixed ropes at Camp III. On the way down, the French climber was so exhausted she actually went to sleep standing up, her long brown hair blowing in the wind. It took two days to descend all the way down to base camp. By the time the party was off the mountain, the date was August 8, more than two months since Fischer had left home. For Scott, once again, the summit of K2 had been snatched from his grasp.

F ischer looked around at the ragged blue mess tent, the garbage pile, the primitive realities of base camp— his home now for almost two months. The climbers had been on K2 so long that many could stay no longer. In ones and twos the members of Vladimir's motley group drifted away as the demands of work and family called them home. With many of the Americans already departed, Vladimir took the remaining climbers by surprise when he announced at breakfast on August 9 that the expedition was over. But like Chantal, who had stayed after her Swiss expedition had given up, some of the team members felt they still had a shot at getting to the top. They were

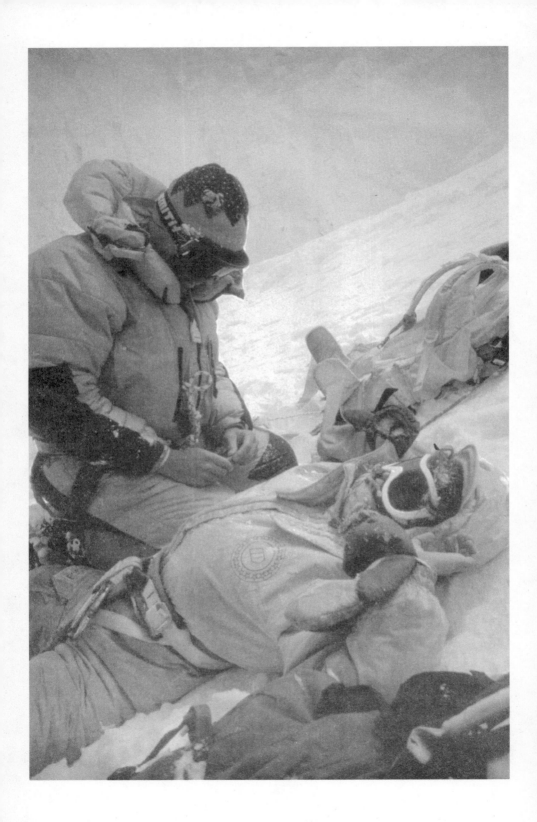

stunned by Vladimir's decision to call a halt to the climbing. Scott and Ed, along with Charlie Mace, Daniel Mazur, and Englishman Johnathan Pratt, decided they weren't ready to quit. Convincing their Pakistani liaison officer to remain, these climbers took over leadership of the Russian-American K2 Expedition after the Russians and the Ukrainians headed home. New Zealand, Swedish, and Mexican climbers from the International Expedition also remained on K2.

Since mid-June, climbers from all three expeditions at base camp had made a series of attempts on K2, mostly as individuals or in pairs. There was little teamwork, and no real organized strategy to reach the top, only the infrastructure of fixed ropes and camps, through which any climber or pair of climbers might take their chances on the weather and go for it. Summit "teams" were formed by convenience, made up of any climbers who happened to be at the high camp when conditions allowed a run for the top. Climbing high on K2 that year, or any year, was not always a team sport.

While the Russians declared the climb over and quickly departed, Fischer had spent three eventful days at base camp. As it had all summer, the weather remained unsettled there. But higher on K2, where the huge mountain penetrated nearly six miles into the upper reaches of the atmosphere, a raging jet stream scoured its upper slopes. Any thought of venturing on to the mountain was put on hold. For Fischer, there was one big open question: was a summit attempt still feasible? The rescue had taken away precious days from the already short Karakoram summer. The season's marginal weather had offered no real period of good climbing conditions, but so far had at least presented no protracted stretches of outright impossible conditions. But autumn was coming to the ice-and-rock wilderness of the Karakoram. Fischer knew the odds were long for success, but with a stubborn resolve he wasn't ready to quit. He turned to his partner. "Let's climb this thing, Ed," said Fischer, "so we can go home."

On August 12, the severe weather on the upper mountain relented. Once again, Fischer and Viesturs started climbing the second-highest mountain in the world from the bottom. Fischer was not demoralized,

Ed Viesturs tends to Chantal Maudit below Camp IV. (Photo by Scott Fischer)

nor even discouraged. This attempt, he knew, would be his last, and he adopted the matter-of-fact attitude that he would not fail. Despite his damaged shoulder, and the time lost in rescuing Chantal, his faith in himself was so strong that he still believed he would climb K2. Ed wanted to climb *all* fourteen 8,000-meter peaks, so Fischer knew that in Viesturs he had a capable and motivated partner. Both climbers totally focused on reaching the top.

Each time during the past two months that the pair had departed base camp to move up the mountain, they faced the heartbreaking work of endless trail breaking in newly fallen snow. On August 12, they began wading upward through deep snow and thin air yet one more time.

There was one salutary effect from all of the up-and-down efforts of the past months: both men were in top climbing condition. Even Fischer's wounded limb seemed sufficiently sound for the work ahead, and his recent forays to the upper camps had restored his ability to function at high altitude. Fischer and Viesturs, after two months on the mountain, were lean but not yet weakened by weight loss. They were well acclimated and aerobically very fit. They had been high—briefly—several times, but not so high or for so long that they had suffered the debilitating effects of the "death zone." They were strong. As they climbed up over the now-familiar ground, the two climbers moved with amazing speed. Starting from base camp, Fischer and Viesturs reached Camp III in one incredible, long day, an impressive feat in itself, covering more than 7,500 feet of climbing at high altitude.

After spending one night at Camp III, they pushed on to Camp IV— this time by a different route, avoiding the avalanche slope. Along the route Fischer placed wands, small bamboo poles, to mark the way to the highest camp. He was determined not to join the ranks of dead climbers who never got down from Camp IV. When he ran out of wands, Fischer used broken sections of tent poles to mark the route.

Finally, on August 13, the two climbers reached the bleak, wind-swept little flat at 26,000 feet. They quickly set up their tent, hoping to go for the summit the next day. But there, in the most dangerous camp on the mountain, the weather again closed in. It began to snow. The falling snow turned to storm, which built in strength with each passing hour.

Snow fell constantly, burying their gear, while a thick, soupy fog enveloped the tent. Fischer knew his grace period was finite. Waiting out bad weather at Camp IV is not something that can be done for long. Above 25,000 feet, the effects of altitude become acute, as one's body deteriorates rapidly from lack of oxygen and dehydration. The hours passed slowly, and slowly turned into days.

The two men were not alone during this weird and dangerous vigil. Charlie Mace from their own Russian-American Expedition was there, as were the New Zealand climbers Gary Ball and Rob Hall. Three Mexicans and three Swedes from the International Expedition occupied tents nearby. All were dug into the small, windswept slope which formed the high camp. It was an elite little group. Few climbers ever get to Camp IV, and it remained to be seen which—if any—would have the energy and will to climb the final 2,300 feet to the summit.

As the hours passed, more snow fell. The wind began to grow in strength, the gusts hammering the cluster of tents. Fischer waited, lost in his own world. Scott thought of his family in Seattle. Despite the fact that he had been on K2 for more than fifty days, he kept himself focused on the summit, only the summit. *If the storm lets up for just one day, I can climb this thing.* He wanted K2, and here was the best opportunity he would have to climb it.

Camp IV on K2 is a near-mythical place, a state of mind, a spook story for climbers. Its legacy of tragedy and death has generated a legend of suffering and peril that is all too real. In the 1986 tragedy, five climbers in the netherworld of Camp IV had slowly died after being trapped by storm in that frozen place where the atmosphere contains only one-third the oxygen it does at sea level, too little oxygen to sustain life for long. On a dozen other occasions, climbers had died, alone or in pairs, in this desolate camp. No one can stay long at 26,000 feet and live. While Scott was well aware that he was in a perilous spot, he was not afraid. He knew that if he dwelled on the fact that any number of things—weather, falls, avalanche, accident—could kill him, he wouldn't be up there. Fischer was mentally psyched and focused on his goal. He believed that what had happened to others would not happen to him.

As the time dragged on, Fischer and Viesturs were becoming alarmed at the deterioration of their bodies. By now they had lost enough weight—at least 20 pounds each—that they were becoming visibly gaunt. But they did not mention to each other, or even consider, the idea of giving up. Eating was so difficult and time-consuming that the climbers simply didn't do it. The lassitude caused by the extreme elevation—pilots put on oxygen masks at 12,000 feet —turned every-day chores such as preparing a meal into Herculean tasks. A candy bar or a high energy food bar counted as a meal. Going out of the tent into the storm was almost unthinkable. They lay in their sleeping bags in a kind of stupor, sleeping fitfully, staring at the diffuse light that came through the tent fabric, hardly talking, hardly stirring. They were suffi-ciently shut down that they were not even bored.

"Mentally we were keyed up," said Viesturs. "It wasn't bad be-cause we didn't let it be bad. It's a mental thing. We were confident—we looked at it as just vegetating, just waiting until we could go. We were committed."

Temperatures dropped at night to 40 degrees (Fahrenheit) below zero. Two days passed—then three. As they waited out the storm in their soporific and unreal high-altitude world, totally isolated and removed, a shout from out in the storm brought shocking news.

"Scott! Ed!" It was Gary Ball, one of the New Zealand climbers in a nearby tent. "We just heard from Camp II by radio. Adrian fell! He's been killed!"

Fischer shook his head at the news. *Has it begun again?* His thoughts went back to 1986 when the climbers had died one by one. Viesturs muttered, "My god." The two climbers exchanged looks in the close confines of their tent. But there wasn't a lot to say. Fischer had hoped he and his partner could avoid the kind of carnage that had occurred in previous years, but perhaps that was not to be. Since their own radio operated on a different channel than that of the Kiwis, the two Americans relied on the New Zealanders for more information.

They learned that two Mexican climbers who had been waiting at Camp IV decided that if they were to live, they had somehow to get down. The two had tried to descend from the high camp during the storm. One of them, Adrian Benitez, fell to his death from just below Camp IV, not far from the spot where Fischer and Viesturs had been avalanched. Climbers at Camp II saw the Mexican as he plummeted

Sunset over Fischer's and Viesturs's tent at Camp III, with Broad Peak on the left, Chogolisa at center, and the Godwin Austen Glacier (Photo by Scott Fischer)

4,000 feet. He was almost certainly killed instantly. English climber Johnathan Pratt and American Dan Mazur tried to reach Benitez, but snow conditions were too dangerous. They saw no movement.

Fischer and Viesturs took the tragic news philosophically. This, after all, was K2. People die on K2 all the time. In fact, it was possible they were camped right now near the corpses that remain at Camp IV from previous expeditions. Although they saw no sign, all the climbers at the high camp knew the dead remained. But Adrian's death would not deter the Americans from their summit bid. Only the weather could do that. Fischer, who had spent more than two months of brutal work to be in a position to make an attempt on the summit, continued to wait for his chance.

145

"We didn't even talk," remembered Fischer. "There's nothing to say, you've long since run out of things to say. We even talked a little about how we didn't have anything to talk about anymore. But the joy of climbing with Ed is that Ed can take care of himself, and that was a new experience for me. I can take care of myself. It seems like on big mountains I'm the one who has to sit up and light the stove all the time. But at Camp IV, Ed did that too. With Ed, I truly believed we could make it."

As the two climbers continued to wait for their chance, they discussed how much longer they could stay at the 26,000-foot-high camp. But both were so focused on the summit that they were reluctant to put a time limit on themselves, or even consider going back down. The very idea of returning to base camp, resting for two days, then going back up—climbing K2 *again*—was unthinkable. It would take another week or ten days. Both climbers had long been ready to go home—but they wanted to climb K2 first.

Finally, as another evening came high on K2, the thick white clouds beneath them thinned slightly, then opened into ragged streamers. The lower peaks of the Karakoram showed themselves for the first time in days, reflecting the beautiful gold of a setting sun off their ridges and summits. Clearly, here was a break in the weather. Fischer could hardly believe his eyes. His powers of reason, partially shut down in the stupor of his stormbound vigil, began to stir with the threads of a strategy.

How long would the weather hold? he wondered. Would it last long enough to permit the weakened climbers to climb toward the summit? There was no way to know. Fischer discussed with his partner the precise timing of the dangerous venture ahead of them. Vladimir had required almost twenty-eight hours for his climb from Camp IV to the summit, a period of time the two Americans believed too long, too risky. Fischer and Viesturs decided that they would go for the summit—tomorrow—but go fast, as fast as they could and as light as they dared. In the confines of the tent, they reviewed the strategy they had formulated months before in Seattle: the more gear they carried, the slower they would have to climb, and the more likely a night out became. Fischer knew a night out on K2 could be fatal. So they decided to take nothing but water bottles, ice tools and cameras. "No sense changing our plans now," said Fischer. Viesturs nodded, but added one ingredient: "If we're not on top by 2:00 P.M., we turn around." Fischer reluctantly agreed.

Their plan was this: by making an early morning start—1:30 A.M.—and by traveling with no packs or bivouac gear, no safety gear at all, they planned to reach the summit and return to Camp IV by nightfall. They believed they could move that fast even though they would not use supplementary oxygen. Fischer privately worried about his shoulder—he could use it to a limited degree, but the pain remained severe when he used his ice ax to climb. And he knew the route to the summit had sections that were technically challenging. But for Fischer, the pain was not enough to stop him. He would ignore it. He would go for it. He felt that his chances were improved by his partnership with Viesturs. The two experienced guides could bank on what had made them successful climbers—their skill, their experience, their fitness, and their combined sound judgment—to get them up *and* down a route known to be a death trap. Scott harbored no negative thoughts that morning. "I knew right then I was going to the top of K2," he remembered.

Before dawn broke on August 16, they were off. Through the fog of high-altitude lassitude they were able to rouse themselves from the warmth and relative comfort of their sleeping bags, get dressed—double plastic boots, full-body down suits, crampons, ice tools, water bottle, and a headlamp to light the way—and start climbing. No other climbers stirred from the small cluster of tents. Stepping out into the cold of that Karakoram night, Fischer saw to his dismay that their weather window was already closing. Chogolisa, his weather indicator, was obscured. But even in the dark he could see big storm clouds gathering in the valleys, moving rapidly up the slopes of the mountain. He could have turned back and no one would call the retreat anything but prudent. He started off toward the summit.

The pair, already higher than many jet airliners fly, continued to climb. Looking slightly comic in their puffy suits of down—Fischer in green, Viesturs in outrageous pink—they climbed moderate slopes on hard snow to reach 27,000 feet. Climbing without supplementary oxygen, the pair labored in the thin atmosphere to keep moving. They saw they were alone. No other climbers from Camp IV had ventured out, at least not yet. But, looking far below him, Fischer saw the dim glow of a solitary headlamp moving upward. At least one other soul was following their footsteps up the mountain. He wondered who it was.

For Fischer, every step was a trial of will and strength, every action a study in slow motion. He did not have to think about the physical part—by instinct he placed his crampons in the snow, swung the ice ax, raised himself up another foot. Then he stopped, took three labored breaths, and did it again.

"For me," said Fischer, "there's no thought process. You just go slow, you realize you're going slow. But the trick is always to keep moving." It all comes down to these few hours, he knew. So many people get this far, and fail—they reach the end of their physical or mental resources and can go no farther. Fischer was in his element.

The effort of kicking steps in the snow was exhausting, so the Seattle climbers traded off in the lead. It was on the steeper, more technical sections where their years of experience counted most, where they climbed automatically, their oxygen-starved brains doing the right thing by rote. Roped together, they knew that if one fell, the other could be pulled off. One mistake could kill them both.

Soon the climbers reached Bottleneck Couloir, a steep gully of hard ice at 27,500 feet that presented some of the most difficult climbing on the route. As Fischer started up the couloir with his ice tools, the climber they had seen below them caught up by climbing in their footsteps. It was Charlie Mace, another member of their own expedition. They tied him onto their rope, and the summit team became a threesome.

Lungs burning in the thin air, Fischer led the way up the Bottleneck Couloir, using an ice ax in one hand, an ice hammer in the other to advance a foot at a time up the frozen, 70-degree slope. Above the couloir, the climbers slowly moved higher through sloppy snow even as the clouds finally engulfed them. Snow swirled through the air, and a thick white cloud hung close. Viesturs was tormented: he wanted to reach the summit but he began to realize that conditions were too dangerous to proceed.

"Scott, what do you think about these snow conditions?" he gasped to his partner. Fischer, frozen vapor forming long icicles in his mustache, was unequivocal. "We can do it, Ed, we can do it. We gotta go on." So on they went, but Viesturs never relaxed, never stopped asking himself, *What should I do? Is this crazy? Will we die?*

"Scott was totally focused," remembered Viesturs. "I finally said, 'Okay, just keep the rope tight.' But the whole thing was really eating at me."

The climbing eased in difficulty as they reached the knife-edged summit ridge. The climbers labored upward, taking turns at the lead. Suddenly, they punched out through the cloud layer into a magical world of bright, intense sunlight, blue sky and dazzling white snow stretching a mere 200 feet to the summit. The climbers were stunned by the sudden transformation, by the austere beauty of the mountain. They took the last, slow steps upward. At 10:50 A.M., well before their deadline and just nine hours after leaving camp, the climbers reached a nondescript mound of snow about ten yards in circumference. They could climb no higher. They had reached the summit of K2.

There was plenty of room on top for the three of them, the first Americans to ever climb the Abruzzi Ridge. They whooped, raised their ice tools in triumph, slapped each other on the back, hugged each other. Ed Viesturs, so choked up he couldn't talk, just shook the hands of his fellow climbers. Fischer shouted with joy and engulfed his partner with big, heartfelt hugs. "All right, Ed, we did it. We did it!"

The climbers looked around to discover that from the second-highest mountain in the world, they could see nothing. The cloud layer was right below them, hiding everything but the sky. It was frightening to be that high and have no view. Even Broad Peak, standing more than 26,000 feet high and just across the glacier, was completely obscured. The climbers could see nothing but each other, which felt weird after all the hard work it had taken to get there.

Scott Fischer was electrified—and relieved—at his success. He knew the thirty-five minutes on top of K2 would be a time he would never forget. But his celebration was dampened by the altitude and the grim fact of deteriorating weather. With the goal of the summit attained,

there was no dodging the reality of their situation: *would they live to share their success with the people close to them?*

"There's no nirvana on the summit," said Fischer. "It's a goal, a goal met, but if you don't get down it doesn't mean a thing."

"I couldn't relax," remembered Viesturs. "I was very worried about the descent with those huge clouds rolling in."

Fischer was ebullient to have climbed a killer mountain widely regarded as the most difficult in the world. But on the summit of that indifferent monster, after fifty-two days of trying, what Fischer felt was not so much elation as a sense of churning. He was thinking not about the exhilaration of the summit but about what he needed to do to get down safely and get back to Jean and Andy and Katie Rose. His brain worked sluggishly but purposefully in the thin air: the summit was attained, the goal met. Now, getting down alive was his new focus. Getting down was all he thought about.

All three climbers knew that descending from the summit of K2 to Camp IV in a storm was going to challenge them as nothing had before. As they began their descent they were immediately engulfed in cloud. Snow again began to fall. In minutes, their footprints were covered by new snow. There was no trail to follow down. The climbers were descending in a thick cloud, a true whiteout. Not only was their route completely obscured, but through the fog they could see no landmarks to guide them. They were living a nightmare, the classic recipe for disaster on K2.

If we screw up here, we die, Fischer thought. To climb fast they had brought no packs, no sleeping bags, no bivouac gear of any kind. The strategy had worked—they had reached the summit in near record time—but if they didn't reach the shelter of the high camp before nightfall, their very lives were threatened. Routefinding was everything now as the trio started down. Fischer, in the lead, heard Ed Viesturs' shouts muffled by the wind: "No, Scott, not there, we gotta go more to the right." Looking carefully, Fischer saw that his partner was correct. He adjusted course and slowly they moved downward.

Scott Fischer on the summit of K2, August 16, 1992 (Photo: Scott Fischer collection)

Through clouds and blowing snow the threesome descended. All three participated in their high-stakes endeavor. It was do or die, and they were fully engaged. At times, two of them huddled together while the third went out on the end of the rope to look for landmarks. There was confusion, and, at times, disagreement over the correct route down. The blowing snow had obscured all traces of their footprints, and the cold landscape of rock and ice and snow made the task of picking out the route difficult. Their lives hung in the balance.

At one point the fear they all felt turned to near panic. Viesturs actually thought to himself, We're going to die. The ghastly descent was made worse by small slab avalanches that fell from above, perhaps the harbinger of bigger slides as the steep slopes accumulated more new snow. There was also the gnawing doubt that they were going in the wrong direction. It started snowing harder. Viesturs was now in the lead.

"We couldn't see shit," remembered Viesturs. "We were feeling our way down, not really sure we were on the right route. Finally we came to a gully I recognized from the way up—and then I knew we were following the correct line. That was a relief, but I was afraid all this new snow was going to crash down on us in an avalanche."

The small snow slides and slab avalanches continued to overtake the descending climbers, but nothing big enough to be dangerous came down the gully.

"Ed was really focused," remembered Fischer. "He was the star getting down. I've got a lot of respect for him. It was desperate, but I always felt we'd get back to camp. You worry about it, but my attitude was, we *will* find camp."

After four hours of descending through the snow and murk, the trio knew they must be near their high camp. But exactly where was it? They shouted into the driving snow, hoping that those who had remained behind would hear, and signal back. Suddenly, Scott thought he heard something. They stopped and listened. There was no sound but that of wind and blowing snow. On they went until—there! Yes! The unmistakable sound of a human voice! "Hey! Hey! Over here!"

The three Americans decended slowly, physically drained now, moving carefully toward the sound. Soon the ghostly outline of the snow-covered tents appeared though the blowing snow. They climbed into camp, but were too exhausted for real celebration. The summit climbers checked in at the New Zealanders' blue tent for a quick hello to Rob Hall and Gary Ball, who were hunkered down against the weather. The Kiwis had waited at Camp IV for their own chance to make the summit. But when the opportunity came, despite climbing with supplementary oxygen, they reached only as far as the Bottleneck before Gary Ball became ill and unable to climb. They had retreated.

Fischer and Viesturs went immediately to their own red tent for a desperately needed drink—they were severely dehydrated—and rest. On August 16, 1992, they had become the first Americans to climb the Abruzzi Ridge. Their round-trip time to the summit and back to Camp IV had been a mere thirteen and a half hours. Fischer felt vindicated about his strong performance high on the mountain despite the injuries he had sustained by falling into the crevasse. His belief in himself had paid off.

But there was little time to savor his safe return to the high camp. The next step in the descent was to reach Camp III and the top of the fixed ropes—but in the long, gory history of K2, that had proven to be one of the most dangerous moves on the mountain. From Camp III, because of the fixed ropes, the climbers would be in relative safety, able to descend in even bad conditions. But the 2,500 feet between those two high camps is where disaster most often strikes on K2. They knew a storm could trap them at the higher camp, or cause them to lose their way on the descent.

Viesturs was still worried that they might be in for a repeat of the 1986 tragedy. Camp IV was not the place to be in bad weather, a fact that was emphatically driven home when the night got off to a bad start. Viesturs and Fischer crawled into their tent, exhausted by their summit efforts at altitude and the stress of trying to find their way down. But, wracked by anxiety for what the next day would bring, they slept fitfully. Suddenly Fischer was jolted out of his uneasy sleep by a terrifying force. Viesturs was awakened by the sound of Fischer yelling.

"Avalanche! Avalanche!," shouted Fischer as the force of snow slamming into the tent knocked him over on top of his partner. The tent collapsed under the weight of snow, pinning Fischer. Viesturs was forced outside in the storm to dig out the entrance. *Now what?* thought Viesturs, who grew more uneasy over what they would face in the morning when they tried to descend to Camp III and the start of the fixed ropes. This wasn't going well. Fischer and Viesturs spend the rest of the night in anxious discomfort, unable to rest or relax.

The two Seattle guides were up early to start the descent in high winds and blowing snow to Camp III. This was the most dangerous part of the descent, and they moved carefully. Fischer's insistence on wanding the route between high camps on the way up proved the difference between living and dying. The few inches of each wand that protruded from the newly fallen snow marked the way. Viesturs was sure that detail saved their lives. The weather was worsening, but the climbers were able to press on through the snow and wind as they approached the last problem: finding the distinctive slot between the seracs through which to descend and reach the camp.

Finally reaching the camp, Fischer discovered that none of the tents remained standing. He didn't care because they would not be here long. Fischer started the stove and made tea in an attempt to rehydrate after the harrowing descent. But both he and Viesturs knew they dared not tarry long. Scrounging among the disarray of the wrecked camp, they located food and fuel for the trip down. The New Zealand climbers Ball and Hall arrived and looked through the wreckage for their video camera. The climbers gathered themselves for the final descent to the relative safety of the lower camps. A combination of fear and relief drove them to move fast.

Fischer and Viesturs zoomed down the fixed ropes to Camp II. They would rest there for their final night on K2, then descend to base the next day. For the first time, Fischer allowed himself to breathe a little easier. He and his partner had pulled off a fast summit day on K2, but they were beginning to feel the cumulative fatigue of altitude and all-out physical effort. They climbed into their tent, hoping to finally get some real rest after the anxiety of the past few days. The other climbers would descend individually, at their own pace, protected by the security of the fixed lines.

Fischer was roused about 9:00 P.M. that night by a disturbance outside the tent. Rob Hall had finally arrived, hours after the others. Fischer was alarmed. The New Zealand climber appeared on the verge of collapse. "Rob was really hammered," remembered Fischer.

Hall told Scott that his partner, Gary Ball was lagging behind. The succession of nights spent above 26,000 feet at Camp IV had apparently taken its toll on both of them. As Fischer prepared to go back to sleep, the weary Hall straggled off to one of the vacant tents located about ten yards away to await the arrival of his partner.

Near midnight, Fischer was awakened again when Gary Ball climbed into the tent he and Viesturs shared. Ball appeared so weak that Fischer grew alarmed. "Gary came in completely trashed," said Fischer. "Ed and I were asleep—this is the first time we've been able to rest. But Gary is in such bad shape he comes right into our tent and just lays there."

Fischer started the stove and made Ball a hot drink. He was coughing up bloody phlegm and was clearly disoriented. He kept asking for a sleeping bag, and he asked Fischer to guide him to his tent. Scott, exhausted himself from the summit ordeal, did not understand what the problem was. "I'm saying to him," Fischer remembered, "'look, it's only right over there, just go to your tent.' He keeps asking for a sleeping bag, and we say, 'Gary, just use your own.'"

As they prepared to go back to sleep after Gary finally made it to his tent, they realized that he probably *had* no sleeping bag. He had stumbled into Camp II without a pack, apparently having left his personal gear higher on the mountain. As the seriousness of Ball's situation sunk in, so did the fact that they would get little sleep that night. Viesturs put on his boots and carried his sleeping bag over to the Kiwis' tent and gave it to Gary.

Fischer checked around the deserted camp and in the storm-caused wreckage of an abandoned tent found an oxygen cylinder left behind by the Swedish climbers. Now the stricken New Zealander could breathe oxygen while he slept, a measure which can often greatly improve the condition of a person suffering from altitude sickness. With Ball taken care of, the Seattle climbers went back to their own tent to rest as best they could.

After a miserable, cold night huddled together for warmth in one bag, the pair were eager to end their discomfort. The mountain climbed, they wanted only to get down safely, and quickly. At the first hint of daylight, both were dressed, with crampons on, ready to descend.

It was 5:30 A.M. when they moved past the tent where Charlie Mace still slept, and then the tent shared by the New Zealand climbers. Scott and Ed hollered a friendly, "C'mon, guys, let's go. We're out of here." They knew that in a matter of hours they would be in the relative comfort of base camp, making preparations for their trek out to Askole. They were more than ready to be off the mountain.

But before he could clip into the fixed ropes, Scott suddenly stopped in his tracks. A feeble voice came from the New Zealand tent: "No, Scott, stay. We need help," croaked Rob Hall in a low voice. "Gary won't come. He can't move!" Fischer stopped and peered into the tent. He saw the oxygen hadn't helped, and Ball had grown alarmingly worse. He had what Fischer thought was a "bad look—the look you hate to see." He was gray and gaunt, the spark gone from his eyes, his blond hair plastered around his head.

Fischer had known both climbers a long time; he had climbed with them in Russia, on Everest, and now on K2. He had to do something. He cajoled, even yelled at Gary to get him up and dressed. "Get up, get up. You've got to do it, Gary. You'll fucking die up here if you don't get moving."

Ball lay listlessly in the borrowed sleeping bag. "I just want to sleep," he mumbled. But Fischer knew it would be the sleep of death, that if Ball stayed behind he would be in mortal danger. The healthier climbers put boots and crampons on the stricken man, and rigged another oxygen bottle. Finally everyone set off toward Camp I. Ed led the way down the ropes. Fischer followed with the debilitated Ball, descending at his side so that he could operate the rappel device for the ailing climber. Hall and Charlie Mace came down last.

Only a few hundred feet below Camp II, however, Ball started to moan: "I can't do it, man, I can't go on." He was fading fast and Fischer grew more concerned. *Not again,* he thought. Once before, in Russia, a companion in similar difficulties had died in Fischer's arms. The New

Zealand climber had the same deathly pallor, the same colorless skin that Fischer had seen before. To Viesturs, Ball looked ninety years old. Struggling with the helpless climber, Fischer was able to assist Ball down the thousand feet of fixed rope to Camp I.

"Ed was sitting there smiling," remembered Fischer, "happy as he could be because we're about to get off K2. He's ready to go full speed back to base camp. I hated to ruin his day, but I knew we weren't going anywhere. I told him that I didn't think Gary was going to make it, and that we had to set up the tent."

Their plans for descent put on hold, Fischer and Viesturs set up the tent to protect the incapacitated climber from the wind and snow that swirled around them. Viesturs crawled into the small tent with Ball, who was coughing up blood and pieces of lung, in an attempt to warm and calm him. Using the Kiwi's radio, Fischer made a call to base camp informing the other members of the International K2 Expedition of the desperate situation. The Mexican members of the team were still shattered by the death of Adrian and were hardly in a position to help. But two Swedish climbers radioed that they would begin climbing up toward the rescue party with more oxygen.

Fischer and Viesturs did what they could for Gary Ball, but it was clear to both of them that he was not responding to oxygen or the lower altitude, the traditional measures for altitude sickness. This news was relayed to base camp. As a last resort, the expedition members at base camp rigged a satellite link directly to a hospital in Christchurch, New Zealand. By patching the hospital through to Camp I by radio, doctors in Christchurch—who actually knew Gary Ball because he is something of a national hero for having climbed Everest—were able to speak directly with Fischer and Viesturs at Camp I. The rescuers were amazed to be talking to New Zealand from Camp I, but the news wasn't encouraging. They learned there was little that could be done on the mountain. Ball must reach medical care as soon as possible.

There were still some supplies at Camp I. The healthy climbers started a stove to make hot food, the first real meal for Fischer and Viesturs since arriving at Camp IV from the summit so many days ago. In an attempt to stay hydrated in the rarefied air, they consumed hot

Scott Fischer assists in lowering stricken New Zealand climber Gary Ball to Camp I. (Photo by Charles Mace)

drinks while they waited for help from base camp. It had grown dark and the weather had gotten worse by the time the Swedish climbers arrived with the oxygen. The new storm was gaining in intensity.

Fischer feared that if they waited at Camp I that night, the weather might make descent impossible the next day. Ball looked as if he wouldn't last much longer. It was clear the evacuation must continue that very night. Gary was, by then, unable to walk at all, so Fischer rigged a lead from his own harness to support the desperately ill New Zealand climber. Just when Fischer hoped that his trials on K2 would be winding down, he found himself in the middle of a harrowing descent through storm down the seemingly endless fixed rope. (The slope below Camp I was so steep that instead of climbing downhill, the climbers could rappel down the fixed ropes.) Coming on the heels of a mountaineering feat that leaves most climbers on the verge of physical collapse, the rescue—at night and in the middle of a storm—was a real test of Fischer's reserves.

"I couldn't believe it," remembered Fischer. "We were so close to being off the mountain. It was a bummer. Because we had just climbed K2, we were wasted, and yet we were still the strongest climbers on the mountain. But those guys needed our help. We had to do what we could."

Not only was the stricken climber clipped into a 30-foot lead rigged to Fischer's harness, but one of the Swedish climbers was tied into Gary Ball via a Jumar off the lead to help guide the helpless climber. Both climbers hung from Fischer, who bore their entire weight as he rappelled down the fixed ropes, carefully controlling the speed of the descent. In the dark and blowing snow, the maneuvering down the steep slope was cumbersome and exhausting. As the rescue party approached the unused advanced-base camp or depot below Camp I, other climbers who had come up from base camp were waiting to help. From that point, two climbers helped lower Gary Ball down the lower-angled slopes.

The rescue lasted through the night. At 3:40 A.M, August 15, 1992, Fischer and Viesturs arrived in the International K2 Expedition's base camp. The grateful and relieved expedition members treated Viesturs and Fischer with generous hospitality, plying them with hot food and drinks. Later that night Scott Fischer and Ed Viesturs finally reached their own base camp farther down the glacier. They had climbed K2, and come down alive.

EPILOGUE

Gary Ball, the New Zealand climber, was evacuated by helicopter from K2 base camp to Skardu, and eventually to Islamabad and on to Christchurch. He fully recovered, so well in fact that he was climbing again in the Himalaya of Nepal a few weeks later. Tragically, however, he fell victim that same season to a pulmonary ailment similar to what had afflicted him on K2. Gary Ball died on Dhauligiri only a few months after being evacuated from K2.

Ed Viesturs, whose fame rose following his ascent of K2, had now climbed the world's three highest peaks—Everest, K2, and Kangenchunga—without oxygen. He was only the fifth person in the world (Balyberdin was another) to have done that, and his stock was rising in the game of big time climbing. In 1993, sponsored by Ralph Lauren and wearing a Polo down suit, Viesturs attempted a solo ascent of Mount Everest by the Japanese Couloir. He was stopped by unclimbable snow conditions. But Ed Viesturs continues to knock off the world's 8,000-meter peaks: nine down, five to go.

Vladimir Balyberdin was killed in an automobile accident in St. Petersburg, Russia.

During the summer of 1993, Scott Fischer journeyed to Ama Dablam, the sacred mountain set amidst the Himalaya in his beloved Nepal. Leading a small group of clients, Scott climbed the mountain in eight days, going fast and light. A few weeks later he led a group of university students to the summit of Mount McKinley in a climb organized to raise money for research to combat AIDS.

Fischer exorcised his Everest Demons in 1994, not only climbing the mountain safely without supplementary oxygen, but spearheading an expedition based on environmental goals. The point of the climb was not merely to reach the top of the mountain but to demonstrate that it was possible to begin reversing the damage caused by forty years of climbing, and its unsavory legacy: tons of garbage littering the mountain from base camp to the South Col.

Fischer's summit day on Everest was in the same fast, safe style as his K2 climb had been, but his 1994 expedition to Everest may best be remembered for its landmark environmental efforts. At the South Col alone, more than two thousand old oxygen cylinders litter the desolate flat. Other, more grandiose attempts to rid the mountain of trash had failed completely. But by simply paying a "bounty"—in cash and on the spot—for old oxygen cylinders and other garbage brought down from the South Col or elsewhere on Everest, the Sagarmatha Expedition cleaned more than 5,000 pounds of trash from the world highest mountain. Even skeptics were impressed. For their remarkable efforts, Fischer and other expedition members were awarded the American Alpine Club's Dave Brower Environmental Award.

In the summer of 1995, Fischer returned to the Baltoro to climb the mountain he spent so many weeks admiring while he was laid up at K2 base camp: Broad Peak. One of the most beautiful mountains in the Karakoram, Broad Peak was Fischer's fourth (of fourteen) 8,000-meter peak. A natural-born climbing guide, he takes as much pleasure in getting other people to the top as he does getting there himself. On Broad Peak, he led five climbers to the summit with him.

For Fischer, his return to the Baltoro was an emotional one. Base camps for K2 and Broad Peak are only a few hours walk apart. During one three-day period, climbers on K2 that year dropped in to visit Scott and the 1995 version of his Baltoro Cafe. The very idea of a decent cup of coffee in the wilds of central Asia was enough to attract members of all three international expeditions, including American, English, and New Zealand climbers. This time Fischer, stocked with a hundred pounds of Starbucks' best, was prepared.

The visitors from K2, who were aware of Fischer's success on the mountain two years earlier, complained to him how difficult the second highest peak in the world was proving to be. They told him their high camps had been destroyed by storm, that there was never a sufficiently long spell of weather to permit a summit attempt, and that they had been there for months and wanted to go home. Fischer, who was in his element—he had already climbed *that* 8,000-meter peak and was busy climbing *another*—could offer little comfort to the frustrated climbers.

"I told them," remembered Fischer, "'Hey, that's K2. Camp III was destroyed by storm for me, too, but if you want to climb K2 you've got to stick around. Keep trying.' They were all bumming out. I know what it's like. But that's the game. It's pretty easy to get tired of it."

As the coffee flowed, Fischer was particularly struck by one climber whose commitment to climb K2 reminded him of his own: Alison Hargreaves. She and Fischer had something else in common: kids. Hargreaves' boy and girl were almost exactly the same age as Andy and Katie Rose. Scott appreciated her strong drive, and her ambition to become the first woman to reach the top of the world's highest mountains.

In the midst of the great mountains he loved, Scott enjoyed hosting Hargreaves and the others who were attempting K2 that year. Among them was Peter Hillary, son of Sir Edmund Hillary, who was leading a New Zealand effort. Fischer also relished his role of old K2 hand, successful K2 climber—and he was happy to share with the others the gist of his own experience: never give up.

When the coffee-fueled socializing ended, the K2 climbers went back to their formidable objective, and Fischer went back to his own 8,000-meter peak. Eventually, a spell of good weather enabled him to reach the summit of Broad Peak on August 13.

"We hit the summit of Broad about 10:00 A.M.," remembered Fischer. "Conditions began to deteriorate around noon, and by the time we had descended to our high camps the weather was getting nasty. At about six that afternoon, a huge storm hit. We had a couple of minor epics, it got a little desperate, but we got everybody in our group down to our Camp I in good shape."

On his way off Broad Peak the next day, Fischer could see the gleaming pyramid of K2 just across the valley. He could tell from the snow plumes flaring off the upper mountain that monster winds were raking the summit slopes of K2. When he arrived at his base camp, there was a knot of people gathered around an extremely sharp 1000-power spotting scope mounted on a tripod. Through the scope, expedition members could see K2 clearly and what looked like bodies near the summit. Tragically, the savage mountain had claimed more victims, and in the usual way.

With all his climbers down safely from Broad Peak, Fischer sent word to Peter Hillary on K2 offering his assistance, if it were needed. But already it was too late. The news from K2 by radio began to change from "everybody's missing" to "everybody's dead."

The storm that had nipped at Fischer's heels on Broad Peak had caught the K2 climbers near the top. On the morning of August 13, Peter Hillary and three others had reluctantly retreated from Camp IV on K2 in the face of what appeared to be dangerous weather. Seven climbers from three expeditions had pressed on toward the summit. At least six had succeeded, but were caught high on the mountain when a windstorm struck ferociously late in the day. None survived. Seven more people had died trying to descend K2, seven more names to be scratched on pieces of metal and added to the Gilkey Memorial.

As Scott listened to Hillary's story, he could imagine what it was like to be exposed to such a storm high on K2. He had been there. The 1995 tragedy on K2 was a stark reminder for Scott Fischer of the dangers inherent in his chosen line of work. He couldn't help but think about Alison's kids. As he prepared for his long march out to Askole, and the flight home to Seattle—and a reunion with Jean and Andy and Katie Rose—he of all people appreciated the extent of the tragedy. Alison's commitment to climbing K2 had left her children without a mother.

Scott Fischer doesn't deceive himself about the danger, but high-altitude climbing remains the focus of his life. He knows how lethal it can be. But he is protected by a strong and innate belief in himself, his skill, his experience—his ability to come down alive when others may not. Like an Olympic athlete, he plays in the big leagues, and he accepts the risks.

"Only an elite international group of people does what I do," said Fischer. "How could you not enjoy it? You go to the most beautiful places on earth, you run into people you know, you do what you love. What a way to live. But, see, that's the whole deal—If you don't live, you don't have any fun at all."

That, more than anything, offers the keenest insight into Fischer's approach to climbing. It's not simply how many big peaks one can bag, it's how many big peaks one can bag and still come home. The past years have seen unparalleled success for Fischer—on K2, on Everest, on Broad Peak. The game of permits and fees, the shifting allegiances and expeditions of convenience, are old hat for Fischer and he accepts them as part of the game. Business is good, his accomplishments have not gone unnoticed. But from his earlier defeats on Everest, he knows that being good isn't good enough—you've got to succeed, and you've got to come back down.

That's the game.

AUTHOR'S POST SCRIPT

On May 11, 1996, as this book was going to press, Scott Fischer died tragically in a fierce storm shortly after having climbed Mount Everest for a second time. He died of exposure and probable high-altitude edema approximately 3,000 feet below the summit when an unexpected blizzard with hurricane-force winds struck suddenly, catching him and other climbers exposed high on the mountain. Scott's friend Rob Hall and six others died in the same storm, making May 11 the deadliest day in the mountain's history.

CHIMNEY ROCK

I registered the pain and
altered attitude of my body
after each collision. Some
were worse that others, I
could tell, some breaking
bones, some not. . . . I was
absolutely aware: it was as
if my body were being killed
while I watched and listened.

W e had the stove going by 5:00 A.M. The dawn came steely gray, cold and still, the sun up but still below the ridgelines. The roar of glacier meltwater tearing down the mountain in midsummer torrents put a layer of white noise on the alpine quiet. The tent was pitched on a gently sloping heather bench, the fuel and cooking pots laid out on a big rock, the packs and the rest of the gear strewn about our camp at the edge of a big snowfield. We were smack in the middle of classic summer high pressure, the kind that brings spells of reliably good weather to the stormy Cascades. The sky was clear, the surrounding peaks big and black where they were silhouetted against the brightening sky. We prepared the usual breakfast of instant oatmeal (extra raisins for me) and coffee, and ate standing up around the hissing stove. I cradled the plastic bowl in my hands, warming them. There were just the two of us, as usual, and not much conversation. We had done this so many times before. We rinsed the dishes with the leftover hot water in the cooking pot. Into the packs went two racks of hardware and two ropes, little else: lunch, a few extra clothes, the maps, and other usual stuff. The plan was to start high, travel light, and move fast. From this camp at about 5,000 feet we figured to be on top of 7,680-foot-high Chimney Rock by midmorning.

With breakfast done and the packs ready, I sat on a big rock at the edge of the snow and with chilled fingers strapped crampons—racks of steel spikes—to my boots. The air was bracing, aromatic with heather and high-country timber. There was the subtle, familiar tension, the pregame jitters, the not-unpleasant mixture of anticipation and anxiety that comes before the climbing begins. Shouldering our packs, we stepped off the uneven vegetation and crunched across 200 yards of frozen snow toward a gully in the rocky shoulder of the mountain. The snow-filled cleft led steeply upward out of our small basin. We quickly warmed as we moved up and out of the sparse, stunted timber. The cramponing and easy scrambling had us gaining altitude fast.

Our route up the mountain was slightly off the beaten path. Our camp on the pretty little heather bench was higher and farther to the east than the basin directly below Chimney Rock's South Peak, which is the usual starting point for the climb. But here on the road less taken the going was obvious, and pleasant. After about 700 feet of climbing, our crampons scraping on the rocks that protruded from the snow, our cleft opened onto a rounded dome of rock and scree from which we stepped onto the broad expanse of the upper Chimney Glacier. We stopped for a drink and a moment to take in the scene. The rising sun illuminated the reddish rock of the mountain above us. We were in the shallow cirque formed by the three summits of the mountain, our view of neighboring Summit Chief, to the east, blocked by the North Peak, the adjacent peaks of Chickamin and Lemah out of sight behind the South Peak. Below us, draining a multitude of small creeks from the surrounding glaciers and ridges, a big forested valley doglegged south, one lake out in the middle distance, a bigger one farther down where the valley turned east. The white ice of the lower Chimney Glacier spread away beneath us. Glaciated mountains punctured by rocky towers marched down the ridge to our right as we faced the valley. In the distance, Cascade mountain ridgelines arced away to the horizon. There was not a cloud to be seen. It was going to be hot, even up this high.

Our slightly unorthodox route put us on the glacier hundreds of feet higher than the standard route, circumventing the icefall and broken ice farther below. In high summer the icefall can present crevasse problems that necessitate long detours.

We checked our maps against the upper mountain before us. Our position was directly under the North Peak, one of three prominent spires that make up the craggy bulk of Chimney Rock. Already above 6,000 feet, we would have only to traverse a mile or so across the glacier to reach the start of the more technical rock climb. As we moved west on the ice we would pass, in turn, the three possible routes we might take to the summit of Chimney Rock: first we would reach the start of the East Face Direct, a midfifth-class route going straight up the big face of the Main Peak; next would be the start of the East Face or so-called normal route, which follows a prominent gully between the South and Main Peaks; and last, a circuitous route called the U Gap that begins on the south side of the South Peak and requires a long traverse on rocky ledges to join the East Face Route high on the face.

As we traveled across the upper glacier we could tell our choice of route was not going to be difficult. The size and condition of the 'schrund—the moat where the glacier meets the rock of the upper mountain—made the first two routes impractical. We stood out on the expanse of ice gazing up at the long rock routes, discussing quietly what was clear just by looking. We adjusted our vector and began the long walk around the mountain to the steep snow chute that would take us up to the col known as the U Gap, hopeful it would prove feasible.

Traversing the glacier was pure pleasure. Doug and I followed in each other's footsteps by turn, sidehilling against the moderate ice slope, enjoying the scenery. We were still crunching along the glacier in cool shadow, but the sun was really working on the peaks, painting the rocky mass of the mountain above us a breathtaking Rembrandt gold. The sky behind was the acute blue of early morning in the mountains.

I was comfortable being here with Doug, the result of years of similar trips into the cursed and wonderful and wild mountains of the Northwest. Our party was small by design, two being the mutually preferred group size for our trips, though conventional wisdom urged bigger parties for the sake of safety. We were well matched in ability and temperament, confident we could deal with the weird and unpredictable turns that events can take in wilderness mountains, and which make traveling in them so interesting. Our specialty, when we had the time, was big mountains in remote areas. We could handle the long approaches and heavy packs, and we enjoyed the scarcity of other two leggeds. In six years of climbing together we had taken minor falls, been lost in slide-alder-choked valleys and caught out in miserable weather, but we

had not had so much as a close call, such was our combined skill, judgment, and dumb good luck.

Traveling together, we could move fast without the conversation or inertia that comes from larger groups. At times we had words over routes and camps and when to cook dinner, but we always seemed to reach a workable resolution without the dark animosity that can come between people when they travel for days in the backcountry. This business of climbing partners is complex, for it's merely prudent to take care in choosing those to whom you're willing to trust your life. But you want to have fun as well. Over the years, Doug and I had found we worked pretty well together, and we did a lot of laughing.

We shared a profession—journalism—as well as a penchant for a good story and a little high-proof whiskey by the fire. We had made our way up major and minor peaks in the Olympics and Cascades, camped in outrageous places, wandered remote little basins and spectacular ridges. Climbing like this in the Northwest is among the best things you can do, and we enjoyed ourselves. Our success rate was high. When climbing day came around we roused ourselves early, moved fast, and generally got where we were going.

That morning high on Chimney Rock was the fourth day of a fairly strenuous outing. From Seattle we had taken the hour-and-a-half drive on Interstate 90 over Snoqualmie Pass, turned off at the little town of Cle Elum, and meandered another hour or so through the national forest to the trailhead at Cooper Lake. Parking the car there, we set off on foot alongside the Cooper River as it flowed prettily through virgin fir and hemlock forest. About seven miles in, just within the boundary of the Alpine Lakes Wilderness Area, we reached Pete Lake. Across the lake we could see the spires of Chimney Rock and its near neighbor, Lemah Peak, rising abruptly from the trees. Both stand almost 5,000 feet higher than the lake and from that vantage point are impressive despite being miles away. We dropped our heavy packs—nearly a week's worth of provisions, plus the ropes and hardware and ice axes, added up to real weight, maybe 70 pounds each—and had lunch while looking up at the rocky peaks.

Peter Potterfield climbing in the Coast Range, 1993 (Photo by Jim Nelson)

First-day packs for extended climbing trips can take the highlight off anyone's wilderness experience. Doug was five years younger than my thirty-eight years, 20 pounds lighter than my 165 pounds, and a couple of inches shorter than my six-foot-one height. A marathoner, his youth and superb fitness enabled him to carry weight nearly half his own. We had done this pack-animal bit before, and did not particularly enjoy it, but it's the price you pay. We squirmed back into our loads and moved on up the valley a mile or so beyond Pete Lake. There we intersected the Pacific Crest Trail, a major thoroughfare of Western backcountry that runs from Mexico to Canada along the spine of the Sierra and the Cascades. We turned right, north, in the direction of Dutch Miller Gap, though our destination was elsewhere.

This section of the Pacific Crest Trail along the northcentral Cascade Crest is well maintained and generally easygoing, but in the July heat our steady uphill progress with our big loads took a toll. We cruised along the valley floor, then labored up the seemingly endless switchbacks on the big ridge separating the Pete Lake drainage from that of Waptus Lake. We were winded and our water bottles drunk dry when, about halfway up the ridge, we left the Crest Trail and set out over rocky, broken ground and sparse timberline vegetation toward tiny Vista Lakes (which don't appear on most maps). There, at dusk, we pitched camp in splendid isolation, feasting and laughing, guzzling the beers Doug traditionally and unbelievably packs in for the first nights of our longer trips. We were giddy to be free of our loads, happy to be, once again, in the mountains.

The next day we explored the rugged country with luxuriously light packs and moved our camp into a little unnamed pass under the Summit Chief massif. We were touring an uncommonly wild corner of the Cascades and, though it was peak season, saw no one. Our intention was to travel off trail at timberline to Lake Ivanhoe, a body of water just south of Dutch Miller Gap, and from there climb a route on the vast west face of Bears Breast. From our new camp beneath Summit Chief, in fact, that massive mountain beckoned to us across miles of hard country. We discussed our options at length as we roamed about. In the end we had to concede that with only two climbing days left before we were due back in Seattle, Bears Breast was out of reach. Chimney Rock was the sensible alternative. We would return another day and do Bears Breast from the other side of the gap.

In the morning, then, back down the mountain we went, retracing our route to the Crest Trail down the boring, hated switchbacks. At the valley bottom I stashed some food, my trail boots, and other gear I wouldn't need, and we found the start of the climbers' track up toward Chimney Rock. Grunting and sweating our way up the steep, brushy, muddy, and unsavory way trail, we reached our high camp on Monday afternoon, July 25, 1988, and pitched the tent on the undulating bench of alpine heather. The next morning, our wristwatch alarms roused us in time for an early start on the mountain.

As we cramponed across the Chimney Glacier with the rhythmic, flat-footed gait such travel requires, each step punctuated with the bite of the ice ax ferrule, it was as if for all our hard work the Cascades rewarded us with their benign aspect. The high reaches of those mountains can be truly awful—gray, windy, wet, cold, colorless—and, in fact, usually are. That's why there are glaciers in the Cascades at the same altitudes at which highway passes are built in the Rockies. Spells of good weather do come in the summer and fall, however, and that morning the scenery and weather both were glorious. Like privileged guests we moved around up there in shorts and T-shirts over polypropylene long underwear, unburdened by sleeping bags, tents, and stoves. It was the kind of day that makes me revel in the tangible sense of freedom climbing sometimes brings—unlike the bad days on dangerous routes when I just feel stupid, the only rational thought coming as a recurring question: "What am I doing here?"

I think all climbers are ambivalent about what they do, but most keep doing it. The allure of mountaineering is something that persistently resists satisfactory explanation, probably because every climber has his own reasons. It nevertheless exerts a powerful attraction. For me it has something to do with being far away in a beautiful place, alone or nearly so, and traveling under one's own steam through rugged country completely unmarked by modern blight. Climbing is the best foil I've found for the onerous realities of the twentieth century. It keeps me in touch with the sun and moon and stars, with wind and terrain, with my body and my abilities, and, quite often, with the texture of my fear. I enjoy it immensely, when I don't hate it.

As we traversed under the summit towers of Chimney Rock—local relief was almost 2,000 feet from glacier to summit—we saw that the mountain was made of slabby, rotten rock—hard, contact metamorphosed breccias with sedimentary interbeds. When Chimney Rock was first climbed in 1930 it was widely held to be the hardest rock climb then done in the Cascades. It has since become a moderate route in the scheme of things, interesting but not terribly technical. But its loose rock is as threatening now as it was in the thirties. More climbers get the chop from falling rock than from falling off; it's a situation to regard with distaste.

With its three distinct summits, Chimney is a sprawling, complicated mountain. Only from a distance does the main summit stand out and give the peak its eponymous feature. Our long traverse took us directly under all three towers. After more than an hour crossing high on the glacier, we passed under the 1,500-foot-high south face of the South Peak and began climbing a narrow snow-filled couloir up to the U Gap, a notch between the South Peak and a high, rocky prominence called South Point. We were able to climb into the 500-foot snow chute without much trouble. It steepened quickly, reaching maybe 55 degrees near the top. We were still in shadow so our crampons bit well into the firm snow, but the morning shadow line was chasing us up the couloir as the sun rose in the sky, threatening to overheat us and to soften the snow into sloppy stuff that would make climbing more difficult.

About halfway up the chute Doug and I discussed the merits of exiting the couloir early to proceed on rock, but decided that continuing up the snow chute to the top was our best route. As we paused fifty feet apart on the steep slope, anchored by the shafts of our ice axes, I heard Doug say, "Uh, we've got a problem."

"What's that?" I said, curious, turning downhill to face him.

He was rifling energetically through his pack, and pointed to a rock the size of a portable television set lying in the snow a few feet from where he stood, downhill leg locked, on the steep slope. "That thing almost hit me," he said. "I'm putting my crack hat on." His helmet would have done

North Peak

Main Peak 7,680 ft

South Peak

U-gap

accident

ledge

Chimney Glacier

icefall

camp

Chimney Rock

STAMPLENAAR

him little good had he been in the way of that rock, but I started digging for my helmet, too. I hoped the slabby slopes of Chimney would send us no more such greetings.

Climbers have a name for such random acts of fate as rockfall and avalanche: objective dangers. Short of staying home, there just isn't much to be done about them. By now a cautious old-timer, with recklessness burned out of me by years of climbing, I try to avoid objective dangers. There was nothing for it here, however. I strapped on my own blue helmet and cinched it up. Hard hats are hot, heavy, and uncomfortable. Like most climbers, Doug and I wore them only when we felt them necessary. But because they are most certainly indicated for wilderness climbs such as Chimney and Bears Breast, we had lugged the things with us for the past 20 miles. Retrieving my ax from the snow, I set out for the top of the gully, taking over from Doug the fatiguing chore of kicking steps in the steep, hard snow. It was 8:30 A.M. We had been climbing three hours.

Finally reaching the top of the snow chute, we left the snow and climbed up to the crest of the small col, where we sat on a couple of big rocks. There we removed our crampons and strapped them—along with the ice axes—to our packs. From here on, we would climb on rock, not ice. Our route traversed the South Peak via a series of small ledges before joining the East Face route about 500 feet directly under the summit. Unroped but helmeted, we set off on an obvious ledge system—the mountain here was made like a Mayan pyramid, stepping back as it went up, and we had merely to connect the wide ledges by easy scrambling.

We made reasonable time around to the south face of the South Peak. There the ledges began to get more problematic, less obvious, and generally a little more tenuous—smaller, downsloping, and covered with loose rock. I didn't like the look of it. Ahead of Doug, I called back to him that our route looked loose and unaesthetic and dangerous. When he joined me, he concurred but suggested we continue on to see what developed.

We stopped on the last comfortably sized ledge to pull out the hardware slings, don harnesses, and rope up for the harder ground ahead. From my hardware rack I selected a likely sized chock, a multisided piece of machined metal alloy with a short sling of nylon rope attached, and placed it into a handy crack. It wedged nicely. I clipped the sling into the back of my harness with a snap link called a carabiner—climbers just call them 'biners—to anchor myself to the mountain. Tied into one end of the 150-foot rope, I pulled out the slack until only a few feet remained between me and Doug, who was tied into the other end. Pushing a loop of rope through the slot on a thick metal disk called a Stitcht plate, I clipped the loop into my main harness 'biner. If Doug should fall now, even if I weren't conscious, the rope could not run through the Stitcht plate and, attached to my anchor, I could not be pulled off the mountain. Doug was on belay, protected from falling. As he climbed, I would pay out rope through the Stitcht plate.

Doug set off on the first lead. We dispensed with the usual signals, such as "ready to climb" and "on belay," because we had done this so often it would have been superfluous. Only when we were out of sight of each other were signals necessary between us. I settled in to belay him as he moved out of sight around a corner.

The morning was unbelievably fine, warm but not yet hot. While the rope paid out through my Stitcht plate as Doug climbed—or rather, moved horizontally around the mountain—I gazed out over the valley and our entire route for the past few days, from Cooper Lake up the big valley to Pete Lake, along the Crest Trail to the hot switchbacks of the big ridge, even part of Summit Chief itself. But as pleasant as it was to be up so high on that perfect Tuesday morning in the Cascades, I couldn't shake the feeling that something was wrong. I had become uneasy about the mountain and the route. It was an odd sensation, and for me an unfamiliar one. I called out to Doug. About a hundred feet of rope had paid out, but there had been no movement for some time. It seemed as if he was taking forever to set up his belay, and I was becoming irritated. My crankiness matched my uneasiness. Soon, though, he was shouting, "Belay on!" indicating that he was safely tied in and ready for me to follow.

I covered the 100 feet or so to where Doug, anchored to the rock, was reeling me in. In that short distance, the misgivings I had expressed to Doug earlier had turned to grave premonition.

"I still don't like this, Doug," I said, and jokingly added, "I tell you, my love of life is stronger than my desire to climb Chimney Rock." I was now experiencing a powerful negative foreboding, but when I looked out over the benign landscape, I could not figure out why. The ledges were loose and unattractive, but we had negotiated worse. There was no rational basis for getting psyched out so, but there it was. Sitting down on the rubbly rock a few feet from Doug and his anchors, my doubts gnawed on me. I declared: "I think this might be my high point."

"Look, it'll probably get better around the corner," he said, as he sat in his belay stance, the rope piled at his feet, a few yards stretched between us. "We're almost around to the standard route by now. Let's check it out, anyway. OK?"

Clearly Doug wanted to press on, and given the perfect conditions I couldn't argue with him. To pansy out now would be bad form—I hated it when climbing partners did that to me. We were more than halfway up and moving well. We were actually ahead of schedule, maybe an hour and a half from the top. The weather was good and the morning young. Reluctantly I agreed to continue on.

There were two routes from Doug's belay stance that looked feasible, though neither was particularly appealing.

"The one on the right?" Doug suggested, as he adjusted the ropes and anchors to belay from a different direction as we swapped the lead. On close inspection, the right-hand route definitely looked more likely than the other to take us where we wanted to go. I checked my gear, cinched up my pack, and climbed past Doug onto new ground. He was ensconced in his stance, back against the rock, the rope piled at his feet. His new belay device, a "Tuber," was unfamiliar to me, but he had shown it to me on our last climb and seemed to like it.

My concentration was now on the rock. The ledge on which I stood was covered with loose rocks, and a little farther on narrowed and became increasingly downsloping, much harder than our previous ground. From there I could go left and up or down and right. My uneasiness did not abate. I wondered if we were off route. Moving cautiously, I set out on the lower of the two ledge systems, angling slightly downhill from Doug's belay. As usual, so long as we remained in sight of each other we dispensed with voice signals.

Leaning out around a corner near the end of the ledge, I could see another ledge, big and grassy, about 15 feet away. The face in between was thin, but looked as if it would go. I figured to make a descending traverse of the face on small holds, and reach the big ledge. From there I could move farther around the mountain toward the normal route.

Thirty feet or so from Doug, I hung a sling on a small horn of rock protruding handily from the face and clipped the climbing rope to it with a carabiner. Since I was actually below Doug, my safety factor had improved. If I fell on the thin section I would essentially be top roped— held from above—and if the sling held, would face, at worst, a short fall. If the sling failed, I would pendulum across the face to a line directly under Doug, but with only 30 feet of rope between us, still not take a serious fall. I moved off around the gentle corner, leaving Doug behind and above as the rope paid out. Out of sight now of my partner, I moved down by strenuous moves on decent holds to the rock face between my protection—the sling—and the grassy ledge beyond. It was harder than it had looked.

Although there were good holds above my head, there wasn't much for my feet, and my boots scraped the rock before I saw some nubbins on which to place the tips of my Vibram soles. Another couple of moves over the thin face, not too bad, and I was halfway. And I knew I was in trouble, for I could see a blank stretch of rock offering no good holds. This climb isn't supposed to be this hard, I thought. We must be off route. By then I had one decent hold for my left hand and nothing but friction on a little bulge for my boots. I thought about trying to reverse my moves back to the narrow ledge, but knew I was kidding myself. I was in trouble and realized I was about to log some air time, a really awful thought. I have fallen only rarely, and then on bombproof-belayed practice crags. The idea of peeling for real scared my mule.

I hung on, looking everywhere for an idea, my left hand cramping up and beginning to slip. There was nothing but a small face hold I had seen before, marginal at best, barely out of reach of my right hand. Better holds just beyond it tempted me to try. I stretched out as far as I could and made a kind of controlled lunge. It wasn't enough. My fingers slid across it and down the rock. I was coming off, as my last maneuver had pulled me out of my previous hold. "Falling!" I yelled, and off I went.

179

It was a bad moment, but I had time to realize that it could be worse—I could have been way above Doug and have faced taking a long leader fall. As it was I expected a short fall before the rope, passing through the sling above, stopped my fall when Doug locked the rope in his belay device.

When I peeled, the attitude of my body was sideways—my head way out to my right side where I had reached for the hold, my left hand coming off the one hold above, my feet sticking out to the left. The face here was quite steep, and I just launched off, pretty clean, straight down. Below, the face steepened to overhanging, so I did not bounce or tumble. But the rope kept running through the 'biner above me as I sailed through space with only minor, scraping contact with the rock. I prepared for the jerk that would come when the rope caught me. But it didn't come, and I wondered why it was taking so long.

Then I smashed against the rock face. The blow knocked the breath from me and completely turned me around. I heard bones break. The violence of the impact was unbelievable, the pain spectacular. Another impact followed in rapid succession, worse than the first. I felt more bones break in my left shoulder, heard them crunch and felt my body give. It was nightmarish. So this is what it's like, I thought. After the second collision, I started tumbling down the steep face. My sensations were of cannon-loud explosions as my helmet crashed against the rock, and sledgehammer body blows as impact after impact jarred and tossed my body. I saw nothing after those last desperate moments looking for holds. I ultimately lost my sense of orientation as I hurtled downward, smashing against the south face as I fell.

I knew I was dying, and felt intense sorrow about that. My life did not flash before me, but I thought of Anne, the dark-eyed beauty who shares my life. I felt so sorry that I would spend no more happy times with her and the eccentric fox terrier that made up our family. I felt anger that my good life would end this terrible way, being pummeled and broken by the fall down the mountain.

The fall seemed to take a long time. A big surge of fear swept through me, blocking thought, but as the fall progressed the shock of dread replaced fear. I hated getting beat up like that, dying like that. The thing was, it wouldn't stop, and I knew no one could take that kind of abuse and live. The impacts continued, they racked and tossed my body, but strangely did not impair my lucidity or stop my stream of consciousness. I kept thinking about Anne, kept coming back to her, and how I wished this thing was not really happening to me. Could this be a dream, a hallucination? No, but it took time for me to admit that I was in the process of being killed by falling off a mountain. Just another dead climber, I thought, nobody's fault but mine. A paragraph in the *Seattle Times*, I read them all the time.

I registered the pain and altered attitude of my body after each collision. Some were worse than others, I could tell, some breaking bones, some not. I began to feel somewhat separate from my body, but I was absolutely aware: it was as if my body were being killed while I watched and listened.

There was a shape to it, starting with the slip and free fall, and then the endless, terrifying rag-doll impacts accompanied by explosive blows to my helmet. Those were, by far, the worst, then there was more painless freefall—pure air time—and then *wham!* Suddenly my fall was arrested. I had arrived at a tiny ledge just as the rope jerked me up short.

A shattering, unnerving quiet replaced the cacophonous noise of my helmet banging against the rock face. It happened fast. One nanosecond I was falling and dying, the next I was suddenly looking out over the valley, suspended from the climbing rope like a puppet, my feet barely touching the small ledge on the sheer rock face. I could hardly believe it. I felt overwhelmed, not ready to believe what had happened. Waves of pain rolled over me. I got a funny, shocky feeling. My field of vision began to shrink noticeably and rapidly. The world appeared unnaturally blurry and bright, but it was getting smaller. I felt ineffably strange, as if I were hardly there at all. Then, I noticed a change: the pain became extraneous, and my attention shifted to my diminishing consciousness and shrinking field of vision. I felt neutral, separate, and thought perhaps this might be death. I was not surprised. I hung there in a peaceful, sunlit silence. There was no hurry.

I don't remember how long I was in that state of suspended reality.

I may have passed out. At some point, however, the scope of my world began to expand, slowly, definitely. A familiar feeling—that accustomed, essential sense of self—slowly reemerged. Squinting into the brightness, I realized that my prescription sunglasses had come off in the fall. But I was not dead. As if to reinforce that fact, the pain returned with a vengeance, shutting out thoughts of other matters. The pain was exacerbated by my awkward bouncing around at the end of the climbing rope.

I knew I must be badly hurt, but had no idea what the inventory of injuries might be. My left arm hung at a bizarre angle. My left leg was twisted outward and throbbing. My pelvis radiated a deep pain where it met my left hip. Each dangling movement registered in multiple points of pain on a scale I had never experienced. I was sufficiently loony that I was unable to truly grasp what had happened, barely able to take in the fact I was not dead. I kept thinking, Man, I am actually here on this little ledge, still breathing. *Unbelievable.*

Everything about my body was racked with pain and seemed oddly displaced or rearranged. I felt woozy and weird. Right then, more than anything else, I wanted to take a load off, to sit down on that little ledge. But there was too much tension on the taut rope, which ran like a steel cable from my harness up and out of sight beyond an overhang back to Doug. My line of sight above was restricted to about 50 feet of steep rock face, the blue rope running upward plumb-line straight. I could not unclip from my harness because there was too much tension on the rope, yet I wasn't quite standing on the ledge, either. Only by standing on my toes could I touch the ledge. Struggle as I might, I could not unclip. I hung there exactly like a doll on a string.

I tried to move my left arm to take weight off the rope so that with my right hand I could unclip the big harness carabiner from the knot in the rope. With that attempt, an explosion of pain ripped along my left arm. The limb literally flapped in the breeze. I reeled and moaned and I feared I would pass out. So this is what they mean by writhing in pain, I thought. I hung there limp, helpless, my full weight on the harness. Turning slowly at the end of the rope, first one way, then another, I stupidly looked out over the valley and felt a more lucid consciousness gradually return. My situation became clear: busted up and possibly dying after a bad mountaineering fall.

"Slack! Slack!," I cried in a plaintive voice, the loudest I could muster but not one I recognized as my own. "Slack, Doug! I'm hurt bad!" If Doug had me on belay, he could pay out a little rope through the belay device and lower me to the ledge. But no slack came. For a long time in the still of that summer morning, there was no reply. There was no noise at all. I hung there awkwardly. Then Doug's voice, small and disembodied, carried down to me:

"OK, but it might be kind of sudden."

I took that in and realized that I must be at the end of the rope—literally. Somehow the belay must have gone wrong. I must have fallen the full length of the rope, 150 feet. Only the anchors into which the other end of the rope was tied prevented me from plummeting entirely off the mountain, and pulling Doug off with me. Doug had no more rope at his end or he could have simply lowered me to the ledge. With my weight on the rope there was nothing he could do except cut it or untie from the anchors, or maybe rig some kind of prussik arrangement. The prospect of Doug's unfastening the anchors and letting me drop suddenly—even a few feet—really got my attention. Such a move could send me careening beyond the ledge and off the mountain, or at least injure me more by dumping me in a heap on the ledge.

"No, no," I shouted back. "Don't do that!"

I was standing awkwardly on my tiptoes, trying to control the twisting and swaying. I was afraid I might pass out. I started to panic. Frantically, I dug for my pocketknife, thinking I might cut the rope above my harness. But I could not get my right hand into my left pocket. My shorts were pulled up and askew by the harness, which was loaded up with my weight. I was sweating profusely and feeling, by turns, faint and overcome by pain. A panicky thought took me over: If I don't do something real soon I'm going to die right here on the end of this rope.

I looked around. The ledge sloped slightly downward, and so was higher where it joined the mountain than it was at the outer edge. If I were able to back up enough I might gain five or six inches of elevation, enough to unload the rope and get sufficient slack to unclip. But as I began to maneuver on my toes, my weight came on my left leg. That same outrageous pain—I was beginning to know it now—blasted out of my hip and knee. I collapsed once again onto the rope, limp, wasted.

I hung on the rope and closed my eyes. I tried to chase the panic, which constantly nipped at the edge of my consciousness and threatened to screw up my thinking.

I either had to do something myself or yell for Doug to chop the anchors and just take my chances. Hanging on the taut rope, I mustered my concentration. Keeping some of my weight on the rope I began to perform a sort of one-legged soft shoe on the ledge, moving backwards on my apparently undamaged right leg and foot. Doing so gained me a few inches in distance and altitude and took measurable pressure off my harness. I was learning how to use my damaged body. With two or three more spurts of grisly dancing I achieved enough purchase on the ledge to heel-toe up the sloping rocky shelf a foot or more, as far as the ledge allowed and just enough to put a little slack in the rope. With my good right hand, I reached around my body, opened the big Stubai locking carabiner on my harness, and pulled out the figure-eight knot at the end of the rope. Free at last from the rope, I crumpled slightly, but managed to keep my balance and hold myself upright on my right leg.

Unroped now, I felt a new surge of fear—that I might fall again. I was balanced on my one good foot on the downsloping rocky ramp of the small ledge, without any sort of safety line. A fall here would send me over the lunch-tray-sized ledge down to the glacier hundreds of feet below. To make matters worse, my pack had slipped off my shoulders but was still attached at the waist belt. It flopped around dangerously, my ice ax with its three sharp ends still affixed to it. The ledge was small. The pack might push me off. But it contained essential items. I couldn't just kick it off the mountain.

Slowly, I reached across with my right hand and unfastened the waist belt. The pack fell down behind my legs. I kept it there, behind my body, so it wouldn't tumble off. Thus encumbered, with my useless left leg flopping in front of me, I began to lower myself with infinite care to a sitting position on the ledge. The maneuver was horrendously painful, but the ledge was big enough to accommodate me, back against the rock face, heels hooked on an outstanding little lip that happened to lie exactly at the edge. I had been moaning softly, making little sounds with my exhalations (they came naturally and seemed to help) since my arrival on the ledge, but bending my left knee into the extreme sitting position required by the ledge made me cry out loud for the first time. Panting, I slid my pack from behind me to my left side, one shoulder strap hooked over my left calf to keep it from falling off. There barely was enough room for me, much less my pack. I squirmed around on the uneven ledge. I thought: this will do.

But the perch was, in its own way, a screaming terror, a tiny ledge hanging in space from the sheer expanse of rock. The exposure was spectacular. The big south face of Chimney's South Peak rose vertically above and behind me, and plummeted down 600 or 700 feet below me to the Chimney Glacier, easing in angle as it neared the ice. Unlike the perfectly smooth granite walls of Yosemite, this rock face was broken, faceted like a huge gemstone, in some places overhanging, in others, slightly off vertical. To my right the wall overhung dramatically, to my left a narrow, shallow chute ran from about five feet above to end just at the left side of the ledge. This small depression, perhaps two feet wide and a foot or two deep at the top, was substantial enough to channel water but almost as steep as the rest of the face. I could see no feature remotely level or flat save for my own tiny shelf. Peering down to the glacier, I could see the line of footprints Doug and I had made on our climb up this morning. It seemed as if that pleasant morning climb had happened on another planet.

Sitting there on the ledge was a big improvement over dangling on the rope, a much less desperate situation. I was amazed that I was still inside my body looking out at the scene of forest, lakes, and mountains. My shattered arm fascinated me. It seemed to belong to someone else. My breathing was rapid and shallow. I wondered if I were mortally wounded in some way that I had not yet noticed.

I wondered what had gone wrong, why had I taken such a long fall. But, I thought, it really doesn't matter now. I've got to focus. I fought against the adrenaline and fear and disorientation, and tried to concentrate. I looked again at my left arm hanging in the dirt, smashed and crooked, my left leg swollen to an alarming size, especially at the knee and hip. I heard bones grinding when I shifted position. But my feet moved, and inside my boots, I wiggled my toes vigorously: my spine must have survived intact. I arched my back, reassured about that. I sat back, feeling better about my chances. If I didn't move or pass out, I thought that I might be able to stay put on the ledge.

That's when I noticed big black blotches all over the rock around me, on my pack and my clothes. Blood was everywhere. My blood. Big swashes, little pools, innocent-looking stains.

I stared at this blood dumbly, then with rising alarm. Where was it coming from? I looked over my body from my sitting position, and saw that the left leg of my shorts was soaked in blood. Feeling around my body, I found it pouring from my left arm. I gingerly examined the smashed limb. Splintered bones protruded from my elbow. Oh God, I thought, I'm going to bleed to death.

"Doug! I'm hurt bad! I'm bleeding bad! Can you get down to me?"

For a long time there was no reply. It occurred to me it had been a while since the fall had happened. Or had it? What time was it? What was going on at Doug's end? Then, his voice reached me, sounding very far away.

"No," he called back, "I can't get to you from here and get back. Can you get back up here?"

"No! No way!" I thought for a few seconds. "Doug! Go for help. I'm hurt bad, I'm bleeding bad. I might not make it. Go fast, Doug."

I was at the very edge of panic. This blood was bad business. My desire to live was overpowering, while my chances of doing so were diminishing. I sat on my south-facing ledge in the hot sun, and a clammy sweat coated me. I had to do something about the bleeding.

My bloody pack was precariously perched, poorly stashed into the little chute beside me, held in place by my immovable left leg. I thought about the first-aid kit I always carried, with its manual of emergency medicine. But what I saw with alarm was that the side pocket of the pack, which held my water bottle, was pointed downhill, threatening to dump the bottle down the mountain. I needed water to live. Gingerly, careful to keep from falling, I reached across my body and with my good right hand turned the pack around. The water bottle was secure.

"Wait!" I cried back to Doug. "Can you lower some water? Are you still there?"

Obviously he was, for his rope still hung beside me, the figure-eight knot from which I had unclipped dangling in space above my head. He called out to wait a second, and I watched the end of the rope rise up and out of sight. Minutes later I heard Doug shout, "Here it comes."

Into view came a water bottle and a blue fleece jacket clipped to the end of the rope with a 'biner. So steep was the face the bottle hung in midair, several feet away from the rock. By rocking the rope back and forth like a pendulum, Doug was able to swing the bottle and jacket to within my grasp, and I stashed them in my pack. He would be able to get more water on the way down—assuming he could manage the technical part of the descent alone. It wouldn't be easy.

"I'll send up the other rope," I shouted back, thinking that with both ropes he might be able to make long rappels and thereby get past the most difficult parts of his upcoming solitary descent. I pulled my red rope from my pack, clipped it to the 'biner and watched as he pulled it out of sight.

"Go fast, Doug," I urged. It felt strange to bid him good-bye. We had never before split up on a climb. Shortly thereafter my calls went unanswered. He was gone.

Alone and bleeding, I looked around. The ledge was unnervingly small. Save for the rock face I leaned against there was nothing but airy space in all directions. I sat vertiginously exposed in full sunlight at more than 7,000 feet on the south face of the mountain. The rock and air were heating up fast. My physical efforts of the past few minutes—stashing gear in the pack, shouting to Doug, squirming around on the sharp stones of the ledge—had left me light-headed and enervated. I gritted my teeth and concentrated on not passing out.

I was shattered by the fall and terrified of falling again. The pain from my leg, pelvis, and arm began to coalesce into a kind of bombardment, which may have helped me stay conscious but also kept me from thinking straight. I was determined to seize control. Blood was everywhere, still pouring from my left elbow and pooling around the little green succulents that grew in a shallow layer of dirt on my ledge. It looked like arterial bleeding to me. I stared incredulously at the smashed bone sticking out from the skin.

I didn't know what to do about the bleeding. But in my first-aid kit—a comfort kit really, with Band-Aids and aspirins and moleskin and antacids and tweezers—was a little booklet bound in survival orange I had been carrying around for a decade. I dug around in my pack, unzipped the little case, and pulled it out: *The Hip Pocket Emergency Handbook*. Sitting there on the ledge with my knees bent, I opened the book on my lap and began to read beneath the hot summer sun.

The table of contents was right on the cover. In the chapter entitled "Bleeding," I immediately found what I was looking for: the top priority for injured people who are still breathing is to stop bleeding. The little book put it this way: "Work fast, be careful. Concentrate only on keeping blood in the body!"

Nothing ambiguous there, and it even gave two suggestions on how this might be accomplished: pressure points and compression. The appropriate pressure point for my elbow was clearly illustrated as being in my armpit. I reached around with my right hand and groped for my left armpit. But my shoulder had been so smashed and dislocated, I actually could not recognize its architecture to find my armpit. Oh no, I thought. Just how bad off am I? The possibility that some as-yet-undiscovered injury might prove fatal still haunted me. But I managed to shrug it off, say to hell with that, do something else. Just keep yourself from bleeding to death.

The next suggestion was compression, so from my pack I pulled out a thin, foot-square, Ensolite-foam sit pad. This item, a prized possession that comes along on every climbing trip, affords a portable, comfortable place to sit on snow, rock, or wet grass. I folded it in half like a piece of stationery and slowly, ever so gradually, began to wrap my left arm from midtriceps to wrist. I simply took my time and moved carefully. I could hear and feel the bones grinding together and could feel them emerging from skin around my elbow. But the pain was not greatly worse than before. My arm was most compliant, as if it had joints every few inches. I removed the rubber Japanese watch from my wrist and let it fall onto the ledge. Soon I had a sort of rude splint fashioned, which wrapped my arm like a hot dog in a bun. A stream of blood flowed out the back.

From the top of my pack, I pulled out the two nylon straps that held my crampons in place. With my one good arm, my teeth, and a lot of contorted wriggling, I managed to wrap both straps around my arm just fore and aft of the elbow. Because the booklet cautioned that a tourniquet could mean loss of the limb, I adjusted the tension just tightly enough to put some pressure against the open wound without cutting off the circulation. It looked to me a decent job: my smashed arm was well protected by the foam pad, and to some extent stabilized. The flow of blood even seemed to slow. The first-aid book also said to never take away compression bandages, just add more—"cloth of any kind." Rummaging around in my pack I found a pair of gloves, which I stuffed inside the makeshift splint. In, too, went some sling material that had been in my first-aid kit for years, finally put to good use, and a spare sock.

I let my head fall back against the rock, and realized my helmet had come off in the fall. It must have been toward the end, for I distinctly remembered my head bouncing off the face. The helmet had saved my life. Looking out over the landscape, focusing into the distance, I could make out hardly any detail. Was my vision damaged as well? Then I remembered my sunglasses had gone their separate way in the fall. What about my regular pair? Deep in the top pocket of my pack, in the black crush-proof case, were my wire-rim glasses. Intact. Slipping them on was a genuine comfort. And what there was to see! My view was outrageous, and under normal circumstances the exposure would have been exhilarating. But instead I felt completely removed from normal sorts of responses. The sun was punishing. I couldn't believe what had happened to me. I was marooned, broken, exposed to the elements. I was scared.

I dug out my water bottle with my good right hand and carefully cradled it against my makeshift splint while I unscrewed the lid. Raising it to my lips I took a small sip, then another, then a big, long drink, then another. Drinking the water was restorative, calming, but I knew I'd have to ration carefully in this heat. Screwing back on the lid, I regarded the bottle's half-full state and carefully put it back in my pack.

My situation seemed unreal. The ledge was cramped, uncomfortable, and paved with sharp, little rocky points, but it was a resting place. I pondered my luck at having landed on the only ledge in sight. Nobody lasts long at the end of a rope. My soft landing—arriving on the ledge exactly as the rope went taut—smacked of divine interference. A full-speed landing surely would have killed me.

I had no room to move, in fact could hardly shift my weight, but I had water and food and clothing. On the other hand, my injuries were probably serious, the bleeding might get worse, Doug might not make it off the mountain. Was I bleeding inside? Was I in shock? Can a person die of shock? Not much I could do about any of that. But I felt that if I kept myself screwed down pretty tight, I could hang on for—what? A day. A day for sure, maybe more.

How long would I have to hold out? I tried to think soundly. If Doug made it off the mountain, help surely would come within two days. If he didn't, no one would miss us for days, and it would take more days for a search effort to be organized. Too long. I had to believe in Doug's ability to get down safely and move fast. I fixed on that. I felt my resolve coming together. I was going to live if I could. I was going to try not to do anything stupid. I put a name to what I was doing: waiting to be rescued. I said it out loud.

Doug and I had discussed our progress shortly before the accident, so I knew the fall happened at about 9:30 A.M. In the dirt beneath my legs I found the Casio G-Shock watch. 11:20. Tuesday, July 26, 1988. It pleased me to be doing something normal, such as checking the time. But it was going to be many hours, even days, before my situation improved, and I had no stomach for the kind of clock watching I was prone to do. I let the watch fall back into the dirt and reached again for the water bottle.

With the midday summer sun cooking my south-facing ledge, the hot rock around me, like a reflector oven, magnified its effects. At more than 7,000 feet the sun baked my brains at solstice strength. But there was nowhere to go. I retrieved my yellow baseball hat, ripped and dirty, from the outside of my pack, and put it on. It helped immensely. My dress for the climb turned out to be most appropriate: the thin polypropylene material of my long underwear bottoms and long-sleeved top saved me from getting badly burnt. But I felt myself wilt under the combination of injury and exposure. I felt weak.

I took another drink. From that swallow, and all the others, I extracted maximum benefit: I held the water in my mouth, letting it soothe

This photograph, taken by one of the rescue climbers from a U.S. Army helicopter approaching the accident site, shows the South and Main Peaks of Chimney Rock. (Photo by Freeman Keller)

my parched throat, rolled it around, savored it. Only then did I swallow. I screwed the lid back on: down to a third of a bottle. If only I had more water. Maddeningly, far below me near the entrance to the steep couloir Doug and I had climbed to reach the U Gap, a stream of glacier meltwater picked up volume in the hot sun. I remembered climbing past that stream in the morning, thinking it would be a perfect place to tank up the water bottles after a long, hot morning on the rock. Now its trickle and splash, utterly out of reach, tormented me.

In those midday hours, the torment of heat and thirst incited me to plot insane schemes to escape my predicament. Maybe, I thought, there's a way I could get down. On the glacier I would be able to recline, wait for help more comfortably, drink water till I burst. Hell, I thought, I'll just rappel down—with one good arm and one good leg, I might make it. Then I remembered I had given Doug my rope. Then I remembered that even if I had the rope it was almost a thousand feet of rock face down to the glacier below. Then I remembered the intense pain from merely shifting around to look over the edge. I remembered I'd fall off if I so much as tried to stand, that I was apt to pass out from pain or shock or loss of blood at any exertion. I kept remembering. I was stuck.

The tumbling fall had put holes in my polypropylene, and I stared in disbelief as the skin under the bigger holes burned so badly that quarter-sized water blisters began to form. Jesus, I thought, that's bad. My whole body was overheating under the dark blue material, exacerbating the wooziness I already felt. I began to fear the sun might kill me. I consciously kept my head turned so that my face was in the shade of my hat bill. But it wasn't enough. I had to find some shelter.

My pack was by now securely stowed by my left side; it wasn't exactly within easy reach because only my right arm worked, but its mere presence was a comfort to me. Its contents already had saved me. The precious water bottles were in the side pockets, my first-aid kit with its medical manual in a top pocket, and a light fleece jacket, windbreaker, and wool hat in the main compartment. My lunch—the remnants of a salami, some Fig Newtons, a small piece of cheese, and some cracker crumbs—was in the lower compartment. Strapped to the outside was my red SMC ice ax, apparently no worse for wear after the fast ride down the mountain.

I thought about the ax, and gingerly began the tedious task of undoing its strap with my good hand. It took a long time. Finally freeing the ax, I placed it across my lap and pulled out my ugly orange Early Winters fleece jacket. These simple efforts so taxed me that I allowed myself a medium-sized slug from the water bottle and a long rest before moving again. Then, holding the head of my ax, I began to probe above me with the sharp end of the shaft. I couldn't see properly, but I did make out a small cleft in the rock right above my head. Into that crack I tried to stick the shaft of the ice ax, but it wouldn't stay put; the crack was too wide and shallow. I tried again and again in different parts of the cleft, without success. Finally, I lucked into finding a place where there was enough purchase on the shaft in the shallow crack to wedge it, leaving the adze and pick protruding two feet or so from the rock face immediately above my head. Perfect. I rested for a while. Then I reached up and draped the orange jacket over the head of the ax. It hung down sloppily, but created a small awning under which I could get my head and shoulders. I had shade.

It remained unpleasantly hot inside my makeshift parasol, but to be out of the direct rays of the sun was a tremendous relief. To celebrate my improved surroundings, I pulled out the water bottle for a victory slug and was alarmed to see it nearly empty. I rationalized before the onslaught of growing thirst: this heat might weaken me to the point of fainting and send me tumbling off. Better to drink it now and be parched during the cool of the night. But not wanting for some superstitious reason to empty the one bottle, I pulled out the nice, heavy, full bottle Doug had lowered. In the shade of my ridiculous shelter, I carefully unscrewed the bottle and drank deeply. Hallelujah! Lemonade! Doug often added fruit-juice mixes to his water, and, thanks to him, I was sitting in the shade drinking lemonade. It tasted great. I think it might have exacerbated my thirst in the long run, but I revelled in the pleasure of those first sips, my head stuck up under my jacket with nothing to see but the labels and the stains, thinking I might just make it.

Without the makeshift shelter, the long, hot afternoon would have taken much more out of me than it did. Even with it, from midday on the sun and heat tortured me. I could feel my strength ebbing. I huddled under the jacket, my head and shoulders out of the sun, and drank all the water I had. Each sip was exquisite pleasure, a sweet surrender. I took no interest in the food in my pack. I put the blue jacket Doug had lowered to me under my butt, to ease the discomfort of the sharp stones on the ledge. Every now and then, lulled by heat and pain into numbness, I stuck my head out from under my shelter and watched the afternoon shadow line creep along the rock face, moving slowly yet steadily toward me. Because the face above me was overhanging, shade would come fairly early, by late afternoon. I hungrily awaited that moment, anticipating the rich relief it would bring.

It was a rare, fine day in the mountains, hot, still, perfectly clear, washed out with the blue haze of high-altitude ultraviolet light common in summer. From my perch I peered out at the panorama. Having climbed above the peaks that earlier had blocked our view, I could now see the jagged summits of Chickamin and Lemah just south of my ledge, to the right. The big valley below was completely revealed: Pete Lake down in the middle of the thickly forested valley, larger Cooper Lake off in the distance where the valley turned east, walled in by a low, timbered ridge. The Cascades stretched on to the horizon to the east and south. That landscape is forever engraved on my memory. But the view held no real interest for me, and conversely, my precarious perch no more terror. I waited impatiently, but resignedly, for the relief of shade. I worried about my condition, particularly the unknown perils of shock. The idea that I might suddenly expire through no fault of my own seemed unfair. I resisted the temptation to root around for my watch to check the time again. Severely overheated, actually sick, the moisture sucked from me, I stuck my head back under the hanging jacket. I took another sip. If only it were a cloudy day.

Some blood was still seeping into the cloth I had stuffed inside the rude splint, but it did not seem a fatal flow. I went through my first-aid kit to see what else might be of use. I found a few of those alcohol wipe pads in foil, and took some pleasure in washing my face. The smell of the disinfectant was pungent. I thought of using some of them on my wounds, but decided it would do no good. The left side of my torso and leg were covered with big bloody scrapes and open wounds, the material from my long underwear tattered and dirty and stuck to the exposed bloody tissue. A protrusion pushed against the skin of my upper thigh, and I feared another bone might show itself. The smashed bones in my shoulder and arm caused me the most discomfort, grinding together ominously with every slight movement. The pain did not relent.

With some surprise I noticed I was still wearing the hardware sling, a half-dozen pieces hanging from it, and carrying slings of nylon webbing over my neck and shoulders. I removed two of the climbing slings and used one to support my left arm from my neck, like a conventional broken-arm sling, and the other to tie my upper arm close to my upper body. There was less movement and less pain that way.

I looked over the hardware rack, and thought maybe I could anchor myself in after all. I had small wired stoppers, medium hexcentrics, and some bigger stuff. I used my right arm to feel around the rock above my ledge for a crack into which I could wedge one of the hexes or stoppers. It's usually possible to get something in somewhere, but I could not. The crack into which I had wedged the shaft of the ice ax was too ill-defined to accept any of the hardware I carried with me. But I had plenty of time, and with my head still up under the jacket I groped around all over the rock with the fingers of my right hand. Finally, I was able to get my two smallest wired stoppers to stay put in sloppy, shallow grooves to my right. Thinking it was better than nothing, I clipped my harness carabiner into the anchors with my last sling, and then clipped my pack to me with another 'biner. But the more I thought about the marginal anchors, I started to worry that if my pack came dislodged it might fall and pull me off the ledge as well. The poor anchors probably wouldn't hold. So I unclipped from my pack. If it went, it went. I was going to stay on the ledge. No dumb mistakes.

When my perch finally came into shadow, I could muster no jubilation, only relief. I took down my parasol apparatus. Stashing the ice ax and jacket, I watched the light over the valley soften into afternoon. There was a swallow or so left in my original water bottle, nothing left of Doug's lemonade. I held off finishing the last bit, knowing the night was going to be a thirsty one. I didn't feel guilty about drinking it all because I didn't think I could have survived the heat without it. I just wished I had more, much more.

As the bright, hot day moved toward muted, warm afternoon, I spoke out loud, to hear the sound of my voice. I looked down at Pete Lake, where Doug and I likely would have jumped in for a cooling swim on our way out to the car. By now, if things had gone as planned, we would have been near the trailhead, an hour or so from a beer and a hamburger somewhere. Instead I was smashed up and possibly done for way up on the face. I thought about my life in Seattle with Anne, my friends, my brother in California—and felt morbid. I saw this kind of thinking as alarming. On the other side of that invasive sadness was a crushing sorrow, regret, and despair that would surely undo me. I tried willfully to avoid it. Pushing those thoughts out of my head, I torqued myself back: endure and do not make mistakes. I sat there.

For diversion, I tried to follow the route of the trail through the trees. I could see the major landmarks, and knew roughly where the trail lay, but could not discern its actual presence beneath the canopy. Across the big, doglegged valley, the bright green of the trees turned black where the lowering sun cast shadows off the big mountains all around me. A raptor rode the thermals, hunting above the higher ground. During the heat of the day, coolness seemed an unattainable relief. Now, out of the direct sun, the temperature was comfortable and I wondered how cold the night might be. I remembered the cold of our dawn start, and I was now 2,000 feet higher than our camp. I wondered if Doug had made it off the mountain. A few hours after his departure, the sound of a huge rock slide somewhere nearby had reached me. I wondered if he had set that off, perhaps been part of it. I felt remorseful about berating him for taking too much time to set up his belay. Those anchors had saved us both. I was angry at myself for my bad judgment earlier on the climb, angry that the belay had gone wrong. I marveled at the power of my premonitions, and wondered if I should have heeded them in the face of logic. I worked the fingers of my smashed left arm. I felt around my pelvis for signs of fractures. I washed my face with another sanitary wipe. I looked out at the softening light.

There was no way to be comfortable on the ledge. Sharp stones made sitting painful, and the ledge was too small and movement too painful to permit changing positions for comfort. Over and over I ran through my small repertoire of options: keep both knees bent, heels hooked over the ledge lip; then straighten good right leg (big relief), hanging right foot out in space; bring foot back on ledge, lock on small lip, and arch back, lifting butt off the ledge, getting a good stretch and brief respite from sharp stones on ledge. Occasionally I'd try to straighten my injured left leg, but the pain made anything more than slight movement intolerable. My arm I kept cinched close to my body, cradled in its protective foam pad. I was grateful to be out of the blasting sun.

As afternoon rolled into dusk, I took out the water bottle. I did so with a sense of fatalism—there would be nothing for it now but to gut it out. I figured I could endure a waterless vigil until the sun started baking my perch the next day. It would happen early. I was already dehydrated from the long day in the sun. I took the last swig of water and immediately felt my thirst begin to build.

A slight evening breeze began to stir, but the temperature remained comfortable, incredibly mild for so high an altitude. Yet I knew the day's heat would dissipate and the coldness of night would soon move in. I checked my clothing: I had a thick wool hat, probably most important, as well as the lightweight jacket I used for my parasol, wind pants, and a light windbreaker. My gloves were currently stuffed into the makeshift splint to stanch the bleeding, so I would have to do without those. I put my hat on.

The day, this amazing, bad day, was drawing to a close. Warm greens and yellows replaced harsh whites and blues. The mountains fell into the stark contrast of warmly lit surfaces and black shadows. I sat alone in my aerie looking out, the beauty of this, my favorite time of day, not completely lost on me despite my troubles. At this latitude in July the night would be short. I figured I'd lose light at around ten o'clock, and get it back by five in the morning. I wondered how it would be, alone on the tiny platform in the huge face in the dark. I felt prepared for what was coming: for the past ten hours I had learned how to sit still on the tiny patch of rock. I worried that sleep or fainting would send me off the ledge, and resolved to remain awake. As there was nothing else for me to do, I leaned back and watched the trees on the east side of the valley go from green to black as the sun set lower. And then I heard it.

The faint and distant rumble of jets overhead had been with me all day, but this was a new noise—smaller, closer. I looked out into the valley and saw something flit quickly across my vision from left to right. I lost it, and the noise faded. Then I heard it again, and saw it: a small helicopter was moving back and forth across the valley between me and Pete Lake. It was five or six miles away, and appeared to have no definite direction. I became excited. Did this have something to do with me, or was this just some sort of random activity in the mountains in summer? It continued to fly back and forth but seemed to be moving closer. As I watched, I realized there could be no mistake. The helicopter was moving inexorably if indirectly toward my ledge. The constant zigzagging up and down the valley appeared to be a means of gaining altitude, not a search pattern.

I watched incredulously as the chopper flew higher and closer, always in my general direction, until it was perhaps a mile away and slightly higher than my ledge. It came closer still, and slower now, looking over the face above me. No doubt about it, the helicopter was looking for me, or at least somebody or something on the South Peak of Chimney Rock. Small and light, like the old whirlybirds, there wasn't much to this machine: just a big plastic bubble and exposed fuselage structure.

I got the orange jacket I had made shade with, and began to wave it in long, slow arcs above my head with my right arm. Between the red pack that was stashed beside me and the bright orange of the Early Winters pile jacket, I figured my position must stand out nicely against the drab red rock, even in this light. They'd have to see me. The chopper came closer, descending at a regular rate, scanning the big south face until it was just above me, maybe 200 feet away. I was waving the jacket like crazy when abruptly the helicopter pointed right at me. It hovered in that spot. I flapped the jacket furiously. I could clearly see the two people inside; why couldn't they see me? Then the passenger leaned far outside the plastic canopy and waved. He was a big blond guy wearing a bright red shirt, and he repeatedly gave me sweeping, friendly, whole-arm waves. I thought I could make out an encouraging smile on his face as he hung out in the breeze. In the other seat I could see the pilot wearing headphones and watching the mountain. As I watched and waved the chopper ascended a couple of hundred feet, and the guys inside looked over the face for perhaps a minute. It returned to hover directly in front of me. I felt the wind from the rotors.

I was stunned as I sat there on my ledge and the realization of what was happening came home. Doug had done it. He had somehow managed his solo descent. And he had reached civilization in good time. Without doubt that was why these guys had come and why they had known exactly where to find me. Now I could be sure that my predicament was known to the outside world. This was a great thing—I was still trapped on my ledge, but no longer lost.

I sat there stupidly gazing at the helicopter. It hovered in midair a few hundred feet from my ledge, carrying, I saw, two basket-style litters, one fixed to each skid. I watched the two people inside look intently over the south face above and below me. Then the guy in the red shirt leaned out into the breeze and gave another big wave. He looked right at me. The chopper was so close I could see his eyes. We both knew there was nothing they could do for me.

With that parting gesture, Red Shirt pulled himself back inside and the helicopter banked steeply and descended, heading back down the valley. I watched it go, silhouetted in the red sky of sunset, then lost it in the dark trees as it flew away. It left behind a great quiet in the fading dusk. To my surprise I felt tears welling up. If only, sometime during the day, I had been able to make it the six or seven hundred feet down to the glacier. These guys could have landed and picked me up, easy as pie. I could be on that bird right now, tied to the skids, on my way to a hospital. I was filled with frustration at my own helplessness. The helicopter's departure made me realize that I was truly marooned, so smashed up I could do nothing to save myself. There was nothing the guys in the helicopter could do either, except pinpoint my location, maybe look over the difficulties in getting me off the mountain.

Once again I had to get a grip on my emotions. The first human contact I'd had since Doug left had come and gone quickly, and I was left feeling small and lonely and disappointed. For all this long day I had wavered some, but pretty much kept my emotions at a distance.

Now I felt abandoned. I so wanted to be carried away by the helicopter. After it left, I had to tell myself to just hang in and gut it out. The right mental state was essential to my survival. The rescue had begun—but it wouldn't be quick or easy.

Any attempt to get me off the face was going to be technical and difficult. I seriously wondered if it were even possible. There absolutely would not be any easy plucking me off the ledge with a helicopter. But at least I knew that Doug had not only gotten off the mountain by himself, he had covered the miles back to the trailhead quickly and found help. I wondered what that trip out was like for him, what he had been thinking. It must have been interesting. I pictured him banging through the door of a ranger station in Cle Elum, exclaiming, "My buddy's hung up at 7,500 feet on Chimney Rock and he's hurt bad." I learned later that Doug had lucked out and had run into a forest service trail crew down in the valley. The supervisor had had a radio, and rescue council pagers had gone off in Seattle as early as 4:00 P.M. Serial reconnaissance was the first step in a rescue, I knew, and somewhere people were organizing, making preparations, launching an effort in my behalf. I was a little embarrassed thinking about that, but I took comfort in it, too.

Darkness was coming on fast. I felt around on the ledge and found the watch: 9:35. The night shift was beginning; it was time to hunker down. I struggled into the orange jacket that had been my flag and my parasol. With my left arm strapped to my body, this was a painful process. I managed to get the right arm through the appropriate sleeve, the other side wrapped around my smashed shoulder and arm. The fabric was stretchy enough that I could pull it closed and zip it up. The wind shirt was another matter. An anorak design, it was tailored more narrowly and would not fit over my battered, trussed-up body. I cut the seam on one side with a pocketknife, which made it possible to get the thing over my head, right arm through the sleeve, and the rest of it draped over my upper body. The hard part of my preparations for night was getting into my wind pants. I debated whether or not to attempt it, but knew if a cold breeze kicked up I could get seriously hypothermic without some kind of protection. It was the kind of mistake I was determined not to make. Fortunately, the Gore-Tex trousers zipped up the outside seams; still, it took twenty or thirty minutes of struggle on the tiny ledge to get the things on my damaged body. I feared the mere effort might cause me to fall off, but it was the prudent thing to do. I pulled the wool hat down over my ears. That was it. I was ready.

I marveled at my intense and growing thirst. I had never before experienced such elemental need and been so helpless to satisfy it. I tried hard to ignore it. The first stars appeared, and the gibbous moon emerged from behind the ridges to the east, but I found that night made little difference to my experience. By now I knew my world pretty well, felt confident I could stay put in it if nothing unexpected transpired. Darkness found me cramped and sore from sitting, throbbing and hurting from my broken bones, stinging from scrapes and abrasions. I was dirty and tired, covered with dried blood and painfully thirsty.

The fingers of my left hand felt cold and tingling, and moved clumsily. I wondered how badly the arm was damaged. The fact that my hand was cold made me concerned about circulation, because otherwise I was not feeling the chill. My gloves were lost to the cause of the makeshift splint, but I improvised by pulling a small nylon stuff sack with a wool sock inside over my bare left hand. I really coddled that arm and hand, keeping it as protected and immobile as possible. Even so, the bones ground away with every slight movement. My shoulder had swollen alarmingly, almost up to my ear.

I thought about eating, but thirst had ruined my appetite. My chief fear was falling asleep, for if I were to lean one way or the other in slumber, I'd tumble right off the ledge. My present lucidity was encouraging, but I doubted I could remain alert through the wee hours.

I was intensely paranoid that the weather might turn at any moment. From wishing for clouds earlier in the day, I had since reversed my thinking. The weather had to hold, or my chances would take a decided turn for the worse. I lived in fear of a mass of low clouds moving in from Puget Sound, grounding rescue aircraft. It happens all the time, so it was no idle worry.

From my high perch, I stared out at the clear, star-filled sky and bright moon. With the valley in darkness, the night sky was the most interesting part of my expansive view. I thought about Anne and our home, the house on Queen Anne Hill with the flowers out front. We were planning to take a few days off on my return to town, to go up to

Vancouver to spend a couple of days together. Throughout the hectic summer at work I'd been looking forward to this week off—a few days climbing in the heart of the Cascades, then a civilized and luxurious weekend with Annie at a good hotel in Vancouver. I certainly had screwed up this vacation. But someone must have contacted Anne by now. She must know. Even though it would be hard on her, I hoped she knew because she'd be rooting for me, and knowing that made me feel less alone.

The time passed slowly, measured by the movements of heavenly bodies from east to west. My south-facing ledge gave me the perfect observatory. In another couple of weeks I could have witnessed the Perseid meteor shower, a phenomenon I had often seen as it came in early August, the high point of the Northwest climbing season. But that night I had only the moon and stars, and the occasional lights of a passenger jet climbing east over the Cascades out of Sea-Tac. I passed the hours looking into the sky, doing my ledge calisthenics, and free-associating through the patterns of daily life, fixing on the glorious, mundane rhythms of home and the people I cared about. I was nagged by the idea that not surviving the ledge would be like disappearing, checking out without any sort of farewell. I never prayed. It seemed bad form to start now, when I had chosen to climb and had gotten myself into this fix with no help from God.

As the temperature gradually cooled, my thirst worsened, becoming a tormenting, painful presence. Each time I swallowed, the parched tissues of my mouth and throat rasped. I sometimes gagged. I continued pulling out the empty water bottles to drain the last remaining drops, even though there was absolutely nothing left in them.

I picked a handful of the small succulent plants growing around the ledge and examined them by moonlight, debating the merits of trying to extract from them some moisture. I worried they might poison me somehow, but in the end my thirst won out. Placing a small handful in my mouth, I crushed them with my teeth and sucked the moisture. There wasn't much in the way of wetness, but they seemed to provide some relief to the parched and gluey tissues in my mouth and throat. When I spit them out, they left an unpleasant and bitter taste. The slight relief was short-lived, but I thought I was ready to try them again if they didn't make me sick.

I reviewed again the inventory of edible items I carried. Five days into the trip there was nothing left offering much moisture. All the fruit and other goodies got consumed in the first day or two. I rummaged around in my pack, looking over the larder, and decided to try a Fig Newton. Might not be so bad, might give me some extra strength and energy for the rest of the long night. I took a small bite, tried to swallow, and the cookie turned to dust in my mouth. The gagging went on for so long I feared I might choke. I was too parched to swallow anything. In desperation I tried another small handful of succulent plants, but this time there was no improvement at all.

Above all, this was the night of thirst. It dominated my consciousness even more than the pain from my injuries. For the first time I knew what thirst really was, and it was a deranging agony. Imagining all the sorts of beverages I might be having at home—cranberry juice mixed with club soda, or large glasses of ice water with a slice of lime or lemon—I conjured up in detail how they would look and taste. Tormented, I longed for a cool drink, and I fought the longing. I tried desperately not to swallow, and swallowed—or tried to—anyway. Despite my determination to remain lucid, my state of mind deteriorated. I reached for the watch: 12:20. Five more hours to daylight. I pinned my hopes on what the morning would bring; by first light, rescue teams surely would be in evidence. With luck, by midmorning I could be on my way. I felt weaker, and worried more now about falling asleep. My vigil, I feared, was on the verge of stupor. I wished I were able to eat something. I needed strength.

In the course of the night I was startled by a small, furious movement on top of me. One or two small rodents scurried across my body. I suddenly jerked upright. That scared me, as a sudden reflex move like that could throw me off my perch. The audacious animals skittered away, but they had given me an idea, or what seemed like an idea. Reaching for my knife, I opened the blade with my teeth, and laid it down beside me. If the creatures came again, I thought, I'll try to catch one, kill it if I can, and drink its blood. I was ready to do it, but I never got the chance. The rock rodents, as Doug and I called them, did not come again.

Late that night, I was surprised by a familiar discomfort: the need to urinate. Surely, the state of extreme dehydration I was in would preclude taking a leak, or so I thought. But it was a fact. I considered for a moment how this might be accomplished in my permanent sitting position. No problem. I simply got one of the empty water bottles, struggled with the fly of my wind pants and layers of shorts and long underwear, and slowly produced about an inch or two of bloody urine. In the moonlight it was as dark as wine.

What occurred to me next is perhaps obvious. There, suddenly, was liquid, right in the water bottle. I knew you could not drink seawater without becoming sick, but, I wondered, what about urine? Didn't that politician, Desai, do it in India? Had I heard stories about people stranded in the desert surviving by drinking urine? Or was it radiator water? Well, I was a guy already chewing on plants and quite prepared to drink the blood of small mammals, so I seriously considered it. I held the bottle to my lips. It was nauseating. I let a little liquid touch my lips. It stung. The thirst I felt was overwhelming, but I could not bring myself to swallow the evil-smelling, highly concentrated, bloody urine. I gagged and gagged. I put the lid back on. Maybe later.

Impatiently, I awaited the graying of the sky, the fading of stars that would come before dawn. But the moon still shone brightly down and the wooded valley remained a dark void. The glacier below, by contrast, was so brightly lit by moonlight that I could have seen people walking on it even at that distance. There was nothing. After peering all day and all night into the void of sky and valley, this scene, I thought, will remain permanently burned into my cortex, like words on a computer screen left on too long.

But now as I looked beyond the glacier into the void of that valley, where the trees were impenetrably black even under the moon, I saw movement. And light.

Actually rubbing my eyes with disbelief, I focused on a small point of light moving slowly deep within the forest of the valley bottom. Could it be rescuers approaching on foot, using headlamps like coal miners? No, it was too far. As I watched, I realized the light was part of a pair. It was a car or truck. And there were others behind it. The vehicles were a long way off, maybe ten miles. I put them somewhere just north of Cooper Lake. But they were real. I watched the slow movement of the lights without euphoria, but with the relief of the certainty that my rescue effort was truly underway.

I thought I knew precisely what was going on. No motorized vehicles could negotiate the trails Doug and I had come in on, but just to the east of that trail from Cooper Lake, and paralleling it for several miles, was a logging road that had formerly been open to hikers and climbers. The forest service had closed that road several years back, adding two or three miles to the hike into Pete Lake and the backcountry around it. Loggers don't work at three o'clock in the morning, so it seemed logical that the road had been opened to provide access for the rescue operation. Even from my distance I could make out the bouncing of the headlights as they moved slowly along the rough road. Incredible. From my perch high on the mountain, I could see hundreds of square miles. I was heartened to see the lights move slowly through the trees. I knew, though, that my position was still at least eight to twelve hours of hard hiking and climbing from where that road ended. If these guys were just getting to the road end, it would be afternoon before climbers could get up to me. That was disheartening. I wasn't sure I could last another six or seven hours under the sun. I was so thirsty. I looked everywhere in that big, dark valley, trying to pick out other lights, perhaps those of people on foot, closer to me. But I saw nothing except the lights on the logging road. They moved slowly.

The night grew colder, my hands and feet became chilled and clammy. I tried to warm them by rubbing the extremities with my right hand. I was glad for the wool hat to ward off hypothermia. Bare heads lose more heat than any other part of the body. Warmth—and dawn—was not far off now. But that would also bring the relentless sun, and I was no longer so sure of what else it might bring. In fact, I felt a new and escalating anxiety about the morning.

I was getting weaker. I was weary of darkness, thirst, and pain. I longed for a drink, for the light of day. Scanning the horizon, I noticed a faint but definite orange glow. Could that be sunrise at last? But wait—it was not yet four o'clock. And that was the wrong direction. I stared at the bright patch of color against the black sky—too far south of east to be sunrise this time of year. What was that? I had no way of knowing that the orange glow marked the site of a major forest fire burning out of control near Snoqualmie Pass. At the time it mystified me, made me doubt my ability to reason.

I began to shiver against the cold. It wasn't the exhausting, killing shiver of being wet in winter, but it worried me. I knew the dangers of hypothermia, I knew I couldn't take too much of this. I was suffering from exposure. I tried to make myself small, to keep as much heat in my body as possible. My legs, hands, and feet became very cold, particularly my left arm and hand. If only I could move around, get some blood flowing. There was no clothing left to put on, nothing else I could do. The mysterious warm glow low in the southern sky continued to perplex me as, teeth chattering, I sat on the ledge. Now I feared my weakened condition might make me careless. I tried to be ever more vigilant.

I had been watching for this event for hours, yet oddly, when it finally came, it seemed to be well along before I recognized it. The black of night had faded to gray. I welcomed the first colorless light, then the band of orange to the east. Ah, and there was the familiar scene of forest, lakes, and mountains. The valley revealed, a tinge of blue appeared in the eastern sky. The rising sun was blocked by the mountain behind me, but I was relieved that it appeared on time and in the right place. The glow to the south was gone. In the valley, the trees were suddenly green. Morning had come, swiftly. As I gazed out over my world, not a soul stirred on the glacier below, nor could I see any activity farther down below. What was taking so long? I said it out loud. "Come on." The helicopter at sunset, the headlights in the night had not been hallucinations. "So where *is* everybody?"

My apprehensions turned to black despair. Thirst raged. My thinking seemed clouded and slow. I felt physically weaker. I tried to calm myself, to muster patience, to wait without anxiety, but I was overcome. I reached down for the watch—the time was near 6:00 A.M. As high as I was, day had fully arrived. Another perfect summer morning was getting on—good flying weather. But soon the sun would emerge from behind the main peak of Chimney and once again roast me. I couldn't believe I was going to have to deal with it again. I felt the sick, over-powering rise of panic. I could not withstand another day under that sun without water. Cold and shivering, I was terrified by the rising sun. *Where is everybody?*

I had no way of knowing that I wasn't the only impatient person on the mountain that morning. At the dusty end of the logging road a man named Bob McBride, sheriff of Kittitas County, was organizing a large and technically difficult rescue involving twenty-five climbers and rescue professionals from four cities, ham radio operators, the Red Cross, the U.S. Forest Service, and two military bases. Six people had been climbing toward my position since half past ten the previous night, many more were waiting to be airlifted to the mountain, others were standing by at various locations. The problem was a lack of air support. The county helicopter—the one I had seen last night—was out of commission. The military would eventually come through, but in the meantime McBride and the growing collection of rescuers were becoming alarmed at the passing hours.

When the sun finally did reach me, its first warming rays brought relief from the cold. This early in the day, the warming was gentle. I felt myself regain body heat. The shivering stopped. But I could feel the sun begin to burn the skin on my face, which had taken a blasting the day before. My lips were cracked and split. I swapped my wool hat for my baseball hat. I wasn't sure I had the strength to rig my shade again. I was disconsolate. I had managed to hang onto my tiny ledge for a full day and night, I had survived the fall and kept myself going, and yet help had not arrived. After mere minutes in the sun, I overheated to the point where I had to struggle out of my windbreaker, and open the zipper on my fleece jacket. I did not have sufficient strength to get out of my wind pants.

I took one last look at the watch—8:30. It seemed remarkable that it had survived on the ledge all day and night. Since it had, I felt I ought to take better care of it, so I put it in my pack. I gagged almost constantly. The raw, parched tissues in my throat tormented me.

With the first puny light of dawn, I had become intently watch-ful. Leaning out over the edge of my ledge, I constantly scanned the glacier below for activity. I searched the sky each time I heard a distant jet, but saw one only infrequently. I tried to pick out the spot where the lights had stopped last night, but could see only trees. I could discern no detail in the forest at that distance.

I leaned back against the face in despair. I could hear the meltwater stream below begin to gurgle audibly as the sun came upon it. The sun was building back up to its ferocity of the day before, yet I couldn't muster the effort to replace the ice ax in the rock above me to rig a sun shelter. Instead, I simply draped the jacket over my head. Soon I was stifled by the heat but was, at least, protected from the direct rays. My thirst was impossible. Hearing another aircraft, I looked out from under the jacket. I saw nothing in the sky. But something caught my eye down on the far edge of the glacier, perhaps 1,500 feet below me and a mile or two away. I stared more intently. There was movement. There were people.

Two tiny figures appeared at the edge of the glacier, so far away I had to squint to make sure it wasn't glacial debris. They moved. Definitely, then, people. Then a third figure, lagging behind, came into view. They looked like climbers—helmeted, small packs, ice axes. They moved incredibly slowly. I could relate. Chugging up that slope was a grunt. I could only hope they were part of a rescue effort. I would not admit the possibility that here were three guys out to do Chimney midweek. But even if they were part of a rescue, it would be afternoon before they could reach me.

I watched them trudge up the ice slope. God, it was going to take forever. I calculated: three hours to the top of the snow chute, then another couple of hours up to Doug's and my previous high point, then somehow down to me, if only a water bottle on the end of a rope. That meant a drink no earlier than 2:00 P.M., almost twenty-four hours since my last drink, and four or five more hours without water in this wilting heat. I put the jacket back over my head.

But immediately I jerked it away. Suddenly there was that sound, the sound I had been listening for since sunrise: the heavy, percussive beat of a big helicopter. I looked around but couldn't see it. There was a huge red dust cloud, however, building in a clearing way down in the valley, maybe eight or ten miles away. I realized that must be somewhere

A U.S. Army Huey lifts off after depositing medic Steve May, Freeman Keller, and Bruce White on the Upper Chimney Glacier. (Photo by Freeman Keller)

near the terminus of the logging road. It was a spectacularly big cloud of dust, spreading and rising, easily visible from my perch. Out of it emerged a big green helicopter. It hovered, rotated and then headed my way. The whop and slap of its rotors grew rapidly to a deafening racket as it flew toward me with impressive speed. With none of the maneuvering of last night's light helicopter, this one fairly screamed up out of the valley toward my position. I recognized it immediately as a Huey, the classic Vietnam-era army helicopter. It was big and loud and to me, in my demoralized state, a beautiful sight.

The Huey flew right at me. As it approached, I could see the red cross painted against a white field. Otherwise it was all drab military green. The noise became deafening as the Huey flew nearer the face, then hovered just as last night's helicopter had. It pointed right at me, wobbling slightly. I could see the pilots in their flight helmets, visors down against the glare of sun. It looked as if there were a lot of people on board, maybe four or five besides the guys in front. I waved my jacket. The pilots acknowledged my wave and looked me over for a good long while, my clothes flapping in the rotor wash. The helicopter then flew higher and hovered again as the pilots examined the face above me. Then, the Huey ascended higher still, and finally disappeared from view altogether. I heard it fly way off to the left someplace, but could not see it. The noise of the helicopter reverberated off the mountain walls of that high cirque and became Wagnerian: loud and spooky, booming beyond belief. After ten minutes or more, I saw it reemerge by the North Peak of Chimney and fly back down the valley. It landed in the clearing, throwing up another big dust cloud.

I watched it disappear into the dust. At that distance it was almost impossible to see, but the moving rotors gave it away. After a few minutes another dust storm arose as the Huey took off once more. This time, it flew not toward me, but off to my left. It soon moved out of sight, booming away invisibly in the cirque as it had before. This was puzzling. Surely they had seen me. What were they doing way over by the North Peak?

I watched the Huey make another round-trip identical to the last, finally settling back into its dust cloud down in the valley. It remained there only briefly, then ascended. This time it flew away—south down the valley. I wondered what these guys were up to. From the two-year stint I had spent in association with a mountain rescue team in Santa Fe, I knew how troublesome technical cliff rescues could be, and my situation was even worse than most. It would be nearly impossible to climb up the face from the glacier to reach my ledge. It was surely impractical—requiring a day at least. The face was covered with loose rock, and two or even four climbers struggling to put up a first ascent could carry no rescue gear. Help would not come from that direction.

Sending climbers down from up above me made more sense. But I didn't see how anyone could come from above without dropping a bunch of rocks on me. Even if climbers were able to reach me, the ledge wasn't big enough for people to gather and work. I could not imagine how these people would go about trying to get me down. The activity I had observed so far from my front-row seat gave me no clue. Putting climbers on top seemed the most likely course of action, but I did not believe that had happened.

I slumped back against the rock. Nothing to watch now but the three climbers moving slowly up the glacier, one continually lagging behind the others. They climbed carefully, deliberately. Climbing up the slope looked like hot work.

I needed to let these guys know where I was—from their perspective, I would be lost in the vastness of the face. Fearing that my voice might fail me, I dug around in my pack until I found the little blue stuff sack that held my lighter, emergency matches, compass, C-rat can opener, and other miscellaneous gear. I pulled out the small plastic whistle and looped the lanyard around my neck. When they got within range I'd blast them with the whistle—which, like my first-aid handbook, I had been carrying around for years without ever having used.

The sun increased in intensity as it rose. My mouth and throat felt like dried-out leather; I could muster no moisture at all. I watched the climbers approach, watched them occasionally drink from their water bottles. I got a great idea.

In my pack was a small ditty bag of various repair items—an extra crampon strap, some ripstop nylon tape, parachute cord, needle and thread, and boot laces. I estimated the guys coming up the glacier would reach the meltwater stream below my perch in about an hour. I would rig up a way to lower a water bottle down to them. Those guys could fill it for me, I could pull it back up and have a drink hours before they could get to me.

The prospect of water filled me with a sense of mission. Frantically, I pulled out every possible piece of cordage I carried, and begin tying them together, an exceedingly difficult task with one hand. I couldn't let the climbers reach the stream before I was ready. I worked like a man dying of thirst, desperately tying together slings, shoelaces, short lengths of parachute cord I used for hanging the packs from trees in bear country. I was using simple overhand knots, but with only one hand and my teeth, it took a long time.

As I worked I began to hear the climbers. At times it sounded as if they were shouting to other people on the mountain, although I could see no one else. But the three I could see were making measurable progress, better than I had thought possible. But so far, no one had acknowledged me. Had the chopper pilots told them where I was? How else would they know? It was time to make sure.

The theory is that the sound of a whistle carries much farther than a human voice, and you're not supposed to shout when you're in trouble, anyway, as it causes panic. I put the whistle in my mouth and gave three shrill blasts, the signal for trouble. To me the whistle sounded incredibly loud, rude almost, ringing out among the peaks and glaciers. To my surprise, one of the figures down below stopped and shouted up at me. I thought I could hear my name, but he was too far away for me to be certain. At that distance, I didn't attempt to yell back. When they got no response they continued their deliberate movement up the glacier.

At last I finished my feverish tying of knots. My lowering system was ready. Everything I could find was tied together into one line. As the climbers moved up the slope, I gave a few more blasts on my whistle. I could see them look up at me. They definitely knew where I was now. I tied the end of a spare red shoelace into a loop on the water bottle just as I heard a faint but distinct, "Hello!" I waved back. They climbed nearer, talking in low voices. I realized there must be another group directly under the face. Suddenly climbers appeared on the glacier immediately below me, 600 or 700 feet straight down. I leaned over. Where had they come from? They were so close to the rock face I could have dropped stones on this new group.

"Are you OK?" someone shouted.

"I need water badly," I croaked. "Come quickly."

"We're coming. We're paramedics. Hang on."

I waved the water bottle tied to my makeshift rope. "Can you get me some water?"

There was no reply. I counted seven or eight people total standing on the glacier. The bigger group, hidden from me before by the steep face, was maybe 20 or 30 yards from the first three. People in both groups were talking to each other. Everyone was looking up at me.

"Are you anchored in?" one of them shouted to me.

"Yes," I lied. I held up my empty water bottle by the shoelace. "Can you fill the bottle for me?" There was another awkward pause.

"Sit still," the spokesman replied. "It won't reach from there. Hang on. We have a shitload of water. We're coming." Four or five of them started up the couloir toward the U Gap.

I was abashed. Jesus Christ, I thought, I must be losing it. In my experience there was no such thing as a thousand-foot climbing rope, much less a thousand-foot shoelace. My water bottle would have dangled down maybe thirty feet off the ledge, and there I was asking those guys, hundreds of feet below, to fill it for me. They must have thought I was crazy. I sat there holding my pitiful homemade rope and felt foolish.

I wondered where the other people had come from. The helicopter must have carried them high on the mountain, depositing them on the flat stretch of upper glacier over by the North Peak. They had not had to sweat their way up from the valley bottom and were moving fast. I figured I might have a drink in two or three hours. I reckoned the time to be around 11:00 A.M., maybe noon.

Meanwhile, I roasted in the sun. My thirst tortured me, my left arm, hip, and leg roared with pain. I felt stunned. Help was almost here, help was coming. My solitary ordeal was ending, and I began to prepare for the arrival of people. I poured out my urine lest my rescuers think me some sort of degenerate drinker of body fluids. I tidied up the little pile of rubble—the alcohol wipe wrappers, some debris from my splint-making. I stuffed my extra clothes back into my pack, stowed away the shoe laces and parachute cord, put my knife back in my pocket, zipped up my pack.

A small group of people had remained on the glacier. I could see them sitting on their packs out on the expanse of ice. They looked up at me. I felt embarrassed to have caused all this trouble. I had never been rescued before. I felt ignoble.

I made no move to protect myself from the sun. What the hell, I reasoned, I can make it a few more hours. I felt a detached curiosity about how the rescue would be implemented, as if someone else were being saved. This ought to be interesting, I thought. My despair was banished.

Occasionally, I heard shouts and scrapes from the couloir, off to my

right. The noises gradually moved higher as the rescuers progressed, until they came from above me. Serious rockfall began to roar off the face to my right, but harmlessly, missing me by 20 or 30 feet. More noises came from above and the falling rocks began to edge closer to me. I could now hear warning shouts of "Rock!" when the missiles whistled past. The sound of a hammer driving in a piton rang out. People on the glacier were gesticulating and talking on radios; they seemed to be directing the people higher on the mountain. Every now and then I'd let fly with a few blasts from my whistle.

Suddenly, from surprisingly close range, I heard a voice from above: "We hear you. Can you show us exactly where you are?"

I took off my bright yellow baseball cap and put it on the end of my ice ax. With my arm fully extended, I waved it around over the edge of the ledge.

"OK! I see you!"

"Come quickly," I said.

More hammering ensued. More rocks sailed past, closer now, a scant 10 or 15 feet off to my right. I heard the electronic squawking of radios.

"Wave the hat again!"

I did so.

"OK. We're coming. Cover your head."

My crack hat had come off in the fall and I had nothing else to protect my head. A pack always makes good makeshift headgear, but there was no way I could manage that. I pulled Doug's jacket from under my butt, placed it on my head, ducked, and turned my head against the rock wall. I got as close to the face as I could. With my good right arm I covered my head and face. A shower of rocks, some mere pebbles, some the size of grapefruit, rained down, but most fell off to the side. All I got was a little gravel and dust.

The end of a doubled rope sailed out and hung in space about 15 feet to my right. The face was so steeply overhanging there that the rope hung free from the lip above until it came back in contact with the rock

Denny Fenstermaker, standing, prepares to rappel down to Potterfield's ledge while Fred Stanley checks the anchors. (Photo by Freeman Keller)

a little below my ledge. The rope was far from reach. As I watched, it danced around as someone above waved and shook it to get out the kinks. I knew that motion well—someone was getting ready to rappel down the rope. And down he came, in a shower of rocks and stones, an undamaged human being. I could hardly believe my eyes.

I thought, so that's how they avoided killing me with rockfall: by descending to my position off to the side of my ledge. But that tactic created problems as well. Sliding slowly down the rope, dangling in midair too far from the face to make contact with his feet, was a stocky young guy in shorts, a T-shirt, and a purple helmet. His rappel was slow and controlled. He descended until he was precisely at the level of my ledge. Still, he was a good 10 to 15 feet away, and he was in a fix. There was no place for him to go. I didn't see how he could get over to me, and there was no ledge or other stopping place for him to alight.

He hung there from his rope, looking over his options. I left him alone to figure out his next move. He finally spoke. "I don't think I can get to you," he said casually. "I'm going to have to go down and climb back up."

I looked over the ledge.

"Boy, that looks pretty hard," I rasped. I had been looking at that cliff for more than a day. It was high fifth class, a tough go. He didn't argue with me. I was dying for a drink. "Do you have any water?" I asked.

"I do," he said, looking around. I wanted water so badly I would have done anything to get it.

"Look," I said. "Throw me the end of the rope. I'll pull you over."

He was skeptical. "Can you do that?"

"I think so. Give it a try."

"OK," he said. But it was awkward. Hanging in midair, he had to hold his rappel with one hand, then gather up the rope below him and try to throw the end of it over to where I sat planted on the ledge. He missed the first two times. On the third try, both strands of the doubled rope came within reach of my good hand and I gathered it in.

My rescuer was a kid of about twenty. He looked strong, but was sweating profusely in the heat. He watched me carefully. I knew that the right side of my ledge had a good lip on it. Putting the rope in my teeth so I wouldn't drop it, I shifted my position slightly so that my good right leg pointed at him, knee bent, the heel locked on the lip. I reached way out, grabbing as far down the rope as I could, and wrapped it around my right hand.

"Wrap it a couple of times," he suggested.

"Ready?" I asked.

"Do it."

If my foot slipped from the lip, or if the lip gave way, I'd sail right off the ledge. There would be nothing to stop me. I couldn't extend my leg, but the big muscles took the force comfortably. I pulled out the slack and felt his weight push my boot heel against the small lip. *Here goes.* With a heave I hauled this stranger toward my perch. The maneuver went fairly well, but it was not quite enough to bring him all the way to the ledge. I tried to lock the rope in my teeth again so I could reach down for another armful of rope, but with his weight on the rope I was afraid I'd lose him, send him penduluming back in the opposite direction, bouncing off the face. He saw what was happening. With me still holding him fairly close, he grabbed the rope between us, pulling himself over the last few feet. He put a foot on the ledge, reached around, found a hold, and pulled himself up. He was here, standing virtually on top of me, his feet on either side of me.

I heard him bang in a pin and clip into it. He adjusted his stance until he was standing on the extreme right side of the ledge, the toes of his boots touching my right thigh. He removed his pack, reached in, and handed me a plastic quart water bottle with a blue top and piece of blue tape wrapped around its middle.

I'll never forget that water bottle, the look of it, the magic weight of it. I heard the rescue guy talk to his buddies above on a small radio as I unscrewed the lid and began drinking. Never has anything tasted so sweet, been so quenching, provided so much relief as that water. I drank in long gulps, stopping halfway through to breathe before finishing it off in another series of gulps.

" . . . he's drinking water now," I heard him say into radio. Right you are, I thought.

"Got any more?" I asked. He handed me another bottle wrapped from top to bottom in, of all things, adhesive tape. I drank it all in one chugalug, leaving a few swallows in the bottle to pour over my over-heated head. God, I felt like a new man.

"Nice to meet you. Thanks for the water," I said. "My name's Peter."

"I know. I'm Mike. No problem."

Mike, struggling to stand on his tiny footholds, got back on the radio to warn his companions of the hot rappel. It was an impossible arrangement on the ledge with both of us there. Mike banged in some more pins and clipped his pack, himself, my pack, and me into his anchors. He took off his hard hat and put it on me, fastening the buckle. He then climbed up above the ledge into the slight depression that creased the face above and to the left of my ledge, and found some footholds. He immediately started hammering in more pitons. The rope started to flap and shake as a second rescuer rappelled down.

Mike and I both hugged the wall as more rocks came zinging past the ledge. I was better protected now with the helmet. As the new guy came into view over the lip, Mike directed him—"OK, a little farther. Stop." He had tied off the end of the rope, so the second guy had a much easier time getting on the ledge. With help from Mike, the new guy scrambled up, putting one foot on either side of me, as Mike had done.

"How's it going?" I asked. "My name's Peter."

"I'm Bruce. You doing OK?"

"Now I am. Got any water?"

He stood there a minute while he clipped into Mike's anchors, then he, too, managed to climb above me and find a some footholds on which to stand. Soon he was handing me another water bottle. I drank it right down. Bruce dug around in his pack some more, and to my surprise, pulled out my blue Ultimate helmet. It was totally roached, with big scrapes and gouges in it, the black trim band gone. But it was in one piece.

"We found it down on the glacier," he said, smiling, looking around in disbelief at the ledge. "Thought you might want it." Mike gladly accepted his own helmet back and helped me put mine on.

The two rescue guys climbed around and above me, into the narrow chute near the ledge, and began placing anchors. They carried a lot of hardware, virtual big-wall racks, and they were driving pins in all over the place. After my solitary vigil, all this was sensory overload in more ways than one. Both had radios, and the entire rescue establishment was on the same channel talking to everybody else. I immediately became very well informed. I could hear my two guys talk to their comrades higher on the mountain, and could hear the people at base camp—down where the chopper kicked up all that dust—talking to people all over the mountain. There was another team waiting at the U Gap, plus the team down on the glacier. Outstanding, I thought, these guys know what they're doing.

A small rock slide announced the arrival of someone new down the dangling rope. Here came a vaguely familiar, helmeted figure carrying a pack with several long, skinny cardboard tubes sticking out of it. He wasn't quite as comfortable with the overhanging rappel as the other guys had been and had a little more trouble scrambling onto the ledge.

"We saw you here last night," he said, smiling. "How are you holding up?"

It was Red Shirt himself. He introduced himself as Steve, a paramedic. Hanging from the anchors Mike and Bruce had placed on my left side, Steve got into the little chute beside me, below the others, and managed to lean down and work on me. The tubes sticking out of his pack were medical gear, and he set about putting needles in my right arm to rig an IV.

"Here. Hold this." He gave me a plastic IV bag of clear fluid.

My formerly solitary ledge had become a beehive of activity. While Steve administered first aid, and resplinted my left arm after praising my amateur efforts, the other guys worked at their anchors. It wasn't easy. I frequently heard the dull thud of pitons being hammered into rotten rock (they ring out when driven into good placements), and the men's vocal frustration at the lack of solid rock. They could work in the vertical environment of the shallow depression above my ledge by standing on holds, protected by the anchors.

Still another person was descending the rope, in the usual shower of rocks and stones. I thought I saw a radio sail by in the rock slide.

Suddenly, in a sickening moment, the latest rescuer came into view in a horizontal position. He was carrying a metal litter broken down into two sections, plus his other gear. The weight of the load had almost turned him upside down during the free rappel, a situation that can lead to a person's falling out of his rappel. Somehow, this guy managed to keep his act together. With considerable help from Mike, he arrived on the ledge exclaiming the excitement of his descent, admitting to losing a radio on his scary ride down. He introduced himself to me as Denny, and I learned he was one of the original three climbers I had seen hours before on the glacier. He had climbed all night to get here while the others had been airlifted up in a matter of minutes by the Huey. Denny was excited. He told me that he was known as the Angel of Death, because so many of the accident victims he reaches are dead when he gets there. He said he expected me to be dead, too.

I introduced myself and told him I was glad to break his string. I asked him if he had any water. He handed me a quart bottle, which I drank right down, saving those last few swallows to pour on my head.

I was feeling better. I had just consumed a gallon of water (a trauma physician later told me that the volume of water had saved my kidneys, barely) in the past half hour. Steve finished wrapping me up and sticking me with needles, and turned on the morphine. For the first time in thirty hours I stopped hurting. I didn't feel high or giddy, just free of pain. But I was still thirsty. I had drunk all the water on the ledge except for Steve's. Having seen me drink everyone's bottle bone dry, he wouldn't trust me with his. Instead, he doled out a few gulps to me, then passed the bottle around. More rocks began to rain down. Somebody else was coming. We all huddled against the face.

Like the others, the new guy glided down the rope, clambered aboard, straddled me, then climbed the face above me to find a spot. Fred Stanley didn't have much to say. Even older than my thirty-eight years, he arrived quietly. He carefully went about checking the anchors and discussing with the others how best to set up the lowering system. He worked calmly, but with obvious urgency.

The guys on the ledge said the best way to get me down was to assemble the litter, put me in it, and in a series of lowering operations, move down the face ledge by ledge until we reached the glacier. There were problems: the litter's support system had not been attached to it, so one had to be improvised out of the sling material on hand. No one was happy about the anchors, either. With all the hammering and sling-tying going on around me, I offered up my own hardware for use. Somebody dug it out of my pack, and my stoppers and hexes went to the cause.

My rescuers were a friendly lot, and brushed aside my apologies for causing them so much trouble. I was still thirsty, but as far as I knew I would be thirsty for the rest of my life. At least I was no longer in emergency need of water. And I was no longer in agonizing pain.

Steve's big syringe of morphine was plugged into my IV; he shot me up at regular intervals. When he forgot, I reminded him. He was humorous and easygoing, and somehow expressed genuine concern for my physical well-being while he worked in perilous circumstances. He had cut away my shirt to resplint my arm and check out my shoulder, given me two bags of some kind of IV fluid, and was almost finished with his ministrations.

The climbers cautiously moved around in the vertical environment of the ledge, connecting the anchors with slings and ropes. These strangers who had roped down to me were outwardly calm—casual to me and to each other. But they were busy, and I detected a certain amount of masked anxiety about the passing time and technical difficulties of the rescue. Two of them, one above the other, were assembling the metal stretcher Denny had brought down. I was a little anxious about how they were going to get me into it. Otherwise, I was calm and curious. I was doped up, but lucid. I watched with detached interest the activity of this group of people working furiously, high in the middle of the huge face. The radios squawked and hissed, carrying conversations between the mountain and base. Concern was expressed about getting another helicopter. Base camp wanted to know when we would be down on the glacier, so one could be waiting for us. It was a question no one could answer. But the day was getting on, around 3:00 P.M., and the time had come to strap me into the litter.

The litter was supported by four nylon slings, one at each corner, which met about three feet up at a big locking carabiner. Into that 'biner was tied one end of a 300-foot rescue rope, twice the length of a standard climbing rope. The rope went from the litter to several belay devices attached to the anchors, so the rescue guys could control the speed of descent by applying friction as required. The system was not a thing of beauty. There were a dozen or more points of attachment to the rock. But it definitely appeared bombproof. Stanley manned the lowering devices while the other guys, hanging from their anchors, maneuvered the litter alongside the ledge. Steve had begun to roll me into the stretcher when Stanley suddenly said, "Wait a minute. Is all the load coming on that green sling?"

Everybody turned to look, including me. I could see how one particular piece of nylon carried much of the weight. It was one of my slings they had incorporated into the system, and I told them that it was sort of old and probably shouldn't be completely trusted.

It took a minute or two to rearrange the supporting slings. But soon the system passed everyone's critical examination. Hanging from their anchors, Mike and Steve did most of the work of manhandling me into the basket-style litter, an awkward and scary maneuver. The jostling caused my injuries to reach up out of the morphine and get me again. But after a minute of awkward struggle, I was lying in the litter. Steve packed some of my clothes and Doug's blue jacket in around me. He then pulled a down jacket out of his pack and covered my upper body where he had cut away my shirt. He gave me a big shot of morphine, then began to cinch down the smaller nylon straps that held me in the litter. At one point I had to stifle a reflexive cry of pain as he pulled on a strap that ran across my shoulder. After a little adjustment, I was totally strapped in, quite snug, staring up at the sky and the sheer upper face of Chimney.

Steve clipped a Jumar ascender—a rope clamp that slides up but not down—onto to the rope above the point where the litter was affixed to it via the big 'biner. That way he could adjust his position relative to the litter. I gathered he was going to make the entire descent at my side, hanging off the same rope that supported me and the litter. Right there next to the ledge, the system worked well: I was lying in the metal litter, Steve hung comfortably at my side from his Jumar, with his legs protruding under the litter so he could hold it off the rock face with his feet. He could more or less walk down the face as the litter was lowered.

A safety line was added to the system: a belay rope tied into my seat harness, then to Steve's, was attached via belay devices to a different set of anchors up on the ledge. If the rope supporting the litter should fail, Steve and I would be suspended from the belay rope by our seat harnesses. I didn't want to seriously consider the reality of a fall from the litter—Steve, me, and the litter bouncing around at the end of the belay rope. But I was glad there was, at least, some sort of backup. Stanley announced that the lower was ready to begin. I asked him some uptight questions about the security of the anchors and the 300-foot rope ("Where'd you get that thing, anyway?"). He looked at me with a crooked grin.

"Don't worry. We've done this before."

After three hours of preparation we were finally off. There was a quick, sickening drop of a few feet, and we dangled around at the end of the rope, bumping into the face just below the ledge. But then things smoothed out. As the guys on the ledge paid rope into the belay devices, Steve and I gradually moved downward. Lying flat on my back, I got my first view of all those people working like spiders on a wall. Ropes zig-zagged through the anchors, and people and hardware and packs hung all around my little ledge. Steve's radio squawked. I heard the people on the ledge report that we were on our way. I heard the guys down on the glacier report that they could see the litter descending.

When we were 20 or 30 feet down, I stared up at that huge face and the tiny ledge where I had spent the past two days alone. I was amazed by the whole affair, not least by the fact that I was inching my way down this vast vertical cliff, completely reliant on a pencil-thin rope in the hands of total strangers.

Strapped into the metal basket, I registered a subtle change in the proceedings. Since Mike's arrival at my lonesome perch, I had been part of the goings-on and preparations. Through the introductions and water drinking and first aid and conversations about strategy, I had been a participant. Now I was something else—Spam in a can, a sack of potatoes, cargo. I didn't mind. As we descended, I looked up at the cliff and the sky and that thin red rope stretching up to the ledge, and I was glad to be making progress at last. I should have been scared out of mind but I wasn't and presumed the morphine had blunted my sensibilities.

As we descended the cliff Steve occasionally asked me how I was feeling. He injected me with morphine every now and then, but mostly

Climbers (from left to right) Fred Stanley, Steve May, Mike Eberle, and Denny Fenstermaker prepare to lower Potterfield from the ledge on which he was trapped. (Photo by Freeman Keller)

he was concerned about driving the stretcher. At times it was quite controlled: as the stretcher descended, Steve merely guided us down the face with his feet. In those places where the face was too steep, however, we hung free in space, at times twisting an uncontrolled 360 degrees. We bumped into things, got hung up on protrusions and little ledges, and rocked from side to side as we descended. At times the rope inexplicably slipped a few feet, and a brief, scary drop ensued. I never got used to it, nor, I think, did Steve. Rocks occasionally whizzed past, but none hit us.

Steve stayed in radio contact with the team on the ledge. Most of the time we were forewarned of any unusual movement or delay. Once or twice I heard Stanley tell Steve, "Hang on now, we've got to pass a knot through the 'biner." Steve and I hung motionless for a couple of minutes while the system was torqued around to let the knot pass, and down we would go again. From virtual midface, my view was spectacular: the sculptured rock rose hundreds of feet up to my ledge, where tiny figures worked the ropes. The vast upper part of the face loomed above them to the blue sky, the cable-straight lowering rope and the slack belay rope flowing gracefully upward.

After literally hours of our slow ride down, we approached another ledge in the face. This one, about 300 feet below our starting point, was much more commodious than mine had been. It was big and flat, with room for all of us. I hadn't noticed at the time, but Denny had rappelled down to this ledge before the litter lowering had begun and he was waiting for us. He guided the litter down to the middle of the ledge, tying us into the anchors he had already established.

When Steve and I were secured, the climbers from above dismantled the lowering system and rappelled down the face one at a time to the new ledge. Then, with more hammering of pitons and placing of hardware, new anchors were placed. Soon, the lowering was resumed. The beginning was the hardest part of each stage of the descent and this new ledge had an even more awkward launch than the first. The litter actually had to be pushed off the ledge, and Steve and I suddenly dropped several feet. But from then on, the ride was as smooth as before, with the occasional pause as the guys working the system made adjustments.

During this second lower, radio conversations increased significantly. The rescuers at base camp indicated they were having trouble securing another helicopter. It was getting late. There was talk about moving faster so nightfall would not catch us on the mountain. One helicopter from the Yakima Firing Range, a military installation east of the Cascades, had been dispatched but had turned back because we would not be on the glacier in time, and the helicopter could not wait. Another was being sought from Fort Lewis, near Tacoma.

It was strange being so well informed since I was a nonplayer, being lowered like a handbag down the face. The news made me start to feel a little anxious. I thought I could detect, too, a rising anxiety among the rescuers with me. It was actually getting dark, approaching the end of the second full day of my ordeal. If we didn't reach the glacier soon I'd have to spend another night out, a prospect I did not want to contemplate. I didn't think I could survive another night.

It was getting cold. Steve and I dangled at the end of the long rescue rope. The strain was beginning to show in his face. We had been at this for six or seven hours. I began to get chilled where he had cut away my shirt, and where the down jacket had come loose. He injected me with more morphine. The rescue people worked away out of sight on the ledge above. To us they were just voices on the radio, but they sounded focused, in control. I developed a real liking for these guys.

The lowering went faster as we neared the bottom of the face. It wasn't so steep there as above, and Steve had better control of the litter. The cliff seemed impossibly huge from my perspective, the plumb-line straight lowering rope disappearing into its vastness.

Suddenly, I heard voices that did not come over the radio. People were climbing up the moderate slabs of the lower face, the same people I had seen waiting down on the glacier. The light of day was failing. I felt as if I had been dangling from ropes most of the day. I had. From about noon, when Mike reached my ledge, until now, eight hours had passed.

The guys who had come up from below were talking to Steve about pulling the stretcher over to the east about 50 feet, where the glacier met the rock face at a higher altitude. Otherwise, they said, another lowering system would have to be set up—and there wasn't time for that. There was a flurry of conversation between Steve and these guys, and, by radio, the team on the ledge. I lay in the litter and listened. I was cold and now I was worried.

Near the glacier the face leaned back considerably. One of the guys began pulling the stretcher out of the fall line, hauling it off toward the east, with Steve helping as much as he could from his position at the side of the litter. I was uneasy about this development. We were still suspended by the rope, and if the stretcher got away from these guys it would pendulum way over very fast, careening out of control. Steve unclipped from his Jumar and began pulling from the end of the

Rescuers rig the second-stage lower. Climbers awaiting the arrival of the litter are visible on the Chimney Glacier, below. (Photo by Freeman Keller)

litter with the other two guys. More people showed up to help move the litter sideways toward the glacier. They leaned into their work, pulling the heavy litter at the end of the long rope. We had literally turned the corner, so far out of the fall line that the rope curved out of sight around a corner of the face. Soon the litter was completely resting on low-angled slabs. Instead of dangling from the rope, we scraped along the rock. Then I could hear the stretcher bottom scrape on ice. We had reached the upper glacier, which sloped steeply downhill from where it met the rock face.

Besides Steve, I recognized none of the others who were around the litter. Here was a whole new group of people. Their radios were alive with reports that a chopper was on the way, and that the "victim"—me— had to be moved to the glacier landing zone some distance away. The guys pulling the litter reported that there wasn't time. "Ask the helicopter pilot if he can land higher on the glacier," the rescuers near me said into the radio. "He will try," came the reply, "but it's getting dark, and windy, too." "It doesn't look good," they said.

Now resting completely on the ice, the litter was unclipped from the lowering rope. Steve unclipped us both from the belay rope. Seven or eight people attached short slings about two feet long to the rails of the litter, and began to drag it sideways to the slope, across the glacier. It was hard work. The rescuers grunted and panted in the thin air, trying to move fast but having to stop for short rests. From my reclining position I watched them lean on their knees and pant. There was genuine urgency in their work. We moved 100 or 200 yards in this manner until the slope relented, but it was still far from level. The light was almost gone. It was past eight o'clock, and we were deep in shadow. I could feel the cold breath of a freshening wind as it blew across the ice. I heard a helicopter.

From my horizontal position in the stretcher, I could see little save the brilliant orange-red sky of sunset. But the sound of the chopper increased in volume quickly. Someone shouted to pop smoke. Someone else said, "He's coming in." With that, the people who had carried me across the ice all turned and knelt beside the litter, surrounding it, leaning over to protect me from the blowing bits of ice churned up by the rotor wash. I stared up into the faces of seven or eight strangers. I was moved by this gesture. Everybody looked alike in their helmets and parkas. Beards and glasses were the only identifying features.

I heard the chopper come in, the sound of it growing as it had on the ledge. It remained at that crescendo level. It was here. Then, to my disbelief, I heard it back off and fly back down the valley. The rescue guys all stood up and watched it go.

I don't remember any radio conversations at this point. I think that, like me, everyone knew that it would be hard to get a big helicopter to land at 6,500 feet on a sloping glacier in the near dark with a wind kicking up. If the helicopter couldn't get in it would take two days to carry me off this mountain, assuming it could even be done. I didn't think I could last that long. I lay listening. I heard the helicopter return.

The people in the rescue team once again knelt beside the stretcher. The chopper sounded even louder this time, kicking up ice like crazy, the noise growing until it sounded as if it were right on top of us. The rotor wash blew like a hurricane, flapping the clothes of those around me. Over the din someone shouted, "Now!"

The stretcher was jerked off the ice, and I looked up to see the open door of the helicopter, two green-helmeted crew members reaching out to take the litter. I was fairly tossed on board, sliding across the floor. The door slammed shut. Immediately we lifted off. But rather than climb upward, I felt the helicopter fall away down the valley in a radical maneuver. It was warm inside the Huey. I lay sideways, head toward one door, feet toward the other. I could see the backs of the pilots' helmets. One crew member sat against the bulkhead looking right down into my face. Another guy sat down by my feet. They were strapping themselves in. I asked the guy above me if he had anything to drink.

It was loud in there, and the guy leaned down and said, "What?"

"Do you have anything to drink?," I rasped. For some reason I thought he might have a soda or something.

He thought for a minute and rooted around in his medical bag. He produced an IV bag and held it up.

"No thanks," I said. "I've already had one of those."

We rode for a while in silence. I looked out the windows at the sunset sky, all I could see from the floor. I was getting tired of looking up at sky. The guy above me pulled out a notepad and asked me my name, address, those kinds of questions. He wrote down my answers.

"Where're we going?" I asked.

"Harborview."

I knew Seattle's famous trauma center by reputation only, but that institution and I were to become intimately acquainted. But on the floor of that helicopter it was enough to know I was on my way. A minute or two before, I had been lying on a glacier not sure I'd survive. Now, I lay there in the vibrating machine, on the wings of an angel, flying full speed toward salvation. I was amazed and exhausted, but I felt very alert. My mood was excellent. I was alive, with good prospects for staying that way. My last morphine shot had been some time before, and the pain was getting bad again. But I could handle it. Wouldn't be long now.

"Can I sit up and look out?" He shook his head. No.

"Where are we?" I asked.

"Three more ridgelines to go." I thought that was a strange answer.

I felt the machine make some turns. I was disappointed to have missed a sunset ride through the heart of the Cascades, but I didn't really mind. I felt more turns. In the chopper window, the top few floors of the Columbia Center, the highest building in Seattle, went by. We're here, I thought.

The helicopter made a series of tight turns, hovered, then hit the ground with a slight bump. The door shot open. My litter began to slide out. Two guys in white shirts with "Shepard Ambulance" embroidered on them were holding the front end of the litter. I was carried across the helipad. It was a warm summer evening. The sky to the west, beyond Puget Sound, still had some color. The ambulance guy looked down at me.

"Get ready for the shortest ambulance ride of your life," he said, and gave a little laugh. He seemed to be in a hurry. As I slid onto the floor of one of those truck-like ambulances, I noticed that the army guys had carried the back end of the litter and were coming along. The doors closed.

We drove perhaps a hundred yards, fast, with sharp turns, then stopped. The ambulance drivers and the army crew members carried me through the trauma center doors into the white-walled, fluorescent-lit realm of the hospital. The army guys down at the foot of my stretcher looked strange in their big green helmets. I was placed on a rolling cart and moved through a doorway. A heavyset man with horn-rimmed glasses came into my field of vision, a normal guy in a shirt and tie, the first I had seen in some time.

"Who should we call?"

"Anne," I said, "call Anne."

I was wheeled beneath a big fixture with a bright light. A man with Asian features leaned over close and looked into my eyes. "I'm Doctor Chen. You're at Harborview Medical Center." Then he was gone.

I could feel myself being unstrapped and rolled out of the litter onto an operating table. Many people seemed to be working on me without saying anything, or, at least, not to me. Someone was removing my helmet, which I had forgotten I still wore. Someone else was cutting off my clothes. Someone else was undoing the laces on my heavy mountaineering boots. I heard the clang of stainless steel bowls and felt needle pricks and blood pressure cuffs. Out of this chaos of activity came a voice that cut through the pain and loneliness of the past few days to speak to my soul. Doctor, nurse, I don't know, but it was a woman's voice, strong and clear:

"We've been *waiting* for you."

With that, I let go. It was over.

EPILOGUE

The night the Army Huey flew me to Harborview Medical Center in Seattle, I was probed and examined, X-rayed and CAT-scanned for hours. Being in the hands of those people, the ordeal on the mountain by then emphatically over, was tremendously comforting. Pain, fear, and unease over my injuries no longer troubled me, because I was exactly where I needed to be. I was eager to have my broken body attended to, saved if it could be. I was hyperalert, watchful, and curious as the medical personnel went about their practiced routine of discerning the extent of my injuries. It was high summer, what the Harborview physicians call "trauma season," and I was in there with the bullet wounds and the car wrecks and lawn-mower-mangled feet.

The cool, sterile room where I was slowly lowered into the bowels of the CAT scan machine seemed to me something out of Jules Verne. But trauma X ray was more interesting, more human, a markedly ghoulish place inhabited by people whose dark sense of humor is inspired by the sad, continuous stream of broken human beings who flow through there. "He *still* isn't straight," one of them said as I lay sprawled on the table. "Put that wedge of foam under him." "I already tried that," said the other. "This is the best I can do. *You* go straighten him out." I was then wheeled in for an all-night session of surgery, and I didn't even mind that. As the anesthesia flowed, I looked forward to the sleep, and the first repairs.

When I awoke at about noon the next day, groggy and swaddled in bandages, sunlight poured through the west-facing windows of my hospital room. Through them, the snowcapped Olympic Mountains rose majestically above Puget Sound. I was quite content to be there. Anne was sitting by the bed, smiling. She has a rare beauty under any circumstances, but on that day, in that wonderfully safe place, she looked to me more beautiful than ever. Once I had confirmed that this was no dream, no hallucination—I was in fact off of Chimney Rock and no longer had to worry about falling off the ledge—I went right back to sleep.

My stay at Seattle's famous trauma hospital lasted more than two weeks. Anne was there every day, and my brother came up from Carmel to spend most of that time with me, also. I was in bad shape, however, and the repeated surgeries were beginning to take a toll. There was too much to do all at once, so the doctors worked in stages. Every time I recovered from one procedure, and I was starting to feel a little better, the "orthopods" would wheel me down for another repair to another part of my fractured anatomy. They called the procedures "ORIFs," for open reduction, internal fixation. Most of my fractures were at joints—shoulders, elbows, wrists and the like—and they were severe. The word the doctors used was *comminuted*. When I asked what that meant, one surgeon said, "Well, your shoulder looked like somebody sat on a bag of potato chips." They would go in, straighten things out as best they could, screw it together, pin it, and sew me up. They used my pelvis to harvest bone chips to fill in the holes and gaps. I had so much stainless steel holding me together I set off metal detectors.

Once my euphoria at being off the mountain dissipated, I began to brood over my broken body. Were my climbing days over? Could I ever move around without pain? What did all this hold for the remainder of my life? I had never been injured like that, never been in a car wreck, and I wasn't happy about what had happened to me. But I was able to get some perspective on my situation.

Gone are the days of lengthy immobilizations following severe traumas. "Move it or lose it," they say, and a few days after the first surgeries they started taking me in for initial physical therapy sessions. To get to the fourth-floor PT department from my sixth-floor room (Six North, the orthopedic floor), the orderlies had to take me down the elevators and wheel me through Four-Center, the rehabilitation ward. Here was the place for people who had suffered spinal cord injuries. Most of the patients in rehab were brand-new quadriplegics and paraplegics, many still in "halos," those big contraptions that sit on the shoulders, screwed into the skull to stabilize a broken neck. I'll never forget that first terrifying ride through the rehab floor, nor the astonished looks on the faces of those people sitting in a wheelchair for the first time, a wheelchair they would never leave. A trip through Four-Center was the guaranteed cure for self-pity. I had been lucky, so lucky.

Not all my family members were sympathetic. "Why do you do that, anyway, climb mountains?" said my beloved uncle. "I always knew you were going to break your neck or something. Now I guess you'll stop." Anne felt the same way. So did I, for a while.

A few days after being released from Harborview, I got married to Anne in our home in Seattle. I was literally propped up like a cardboard cut-out, but I was there. Thirty-eight seemed to me sort of old to get married for the first time, but it turned out to be a good decision, another example of how the accident—clearly a bad thing—brought unexpected meaning and pleasure into my life. My time with Anne since the accident has been rich in a sharing and happiness that can come only from a lifelong commitment, of which I had been wary, even fearful, before. The air time on Chimney Rock changed the way I thought about everything, including marriage. For me, after Chimney Rock, there was a strong sense that life is uncertain, highly so, and the only rational approach is to enjoy each day as it comes and don't sweat the small stuff. I gather that's a common reaction among people who have narrowly escaped a fatal injury, but still, that simple realization seemed very strong, almost irresistible. What is curious to me is that it takes traumatic violence to reveal such a simple fact. Friends have asked if that's a temporary reaction, if it wears off after a while and then you sink back into being bummed out by rush-hour traffic. The answer to that, after seven years, is no, at least, not completely. A close brush with violent death can really give you the range, can make you value the good things in your life, and even enjoy them more.

In those first years, other significant changes ensued as a result of the accident. In fact, my life seems to fit into two categories: before the accident, and after. Within a year I had quit my job as a magazine publisher and gone back to writing full time. While not necessarily a smart financial decision, it has been a personally rewarding one. As they used to say in Harborview, nobody on his death bed ever said, "I wish I had spent more time at the office."

The surgeons at Harborview had done a good job, considering what they called the "quality" of my injuries. But I was a mess. I had to have my suits retailored because one arm was a couple of inches shorter than it had been, and I seemed to have lost about half an inch off my six-foot-one height. There was endless trying, painful work at physical therapy—James Brady was onto something when he said physical therapists get their text from the Marquis de Sade. Slowly, I was learning how get around and do everyday things. I could quit taking painkillers and start trying to get strong again. The accident left a lasting legacy of pain and discomfort, and an ensuing grief over my lost fitness. Nerve damage has prevented me from regaining the strength I had in one arm, and the joint fractures have led to nagging arthritis. I want my old body back, but have come to terms with the fact that it's gone for good.

The fall took my nerve in more ways than one. I started climbing again, but routes which had once seem good, easy fun now struck me with a dark ominousness. The pleasure of moving quickly and confidently up a rock route was replaced with a tentativeness. In the back of my mind I found myself wondering if that last piece was really as solid as I thought, or if that flake was going to come loose—and that kind of thinking really precludes smooth, joyful climbing. I think that once you experience the terror of a bad fall, it never really goes away. I still climb, sometimes even hard (for me) rock climbs, but inevitably I have drifted toward glacier climbs, mountaineering, and alpine travel.

Another good thing to come out of my new, worried climbing style was the seeking out of other venues, which is how I discovered the red rock country of Utah and Northern Arizona. Canyoneering through that beautiful landscape is perhaps the most outrageous fun I've had in the out-of-doors. Climbing skills are called into play—a rappel into a canyon, a short rock climb out—to the extent that, without them, where you could go in the desert would be tremendously restricted. But those are only occasionally needed. Mostly that landscape calls for good judgment, navigational skills, and the ability to travel through incredibly rugged, untracked country. Had I not been gimped up on Chimney Rock, I'm not sure I ever would have found my way down there.

As I healed, the events of the accident began to intrigue me. As a journalist, I knew how to do research. It was only natural for me to look for the people who had been involved in the rescue, and try to learn something about what had happened. For me, it was part of a long, complicated healing process. It quickly became a story, however, because I discovered that while my own experience had been kind of interesting, there were other remarkable episodes to come out of that incident. While I had been marooned on the ledge, alone and isolated, aware only of the action I could see, events all over the state had figured in my evacuation from the mountain.

The effort to get me off Chimney Rock had involved a hundred people, from climbers and law enforcement officials to army helicopter pilots and ham radio operators. A lot of them told me it was the most dramatic rescue ever pulled off in the Cascades. One said later that he was sorry I was the one who took the hit, but he wouldn't have missed it for anything.

The rescue was complicated, dangerous, and expensive. Peeling back the layers, it became clear that most of the players were aware only of their own contributions, not necessarily how those fit into the bigger puzzle of interlocking pieces. What struck me was the scope of it, the sheer scale of the operation. Gradually, over time, I started putting the disparate elements and individual episodes together. The result was a large, complex mosaic of selfless effort, at times heroic, in extremely dangerous situations. The most interesting element was the human one, as the critical details that resulted in my survival were implemented not by faceless organizations but people, people whose resourcefulness, quick thinking, and physical prowess came together in success—but just barely. More remarkable still, these people, in most cases, did not even know each other, and most of them weren't paid for their trouble. And they had to figure out a way to work together in the absence of any formal structure, to somehow coordinate efforts with efficiency and dispatch, as if they had practiced for it, to pull off a difficult rescue under extreme circumstances of altitude, technical problems, and time constraints.

The whole operation was organized by Sheriff Bob McBride of Kittitas County. The heavyset McBride is a laconic, understated character right out of central casting, a twenty-seven-year veteran state trooper who was virtually drafted into his job as chief law enforcement honcho of the rural Cascade mountain county. To McBride and his deputies fell a complicated and critical management and supervisory role that was fraught with rich opportunity for wrong judgment and even deadly mistake. The way events ultimately unfolded show that the Kittitas County deputies performed with skill, intelligence, and rare common sense, with hardly a wrong move in the whole, long game. McBride enlisted the help he thought he needed from four neighboring counties, a half-dozen mountain rescue organizations and the U.S. Army. He and Undersheriff Carl Christensen used charm and a disarming power of persuasion where conventional methods failed.

It seemed to me that nobody realized the crucial role the sheriff played in my salvation and, except for a few people in the Cascades that July day in 1988, no one ever knew how competent those guys were. It seemed a matter of little interest. After all, who cares?—unless it is your hide brought down from the mountain.

The more I learned about the details of the complex chain of events, the more I realized how lucky I had been to get down alive, and how much the successful outcome owed to a hundred separate incidents of courage, resourceful improvisation, and sheer, practiced competence.

It all started with Doug. He's not a big guy, but he is extremely fit aerobically. He runs marathons and routinely carries big loads. I tend to pack light, but even on seven-day climbing trips in the North Cascades Doug carried all manner of things in addition to the requisite heavy gear—ropes and racks and ice tools. Doug always amazed me by pulling out of his pack towels, binoculars, candle lanterns, shovels, and, best of all, beers.

After leaving me on the mountain, Doug was able to negotiate the technical part of the descent without problems. As he crossed the glacier immediately beneath where I was stranded, he said he was tempted to look up and see what was going on, but he was afraid I was watching him and would have scolded him had he tarried to take a look. (I never saw him.) Stopping at our tent on the way down, he stashed some gear there and then began to smoke it out to the trailhead to get help.

It was almost 17 miles from our high point on Chimney Rock to the trailhead near Cooper Lake. But Doug got lucky after about 14 miles, and ran into a handful of people and what looked like a donkey or a mule. These guys all had uniforms on, so he figured they were feds.

They were, in fact, a Forest Service trail crew near Pete Lake. (The Alpine Lakes' wilderness designation prohibits power equipment from being used for trail mainenance.) The trail crew foreman had a radio, and at Doug's request he called in the first report of the accident to his supervisor. Kittitas County Sheriff logs show that the first call came in about midafternoon. The accident had happened at about 9:30 or 10:00 A.M., so Doug made awesome time. Sheriff Bob McBride told me what happened next.

"It was a good thing the trail crew had a radio. Otherwise it would have taken a lot longer. Doug probably would have had to hike all the way to Cooper Lake, then drive to the ranger station at Salmon La Sac. But the Forest Service guy called his office in Cle Elum, then the Forest Service notified the sheriff's office. Our dispatcher took the call here at 2:30 on Tuesday afternoon.

"We dispatched a patrol deputy to Cooper Lake to make contact with Doug and sort out the facts of the incident. Deputy Papineau found Doug, and that's when we learned the accident had happened high on the mountain. It wasn't going to be easy to get you out of there, and I knew we'd need help. So the next step was to call the State Department of Emergency Management in Olympia (Washington's state capital) to obtain a search number. We do that so everybody involved in the rescue is then, by law, covered by insurance.

"Next, we put in calls to our local mountain rescue people"— Kittitas County Mountain Rescue, an informal group based in Ellensburg—"looking for Gene Prater and Fred Stanley. We couldn't find them right away, so we also notified the Seattle Mountain Rescue people. We got the Forest Service to unlock the gate on a logging road that put us a little closer to the mountain. By 5:10 P.M. the day of the accident, my undersheriff had established a rescue base camp at the end of that logging road.

"We did one more thing. Doug gave us good information, but we really didn't know exactly where you were. That was the first thing we needed to determine. So we also called the Chelan County Sheriff, and requested their helicopter do a fly-by of the mountain. Pete Peterson is their pilot, and he said he would get going immediately."

Chelan County, home to the cities of Leavenworth and Wenatchee, lies just north of Kittitas County. The crest of the Cascade mountains forms the border between the two counties, so they often assist each other on mountain-related incidents. Captain Pete Peterson, a Chelan County chief deputy, is both the county's SWAT team commander and its helicopter pilot. He spends a lot of his time flying around looking for marijuana, but since his county lies in the heart of the Cascades, he is also a key figure in mountainous-terrain search and rescue. He told me what happened when he got the call from McBride:

"We have the only helicopter around, so it's not uncommon for other counties to ask for our assistance. I was in the office when the call came in from the Kittitas County sheriff that they had a report of an accident on Chimney Rock. They knew only your approximate position, but they needed to find out exactly where you were—and, if we could find you, to assess the best approach for getting you off. Before leaving for the airport at the north end of Wenatchee, I called Steve May. He's a member of the county mountain rescue group and a professional medic"—Steve works for an ambulance company—"to ask if he could come along.

"I met Steve at the airport, where the county stores all of its rescue gear. We cranked, and flew toward Chimney Rock, communicating with Kittitas County on the way. The helicopter is a two-seat Bell 47, turbo-charged, which gives us the altitude. I know the terrain around there pretty well, having flown for sixteen years in the mountains around Wenatchee. But I was *not* familiar with Chimney Rock. We flew first to the rescue base camp and landed in a big clear-cut at the end of the logging road. The Kittitas County deputies advised us of your approximate location. So Steve and I got back in, got airborne, checked the position of Chimney Rock on the map, and navigated on our own up the valley.

"We were operating near our altitude ceiling, so I didn't have enough power to hold us at hover. To get enough altitude to even get near you, I had to fly around the back side of the mountain and go up and over to the other side. Wind goes downhill on the lee side—the south side in this case, where you were. So first I flew around the north or upwind side of the mountain, climbed up with the help of the up-drafts on that side of the mountain, flew through the notch between the peaks, and let the downdrafts on the lee side carry us down. We initially thought that if I could land on the glacier, we could carry some gear up to you, maybe even get Steve May up to you. That turned out not to be the case, not even close. But at first we couldn't find you at all. That South Face of Chimney is really huge, and we just couldn't see you."

Steve May, the guy I had seen that first night waving from the helicopter—he will always be "Red Shirt" to me—recalled what that first fly-by was like for him:

"When Pete called, I grabbed my rescue pack and met him out at the helicopter pad on what we call the Sunnyslope Area. He and I have probably been on twenty rescues over the years, including some pretty hairy ones around Mount Stuart. I trust him implicitly, and his ability to fly safely. In fact, I always enjoy his calls because I know it's going to be exciting.

"This time Peterson was asked to fly up to Chimney Rock to take a look, see if there was any chance of getting to the injured guy, maybe even get him out. Of course that was you. We didn't really know where you were, though; it seems like we never do when the first call comes in.

"After we checked in at base camp, we got back in and flew for what seemed a long time before we located you. It was going into dusk, and the mountains were beautiful. We were looking all over that side of the mountain, but just couldn't find you. Pete and I were saying, 'Where is that guy, he's supposed to be right here somewhere.' Then we real-ized that the tiny red dot we could just make out in the middle of that big face was probably you. We flew really close. The mountain is so steep there that we could get in extremely close. I remember waving to you to let you know I could see you, that we now knew where you were. We knew right away that we couldn't get to you. No way. There was no place to land, and even if there had been we couldn't have gotten to your ledge.

"I could see you waving back. That's when I leaned out and made as much movement as I could to make sure you saw us—and also to get as good a look at you as possible. I was trying to figure out if you would be able to survive up there for a while, because you were in a place where evacuation was really difficult. It started getting real windy up there, blowing us around like crazy, so we beat a hasty retreat back to Wenatchee. We notified Chelan County and Kittitas County and everybody else as to exactly where you were located and what the situation was. I knew right then this was going to be interesting."

Peterson added: "I spotted you initially and pointed you out to Steve. You were a lot higher than we expected. In fact, it was about as high as we could fly. So I asked Steve to pay particular attention to what you were doing while I concentrated on flying the helicopter. We talked about you quite a bit. Steve was saying that he saw you waving, that you didn't look like you were dying. We went by again, and it seemed that you were going to be okay where you were, at least for a while. There was nothing we could do about it anyway.

"Sometimes we can lower food, gear, et cetera with ropes, but with the winds that day I couldn't slow it down any more even to look at you. If we moved out far enough from the mountain so the wind wasn't a factor, we couldn't see you at all. So we made just those two trips, and then I took Steve back to Wenatchee. There was some talk of my returning the next day, but we all felt that we needed the bigger military helicopters to get enough climbers up there to help. It was clear that it was going to take quite a few climbers to get you down."

Now that McBride and his deputies had a fairly good idea of the situation, he needed to organize his forces. While Pete Peterson and Steve May had been flying around Chimney Rock, calls had already gone out that afternoon to mountain rescue volunteers in Ellensburg, Seattle, Wenatchee, Everett, and Olympia, and apparently other places as well. Some of those organizations were asked to stand by, to prepare to send people if more were needed, but others began immediately sending volunteer climbers toward the mountain. Kittitas County, Chelan County, and Seattle all sent teams out that night.

At the time, Seattle Mountain Rescue Council (SMRC) volunteers carried pagers, which were actually small talking radio receivers controlled by the King County Police from its emergency dispatch center. When the call came from Kittitas County, a general page went out. One of the first of the Seattle climbers to get the call, Denny Fenstermaker, told me what happened.

"Late Tuesday afternoon, around five or so, my pager went off. I was at my house in Lynnwood at the time, had the day off from my job as a Seattle firefighter. It's a voice pager that announces the number of the call. So I called in to the in-town field operations leader, who that day was Jim Cleary. He said there was an injured climber on Chimney Rock, so I checked the *Alpine Guide*"—Fred Beckey's famous Cascade guidebook—"to get a better idea of the approach and the climb. Like most of the mountain rescue volunteers I keep my gear packed and in the car, so I just jumped in and headed for the rendezvous. On that particular night, the first people who responded to the page were to meet at a previously designated place known as the Eastgate Rendezvous— it's the Safeway Store on Interstate 90. I got there about 10:00 P.M., and met up with Pete Bustanoby, Tim McGruder, and Steve Jewett. We drove up toward the mountains and finally on to Cooper Lake campground. From there we were driven down that really rough logging road the forest service had opened to the rescue base camp.

"We arrived at approximately 2130 Wednesday, and the Kittitas County Sheriff deputy gave us a brief description of the situation. By 2230 the five of us—we were joined by Jim Baker who had driven directly to the trailhead by himself—formed the FART team [Fast Alpine Response Team] and began to hike in by headlamp. Pete Bustanoby of our group had the duty as field operations leader, so he was going to communicate by radio with the Seattle Mountain Rescue radio truck when it arrived at base camp. That night we started up the trail."

"We got as far as the Crest Trail, and hiked a little farther until we got to the place where the climbers' track up to Chimney Rock leaves the trail. We had to bivvy there because there's no point in trying to crash up that ridge in the dark. We bivvyed out maybe two or three hours, but really didn't sleep much, maybe a little. We weren't there long. At first light we started climbing."

Another Seattle climber, Ed Boulton, also took the page Tuesday afternoon. "I had just come home from jury duty when my wife, Hille, told me my rescue pager had gone off. I grabbed the phone and called Jim Cleary, who told me to go to the Eastgate rendezvous ASAP, as five people were already en route. I was a little nervous about skipping out on jury duty but left anyway. I grabbed my gear and took off, but I just missed Denny Fenstermaker and the others. They had already left. So I called Jim Cleary, and he suggested I return home and leave with the next group at first light. That's what I did."

Meanwhile, Fred Stanley, a veteran Northwest climber who lives in Ellensburg, about 80 miles east of Seattle on Interstate 90, finally got the call.

"I was at home that evening around 6:30 when I got a call from Pete Bustanoby from Mountain Rescue in Seattle. He asked me if I knew what was going on over here. He thought I'd know because I'm in Kittitas Mountain Rescue. I didn't. I think the sheriff's office had tried to find somebody around here, but had no success, so somehow Seattle got the first call. The Kittitas County sheriff's office eventually got in touch with me to let me know about the incident on Chimney Rock. Then Pete Peterson called to fill me in on what he had found out on his helicopter flight up to the mountain. That's how I got the initial information.

"Seattle asked me if I would try to get some other people from Ellensburg to go into Chimney Rock the next morning. We knew by then that some Seattle people were going in that evening, but it wasn't clear how far they were going to get or what equipment they had with them. The distance in was significant enough that any climbers going up in the dark probably would not get up on the mountain that night. From what little I knew at that early stage, it seemed we'd need helicopter support to get enough people up there in time.

"Anyway, I got ahold of Mike Eberle, also from Ellensburg. We left town early the next morning and drove out to the Cooper Lake trailhead.

The sheriff's office had opened up the logging road. We got there, to base camp, about 5:00 A.M. Wednesday. The sheriff's deputy was there, I think the Seattle Mountain Rescue radio truck, maybe a few others. But all of a sudden a lot of people started showing up real quick, from Chelan County, from Seattle, even from Olympic Mountain Rescue."

Steve May, having been deposited back in Wenatchee by Pete Peterson's Bell 47 after their recon flight on Tuesday evening, joined up later that night with Bruce White and Freeman Keller. The three Chelan County volunteers drove toward the expanding rescue base camp.

"Peterson and I landed, then I packed up some medical gear—a lot of it, because I figured you'd need it. Freeman, Bruce, and I then drove through the middle of the night—2:00 or 3:00 A.M.—so we'd arrive at base camp before daylight. We left Wenatchee and drove over Blewett Pass through Cle Elum to the base camp near Cooper Lake. We had been given ground directions about how to get to the end of the road they'd opened up for the rescue, but it was hard to find at night. When we finally arrived, there were several sheriff's deputies from Kittitas County, and a few people from Seattle Mountain Rescue. Some of them were setting up their mobile radio truck. I was glad to see Fred Stanley was already there. Fred is a guy you want to have on something like this. He and Mike Eberle had driven over from Ellensburg. It was still dark, and a lot more people started to arrive."

By Wednesday morning, Sheriff McBride and his deputies had mustered a sizable force, at least at their base camp. Only the Fast Alpine Response Team from Seattle Mountain Rescue was already climbing toward the mountain. Other rescue volunteers from around the state were arriving at the base camp in increasing numbers. The rescue was turning into a strategic challenge, and an organizational one. Fred Stanley described to me how the crucial early strategy was formulated that morning:

"In Washington, the sheriff is responsible for organizing the rescue, and Carl Christensen was the deputy in charge. But at that particular point the deputy knew he had a difficult technical rescue on his hands. He depended on people from the rescue organizations to take charge of their own people, and to decide what happens up on the mountain. As dawn broke, I did a lot of talking with Undersheriff Carl Christensen.

243

Five or six Seattle people had headed in toward you the night before. We were hoping that they were making good progress but were not sure if the Seattle radio truck had radio contact to find out how close they were. Our information was they had hiked in as far as they could, and were waiting for first light before moving again.

"At base, I emphasized to the deputy that because of the distance in to Chimney Rock, the growing group of volunteer climbers forming at base camp wasn't going to be much help to the people on the mountain unless we got helicopter support to take more people up there—and get them up there quickly. I was extremely concerned about the passing time. We didn't know what kind of shape you were in. Even if we got immediate helicopter support to take climbers high on the mountain, it was still going to take a significant operation to get you down to some place where we eventually could fly you out. I knew it was going to be an all-day operation just to get you off the face.

"I talked to Carl about how many people we needed on the mountain, and how many people we needed as backup at base camp. I tried to find out what the initial group"—the Seattle FART team—"had with them in the way of gear, and where they were.

"That's when I found out there was a big problem. Army MAST [Military Assistance to Safety and Traffic] helicopters will fly injured people, but they don't like to transport rescuers and they won't do body recoveries."

Stanley had convinced Christensen that helicopter support was crucial to a successful outcome. Rescue lore is full of stories of how supervising law enforcement agencies on a few unhappy occasions have hindered complicated operations by failing to take the advice of their own rescue experts. In some states, deaths, law suits, and operation paralysis have resulted from such turf wars and bad feelings. But that was not the case here. Christensen took Fred Stanley at his word. As the officer in charge of the rescue—McBride had not yet arrived—he began trying to convince the army that a helicopter was desperately needed.

"Over here in Kittitas County," said Fred Stanley, "things are more informal than maybe in other places, mainly because there are very few rescues. But we have enough contact with sheriff's deputies that we can work pretty closely together without a lot of organizational problems."

By then, Ed Boulton had arrived at base camp with other volunteer climbers from Seattle. He had a ringside seat for some of the uptight moments early on.

"I arrived at base camp in the early morning with Mike Maude and two others from Seattle. At that time the sheriff was engrossed in a spirited conversation over the radio with MAST at Grey Field near Fort Lewis. The MAST commander was arguing that they did not transport rescue workers, only persons threatened with loss of life in remote places. Deputy Christensen said he knew that, but argued strongly for a helicopter on the basis that if he couldn't fly climbers to the mountain *right now,* it would be too late to bother after the guy died."

Eventually, Christensen successfully argued his point, and the army agreed to send a helicopter. By then, it was a matter of how long one would take to get there. Military helicopters large enough and powerful enough to fly at the altitude of Chimney Rock could come from two sources in that part of the state: Fort Lewis, a large army base near Tacoma, and the Yakima Firing Range, a vast, empty landscape on the east side of the Cascades in which the army conducts large-scale maneuvers and artillery practice. The first helicopter sent to Chimney Rock that day was dispatched from the Yakima Range. In the forty-five minutes it took for the helicopter to fly from Yakima to the base camp, Stanley and Christensen put the finishing touches to their assault plan.

"We together decided that we needed to get a paramedic in to you as soon as possible," remembered Stanley. "And since it turned out that Steve May was not just a paramedic but the only one there who really knew where you were, it was obvious that he should be the first in. And it was my opinion that since he was from Wenatchee, the people he was used to working with should go in with him. That was Bruce White and Freeman Keller."

There was, by then, a large crowd at base camp, perhaps thirty volunteers. While everyone waited for the helicopter, people took turns looking through a powerful spotting scope that had been set up at base camp. They could not only see me stranded up on the face, a good ten

245

air miles away, they could also see Fenstermaker and his FART team begin to ascend the lower sections of the glacier. Boulton said it was kind of neat to see me way up there on the mountain, but that the volunteers were all worried that the helicopter negotiations had cost a couple of precious hours.

The Huey arrived at about 10:30 A.M. on Wednesday, circling the valley before landing in the clear-cut at the end of the logging road. The rotors kicked up a huge dust cloud which was visible to me up on the face, and got the people at base camp fairly dirty. The volunteers were ready and waiting for the airlift. In accordance with Fred Stanley's advice, Bruce White, Freeman Keller, and Steve May went in on the first ship. From my perch, I watched that first helicopter lift off and head toward the mountain. That was really exciting for me, because on the first load the army pilots flew to my location to have a look, hovering there for a minute or two before flying away to off-load the climbers. They were eventually landed on a reasonably flat place on the right side of the glacier where I couldn't see them. The Huey returned to base camp for more climbers.

Fred Stanley and Mike Eberle from Kittitas County, and Ed Boulton from Seattle Mountain Rescue, flew in on the next load. The helicopter made three trips altogether, ferrying eight climbers to a spot on the glacier about a thousand feet below where I was stranded. The landing zone was around the corner where I couldn't see what was happening.

Meanwhile, the FART team—Fenstermaker, Bustanoby, Jewitt, McGruder, and Baker—had been climbing since first light, first up the wooded ridge to the gullies at the base of the glacier, then through the icefall and finally onto the lower glacier itself. The five climbers were already tired as they began climbing the glacier. But they were steaming at maximum speed, ignorant that other climbers already had been airlifted above them.

"The five of us started out before dawn," said Denny Fenstermaker, "but we became somewhat separated on the way in somewhere on the ridge. Two people got off route and got onto the moraine or something. So three of us were more or less together when we reached the glacier. We just kept going. We were moving pretty fast, considering.

"It was on the lower slopes of the glacier that we first heard your whistle. We heard you long before we saw you. Finally, we could just pick you out way up on the face. I guess it was about noon when we reached base of the rock face. Just as we got up to the base of the rock, God, ten people or so appeared in front of us. I remember thinking, 'Where in the hell did those guys come from?' We didn't see the helicopter, didn't even hear it. I guess it came in when we were down in that narrow gorge at the bottom of the glacier, but I can't believe we couldn't hear the Huey making four trips. The only person I knew among these new guys was Fred Stanley, and that more by reputation than acquaintance, and several other people there from Seattle, including Ed Boulton."

"When we got out of the helicopter," remembered Ed Boulton, "we could see Denny Fenstermaker, Jim Baker, and Pete Bustanoby just coming up over the top of the icefall, after climbing all night. I was fresh and enthusiastic. I tried teasing them a little, like, 'Hey, what kept you guys?' but my humor was not appreciated." Boulton saw something lying out on the glacier a few yards away. He walked over to the object, and found that it was a blue Ultimate climbing helmet, shattered, totally roached. "There was no mystery about whose it was because I turned it over and saw the name Peter Potterfield written on the inside."

From their position now high on the glacier, the rescue climbers needed to ascend the snow couloir Doug and I had climbed up to the saddle in the ridge crest (called the U Gap), then follow the route up and around to the point where Doug was belaying me when I fell. Fred Stanley recalled the meeting of rescue teams:

"All of us who were taken up in the Huey gathered together on the glacier. We had quite a bit of gear to carry up. I had three or four ropes in my pack, and I distributed at least one to somebody else. The situation was that everybody who was available was going to go up at least as far as the top of the couloir to carry equipment.

"When the Seattle climbers who started out with Denny arrived, there was a question of who was going to go higher. It was a matter of how people were feeling at the time, and at that point some of the people who had been traveling all night were pretty tired. They were fine with the idea of waiting on the glacier to help later on. We tried to figure out who could move the fastest, who were the quickest rock climbers. It ended up that Denny Fenstermaker climbed up the couloir with some of us who had been ferried up by the helicopter."

"I wasn't surprised Denny kept climbing," said Ed Boulton. "The guy is a total horse, just goes all day with a huge load. He does all the high-angle rescue work off buildings for the Seattle Fire Department. Here he's been climbing all night and he still leads the way up the couloir."

Of the climbers on the mountain, Denny Fenstermaker, Ed Boulton, and Mike Maude from Seattle joined Bruce White, Freeman Keller, and Steve May from Chelan County, and Mike Eberle and Fred Stanley from Kittitas County. They started to up the couloir.

"We wanted to get Steve May up to you as quickly as we could," said Fred Stanley. "So Mike Eberle went ahead to try to pick out the route. Denny was roped with Mike; next, Bruce White was roped with Steve. Freeman and I were roped together, and we had the litter. Ed Boulton and Mike Maude were right behind me."

The meeting on the glacier of those relative strangers clearly might have become an uneasy situation. These were climbers, a notoriously independent breed, with no clearly established organization. But it all turned out extremely well. With almost no conversation at all, a reasonable and rational plan of action was decided upon in a matter of minutes. Eight climbers, ranging in age from twenty (Mike Eberle was the youngest) to sixty-one (that would be Ed Boulton) were heading toward the couloir, and by this time I had seen them coming. I could also see the three or four climbers who would remain on the glacier to provide information to the climbers higher up, and to assist with the litter-carry later on.

As the eight climbers headed for the couloir, they crossed the glacier right under the face and just below my perch. Finally they were within earshot. I apparently was already flaming away. That made a poignant moment for Steve May as he got close enough to hear me, or rather hear something other than my whistle: "One of the things most striking to us, as we were ascending the glacier up toward the foot of the couloir, you were like 800 feet above us, yelling at us, delirious, asking us for water, making us think you were really losing it. We felt so incredibly sorry for you at that point, and we really moved as fast as we could."

I could tell when they were climbing the snow couloir by all the noise they were making—talking and scraping. A few minutes later I could hear them knocking off rocks as they climbed above me. Denny told me what it was like as they got to the site of the accident.

"Like I say, it was just kind of separation by ability and endurance, and so I went up the couloir with the Wenatchee and Ellensburg guys and some of SMRC people—Ed Boulton and Mike Maude—while some of the people who had hiked up with me stayed behind on the glacier. At the top of the couloir, in the saddle they call the U gap, we were sitting up there with Fred and other people waiting for everyone to get there. There wasn't really anyone in charge per se, just a kind of informal pecking order developed, and we decided who would go higher up as there wasn't any point of having a hundred people up there."

"At the top of the couloir," remembered Ed Boulton, "Denny unloaded his snow and ice-climbing gear, and his cooking gear at the saddle. We began climbing the rock face to the Southwest Shoulder. It seemed almost straight down and slightly overhanging to where you were hanging onto the ledge. We couldn't see you. I was carrying a 300-foot, 11-mm rope I had taken from the SMRC truck. It was a special lowering rope, twice as long as a standard rope and without the elasticity of climbing ropes. But I was spooked by the down-climbing. I asked Fred Stanley, 'Fred, do I really have to go down there?' He looked up as he easily moved across the near-vertical face and replied, 'Ed, we need that rope.' I shut up and climbed down *very carefully*.

"Mike Maude belayed me, but he didn't bother to set up an anchor as we were moving as fast as we could. Your mind plays tricks on you and I imagined falling and pulling Mike off his stance and both of us falling 800 feet. Nothing happened, of course, and I reached the ledge where the other guys were setting up anchors so they could rappel down to you."

"We followed your climbing route around to the top belay point," said Denny Fenstermaker. "We knew we were there because we could see the tied-off red rope." (That was my rope, the 9-mm Doug and I carried on most climbs as a backup. He had hauled it up from my ledge, and I figured he'd use it to make double-line rappels on his solo descent. But it turned out he wanted to travel light, so he left the rope to mark the site of the accident.) "The people waiting on the glacier below got on the radios. They could see the whole face, both you and us, so they could tell us pretty closely where you were in relation to us. But the mountain is so overhanging there that until we actually came over the overhang there was no way to tell exactly where you were. It was kind of a difficult point to come down, really not good at all.

"Surprisingly, I didn't feel really tired although I'd been climbing all night. In fact, we zipped up there as fast as we could, unusual for a climb to move that fast. We knew you were in bad shape. By then, up on the face, I figured it had to get easier—it was all downhill from there! I was just ready to get on with it, see what the situation was with you."

"At the point where Mike Eberle led everybody up to the tied-off rope," said Fred Stanley, "Fenstermaker was in touch by radio with the Seattle guys down on the glacier. I was a couple of hundred feet behind with litters and extra ropes and what not. By the time I got to the tied-off red rope, they had already set up some anchors for rappelling down to your ledge. In fact, Mike Eberle was already going over the edge.

"We were discussing everything at that point. The question in my mind was how many people to put down there on the ledge with you. If you send too many people you spend too much time just getting them down. And time was clearly critical. It was a matter of how many people would be needed to rig the lower. Everybody was moving around real carefully so we wouldn't drop rocks on you."

Mike Eberle was the first of the climbers to rappel down to my ledge. I don't think any of them realized that the mountain was so overhanging at that point that it would result in a really hot, overhanging free rappel. Mike had to pendulum big time to get to my ledge, and I remember that as soon as he got there, he radioed the others to be prepared.

"I remember coming down a good 10 to 15 feet off to one side of you," Mike Eberle said, "to avoid dislodging any rocks. The whole face was really loose and rotten down there. So there I was hanging at the bottom of the overhang, and I heard over the radio the guys down on the glacier saying to the other guys on the ledge above, 'He's too far to the left, he's going to have to pendulum over to reach the guy.'

"But it really wasn't that big a deal. I had to try several times to get far enough over, but eventually you got onto the rope and I got onto your ledge. You were pretty bad off, but, frankly, not as bad as I thought you'd be. One thing I noticed right away—you were in pain, you were really hurting. But mostly it seemed to me you wanted water, a lot of it. I gave you all I had, but I was getting concerned about the rotten rock. It was awful, and I couldn't really get anything in right away that I felt good about. I knew the EMT was coming down next, so I was paying attention to the anchors more than you. I also wanted to let the guys above me know that they were in for a radically overhanging rappel."

When the warning was received by the climbers higher up, Ed Boulton, who wasn't going down to the ledge, set up a belay off the anchors so he could safeguard the climbers who were rappelling.

"I clipped into the anchors," Boulton said, "and prepared to belay the rappellers. Second down was Steve May—we wanted to get the medic down there as soon as possible. Mike Eberle had already warned us about the rappel."

"When I was descending down and around to where you were," remembered Steve May, "I couldn't believe what a horrible, horrible, horrible rappel that was. We all agreed it was the worst we'd ever done—we were all carrying too much weight and the overhanging rappel tried to turn us upside down. It was days later before we all admitted that that was a very scary descent.

"But when I first saw you I was impressed by your injuries; you were really hurt bad. I get tunnel vision in situations like that, and tend to focus in on injuries so much I kind of lose sight of the bigger picture. I totally left the technical aspects of the rescue to the other guys while I worried about you. I watched you consume a whole bunch of water; there wasn't anything else we could do about your kidneys at that point, so I just concentrated on your injuries.

"When I got a good look at them, I was concerned. You were seriously banged up. But what impressed me the most was how resourceful you had been—you had stayed put, you had handled the mental aspect of hanging out on that face for a couple of days, and had protected yourself. I thought this guy knows what he's doing and will be cooperative. That's always a concern. I've seen people revert to three-year-olds—it's impossible to deal with them. At least we didn't have to deal with that."

"We knew by radio what was happening on the ledge," said Ed Boulton. "Steve was working on you while we carried on a continuous but meaningful radio conversation as the situation developed. Down at base camp the radio truck received the radio communication from the mountain and replayed it by outside speakers so all the people down there would know what was going on.

"Mike Eberle told us that he had finally got some decent anchors in and that it was okay to send the other guys down. Bruce White went down next, but before he roped off I gave him the helmet I had found on the glacier. With all the rocks falling off, it seemed like a good idea. Next down was Freeman Keller. I was still belaying the rappellers. Mike Maude was belaying me from way up on the ridge crest where he remained working, totally alone, all day."

Denny was next to rappel down the rope, carrying both halves of the metal litter. He already had a full mountaineering pack, and the litter turned out to be too much. He freaked out everybody on the ledge when he emerged over the overhang upside down.

"By the time I came over to the site of the accident," Denny said, "the first couple of guys had already rappelled down to your ledge. At that point we decided that Ed Boulton should stay on top to belay those going lower. Then I went down. I tend to carry a big pack, anyway, with a lot of stuff, so it was not a big deal for me to take the two halves of the litter and tie those on my pack as well. It did make for an unwieldy load. I think now it would have been better to let the litter hang below my harness.

"But at the time, the weight of the litter pulled me over. It made for an exciting rappel." When he went upside down, an eight-hundred-dollar Motorola radio dropped from Denny Fenstermaker's pack and went crashing to the glacier below. There were so many radios on the mountain that its loss was not critical, but the incident did result in new procedural rules for carrying radios for members of the Seattle rescue group.

"By the time I got down to your ledge," said Denny, "things were starting to shape up. You were obviously busted up pretty bad and kind of mentally weird. But you didn't seem to be in your death throes. You were talking. Pretty happy to see us, it seemed. We hadn't really decided if we were going to try and lower you down or raise you up. But I guess the guys who got there first had pretty much realized that down was the best direction."

Fred Stanley was one of the last people down to the ledge. "I felt that you didn't look too bad," he said, "as far as being coherent and able to help move yourself around. I expected worse, and was frankly surprised you were able to assist as well as you could."

"For me," remembered Denny, "it was kind of strange because I was the outsider in that group, the only guy from Seattle. They were all from Chelan or Kittitas County. I didn't really know any of those people. Not knowing the people and their capabilities, and personalities—well, it can get a little complicated in a difficult situation like that. But it went pretty smoothly after a little informal sorting out who was going to do what.

"Fred and I were really sweating the anchors on that thing. Man, it was pretty bad. The rock was just grossly inadequate, but we had no choice. It was clear what had to be done and everybody went to work trying to get some protection in that would take the load.

"After a while we had two sets of self-equalizing anchors of four or five pieces each. You'd think that would be pretty good, but the whole thing was so shaky we had to actually back it up with the rappel line from above. We still weren't really happy with it. We were real concerned, in fact. We had a lot of stuff in, a ton of stuff, and we all felt we could just pull it all out, the pins, chocks, everything. That's why we tied into the rappel rope from above, just for a little extra security. The rock was all downsloping, with shallow cracks, it just didn't lend itself to anchors."

While the climbers on the ledge tried to set up workable anchors, the climbers above them, and those waiting below on the glacier, and everybody back at base camp, listened to the events unfold via radio. "The conversations from down on the ledge were quite interesting," said Ed Boulton, "and we could follow the action as they did their work, move by move, and gave each other instructions. I never did figure out who was in charge of the lowering party. I think they were all in charge."

With the anchors finally in place, the climbers on the ledge prepared for the lower. They put together the two halves of the litter that had almost pulled Denny from his rappel, rigged the belay devices in the lowering system, and prepared to lower me using a 300-foot rope. Before that, Bruce White went down first, rappelling the route to clear as much loose rock as possible from the line of descent, and to assess where the next lowering point would be. Once he found a reasonable ledge, a big, flat one, in fact, he stayed down there to assist Steve May when he arrived with the litter—which would be many hours away. Steve, who hung right at my side, suspended off the haul rope with a Jumar ascender, recalls the lower vividly:

"While we were going down together on the end of the rope, we talked a little at first, but the farther we got down the less we talked. The Demerol seemed to take the edge off, but it really didn't seem to completely ease your pain. I think you might have gone to sleep a couple of times for a minute or two. My arms got pretty tired because there's a fair amount of manipulation with the basket. Everybody was getting tired, I was *really* getting tired, and it seemed clear we weren't going to make it down to the glacier in time to get you out that night. That was a depressing thought."

Mike Eberle handled the actual braking during the lower. "I actually did the lowering," he remembered. "We had a system with multiple carabiner brakes that went to a figure-eight device off my harness. If one of the belay brakes had failed, it would have been no problem because we had so many.

"I was essentially just a belay anchor for Steve. If he said, 'Hey, stop for a minute I've got to give Peter more Demerol,' I could stop both of you, no problem, by putting a little tension on the figure eight. The lower wasn't difficult, it just took a while."

Boulton followed the progress by radio. "I was impressed by how relaxed everybody appeared to be, even if they weren't. The radio calls were things like, 'Okay, there'll be a delay as we pass this knot through the 'biner.' A couple of times Steve May called out, 'Stop for a minute, we're doing drugs down here.'

"The operation took hours. When the litter finally reached the second ledge, I was told to drop the belay rope, which was the last connection between me and Mike Maude up higher, and the climbers below on the ledge. I carefully did so, avoiding entanglement as it slithered away. The umbilical cord was severed, so the lowering team had no choice now but to go down. Then Mike Maude belayed me from above as I climbed up. The last word I got from the lowering party was, 'Don't kick any rocks on us!' So I climbed up carefully, like I was walking on eggs, trying to avoid dislodging rocks. After reaching the place where Mike Maude had spent all day belaying everybody, we both climbed over the shoulder, and down to the saddle at the top of couloir. We picked up the equipment Denny had left there, and started descending the steep snow finger. We reached the glacier as dusk was approaching, and walked over to the point where you were being lowered off the second ledge."

When Steve and I had been lowered down the face to the second ledge, about 280 feet below my original ledge, the climbers still on the ledge above began to rappel down the haul rope to the new ledge. Then Fred Stanley came down last, using two 165-foot climbing ropes tied together. (He had to stop midway and clip his rappel device past the knot in the two ropes.) A lot of hardware, theirs and mine, was abandoned at the original anchors.

The second part of the descent was lower angled, making it somewhat easier, but there was building anxiety about nightfall and the prospects of getting me down, getting me to a suitable landing zone, and getting a helicopter. Steve May was done in from horsing that litter around all day at the end of that long rope.

"We were in that lower for hours," said Steve, "and near the end I was pretty beat. But most of all I was worried how I was going to manage you through the night. I definitely didn't have enough Demerol to keep you medicated for the whole night. I didn't have enough of anything. I didn't think you were going to make it another day. We had to get you out that night, but I remember thinking during the final stage that we were not going to make it. That made me sort of mildly depressed. I knew we were all getting really worn out, hungry, thirsty. But to do all that work and not get you out. Everybody seemed to realize that, everybody got sort of quiet."

"On the second lower," remembered Fred Stanley, "there was a lot of radio communication trying to line up helicopters, and trying to figure out when we would reach the glacier. It got to the point where we were getting distracted. I can remember picking up some extraneous radio traffic—sounded like it was coming from a trucker on the highway or something, I don't know what it was, but it interfered a little bit. In fact, some of the radio traffic seemed to me unnecessary, at least for those of us on the mountain. I remember feeling, 'Leave us alone and let us get on with it.' It seemed like some of us on the mountain were having to stop what we were doing to make some radio communication."

There apparently had been real trouble in obtaining a helicopter for the evacuation. Communications between base camp and the MAST service at Fort Lewis had deteriorated, so all communications between base camp and MAST had to be relayed via a ham radio operator in Seattle named John Pollock. As the lower proceeded up on the mountain, Sheriff McBride, who was now on the scene, and Deputy Christensen were trying to convey the urgency of the situation to the military authorities through Pollock.

"The base camp was out of range of any repeater," remembered Pollock. "So I was using my low-band frequency gear to talk to the guys in the truck. I often help them out when their FM gear can't get through. The only reason I am able to get through to the truck is because a while back I used a slingshot to put a wire antenna up in the top of a huge fir tree on my property in Seattle. That permitted communication with the truck, which was down in the valley. I was using the telephone to talk with Fort Lewis.

"That night, we thought everything was squared away. The chopper was on its way and should make it just before dark. But then I was told the helicopter was being recalled to Fort Lewis. The army was diverting the chopper to pick up a soldier with a broken leg at Fort Lewis. I was talking with the sergeant down there and he's talking with the chopper pilot. It doesn't look good, but I live with a major in the Air Force, I've seen her work the system. So I used some persuasion.

"'Sergeant,' I told the guy, 'listen, the injured soldier can be evacuated by ground transport, the guy in the mountains can't. We need your help. You've got to do it.' He finally said, 'Makes sense to me,' and so the chopper once again headed for Chimney Rock."

Eventually the litter reached the foot of the face. Ed Boulton and Mike Maude were, by then, on the glacier waiting for it. "We had climbed up to the 'schrund, the moat where the glacier meets the rock face and the foot of the wall. A length of rope had been rigged to hang below the litter. When it came down far enough, we pulled on the tail of the lowering line, trying to swing the litter over and across the moat to the glacier."

Some of the people on the second ledge rappelled down the haul line to join Steve May and the litter party on the glacier. Some of the other climbers, still on the second ledge, took a while to dismantle the system and rappel down on newly rigged ropes that could be pulled down from the glacier. Denny was one of the first down, and he joined Steve May, Ed Boulton, Mike Maude, and some of the other rescue volunteers who had been waiting on the glacier since noon.

"I rappelled down to the glacier as soon as you guys were down there," Fenstermaker remembered. "Then the concern was to move you a quarter mile, maybe a half mile, to get you over to the flat spot on the glacier where the helicopter could land. The litters are designed to slide pretty well, so we just dragged you along. Fortunately it wasn't far. It was getting dark though, dead dusk at least by then. Everybody was getting a little worried."

The concern of the rescue volunteers on the mountain was now to get the litter to a place the helicopter could land in time to meet the Huey arriving from Fort Lewis. But it was getting dark quickly, and everybody was afraid they would arrive too late, or the helicopter would arrive too late, and that after all that work they would miss the small window of opportunity by a few minutes.

"When we hit the glacier," said Steve May, "there was no resting. We all horsed you across the glacier. We were virtually out of daylight, knew we had twenty or twenty-five minutes at best to get you to the landing zone a half mile away, and, frankly, we didn't think we were going to make it. There were maybe six of us, and it was a pretty hard pull, mostly traversing, slightly downhill in places."

McBride had been monitoring the lowering progress with help from Pete Bustanoby, the Seattle Rescue field operations leader and a member of the original FART team, who had been at the base of the cliff since noon after having climbed all night to get there. He and McBride had called for the helicopter. But timing was everything. If the helicopter got there before the litter reached the landing zone, the Huey might burn off too much fuel waiting to land and have to turn back. If it arrived after dark, that might preclude any air evacuation at all. They were walking a fine line. By then, the die was cast. The evacuation Huey was on its way.

The excitement, however, wasn't over, nor was the uncertainty. In fact, the rescue climbers on the ground were not aware of some of the most dramatic moments of the day, which transpired in the cockpit of the Huey. At that moment, Captain Gregory Krueger, United States Army, was navigating through the peaks of the Cascades as darkness approached.

The exhausted rescue volunteers had finally reached a section of the glacier at about 6,800 feet, near the landing zone used that morning. The glacier, at that point, still had a decent slope to it, but it was the best they could do, and the climbers reckoned it was flat enough for the Huey to land. After this long day of coordinated effort, the closing moments churned with anxiety for the beat volunteers. Would it all come off? they wondered. Would they be stuck out there all night or have to carry the litter down the mountain? Nobody wanted to even consider that. Steve May said he saw me fading. He was afraid I wouldn't make it.

Gregory Krueger had not been involved in the earlier flights to ferry climbers up the mountain. He didn't know exactly where it was, and so was navigating on his own through the dangerous mountain terrain, attempting to located Chimney Rock in the near dark. What happened in the ensuing few minutes makes for a little known part of the story, a drama played out mostly between Krueger's ears as he guided his big green helicopter toward the mountain. He was known in his flight unit not only as a good pilot but as a really exceptional disco dancer. His moves in the dark around Chimney Rock must have rivaled anything he'd ever done on a lighted dance floor.

"I had flown in the Cascades since 1985," remembered Krueger, "so I knew the area pretty well. We had been diverted from another mission, so as we headed for the mountains we were carefully checking our course and weight—how much fuel we had. The plan was to land at base camp, get a better picture of the situation, then try to get the guy off the mountain. I didn't think that altitude would be a major factor when landing at base camp, but I was concerned about landing higher on the mountain. The important thing as we approached was to check the maps, make sure we were going to the right place, and watch out for terrain obstacles. I knew we had an extended period of light, it being July, but I didn't know if we could get the guy off before dark.

"When we got to the site of base camp, I set down on the logging road. We kicked up a lot of dust and dirt, really a mess, so we shut down and got out. I spoke with the coordinating team, and they told us what the situation was. They lent us some big binoculars, so we looked through them, and even in the gathering dark we could actually see the rescue team dragging the litter across the glacier. That helped a lot, because Chimney Rock is a big mountain, and being able to see what was going on pinpointed the location for us. The rescue team was in the process of dragging the litter over to the spot where we thought we could land. We remained at base camp a few minutes, listening to the radio transmissions.

"The climbers on the mountain finally notified base camp that they were nearing the landing zone. But by then the whole thing was changing—it had grown much darker, almost too dark to fly. I had serious doubts about getting you off the mountain at that point. I mean, I had no idea about the winds higher up, or the terrain. There were a lot of unanswered questions. I just thought, the guy's hurting, let's give it a try. My copilot was a total rookie; this was his first flight with me. He was game, and he was in for a flight he'd never forget.

"We took the aircraft up and circled the valley a few times, checking the wind. What I was going to have to do was get close to the landing zone and pull the helicopter in and out of ground hover. You see, when a helicopter is hovering next to the ground, that's called 'in ground effect.' That's good. When there is no ground effect, it's much harder to hold a hover, it takes a lot more power. My plan was to get in close, do the hover, see if I could maintain altitude position. If I could, then I'd know the aircraft had enough power at that altitude to attempt a landing at that weight. Otherwise, I can't go in. It's that simple. All you get is one chance to find that out.

"By then we've burned off enough fuel, we're light enough that I think we can fly and work at that altitude. You have to remember that as rescue aircraft we carry more equipment on board—backboards, cold weather gear, blankets. It adds up to a lot of weight, the equivalent of a person or more. Those are the types of things you have to think about. I felt that everything was looking good at that point. When you do this for a living, you really want to help out, do the mission. We traversed a little bit in the canyon, everything seemed pretty stable, performance seemed to be at par. I was frankly surprised I had not felt updrafts or downdrafts by then, but I hadn't. So I started in.

"We had gotten a good look at the terrain. The glacier was there in the basin running roughly east/west. We came in from the south, with that small peak to our right. I started in on the approach, and for the first time I experienced winds—we got caught in a downdraft that dropped us several hundred feet. But we were still high enough that losing a couple of hundred feet wasn't critical, so we continued in. My copilot's eyes were as big as saucers.

"Eventually we got in close, real close, to the glacier, under a hundred feet. I was just about at the point where I'd go into ground-effect mode, when suddenly I lost tail-rotor effect. *That* is serious. When you lose tail-rotor effect, the tail rotor can't compensate for the torque of the main rotor. When that happens, you lose control. I had full left pedal in but couldn't keep the helicopter from spinning on its own axis due to the torque of the main rotor. So I've got the pedals all the way to the stop, and I'm still starting to rotate. Flying a helicopter, I tell people, is like being a percussionist at a drum set—sitting on your ass with both hands and both feet working away, just busy as hell.

"That's a critical situation. Your first thought in a situation like that is saving the aircraft and the crew—getting the aircraft back into stable flight. You don't think about the injured guy at that point. All you can do is try to get enough forward airspeed to keep the helicopter from spinning on its own axis and crashing into the mountain. That's when I backed off. When you're flying in the mountains like that you always keep an exit route open so if something goes wrong with the approach, you have a way out. I was able to get enough speed up by going slightly nose down and losing a little altitude as we backed off down the valley.

"Our post has an operating ceiling of 7,000 feet for the Hueys, and the glacier landing zone was just about at 7,000 feet. We were definitely at the upward end of our operating altitude. In fact, at that time it didn't look good. But I hadn't given up. It was definitely an adrenaline rush, but I hadn't seen anything so bad as to make me concerned about losing the aircraft.

"In any critical situation I'll keep trying to get the guy off until the fuel situation gets serious. But one thing about mountain flying is that the winds are very changeable—each approach may be entirely different. The first thing you want to do is to make some decisions and re-evaluate the approach. Was that the best angle and direction of approach? Is there another way in?

"The trouble was, up there we really didn't have any options. Those big faces of Chimney Rock eliminate two-thirds of the possible directions, plus there's the small peak to the east. I didn't have much choice. Coming in from the north, over the ridge of the mountain, wasn't an option. If you tried to come in over the ridge, you'd have to decrease power to get down, but you'd have to pour on power to stop descending on the other side. So there it is getting dark, I'm trying to take all this in and make sense of it while I figure out a way to get this guy off the mountain. One big concern was that I knew I wouldn't have many attempts—because of the fuel situation, there would only be two or three attempts, max.

"After we got blown off on the first try, we came back up the valley. This time we knew what to expect whereas on the first approach we had no clue. I flew in at a little different angle so we didn't have to make such a tight turn to reach the glacier—I wanted to come in straight but we couldn't do that because the small, rocky peak to the east blocked the route. We already knew from our first attempt that there was a downdraft 100 to 200 feet out from the face, maybe a little more than that. So I got ready to compensate for it. When you're expecting it you can compensate for it. That's why a couple of reconnoiters can make all the difference.

"So this time we came in, made the turn, and waited for the downdraft. It didn't happen, or at least it was much less severe. In fact, *all* the conditions were less severe. That's the way it is with mountain flying. This time, we got lucky. But as we got in closer, things became really critical. My copilot was watching the gauges and was calling off torque, and power and rate of descent. He was doing great. The first thing I needed to do was to get the aircraft down into ground effect.

"When flying helicopters, there's a transition from the clean air of altitude to the dirty air of ground effect. That's called 'effective transitional lift,' the transition from flying to hovering. The aircraft kind of shudders. It happens on takeoffs and landings, too. So to deal with that, I got into ground effect slightly short of the landing area—and just flew it in from there in ground effect. That's a little risky. You don't want to go into ground effect too soon because you expose yourself to a sudden downdraft for too long.

"As we got down close I was surprised to see the angle of glacier was much greater than I anticipated. Wow, I thought, that's pretty steep! I could see the rescue guys off my right front. I put the aircraft right onto the snow, slowly let it settle in. But as soon as I did that the aircraft started to slide right down the glacier because of the steepness of the slope. That's bad because the back end of the skid could dig in and flip us over. I elected at that point to pick the aircraft back up, and put the tail in an upslope situation—which, by the way, is not the preferred attitude for a landing on a steep slope. It's dangerous as hell because the tail rotor can catch the slope. I essentially just picked up the tail and did a 180 to turn the tail away from the rescue team and held the helicopter light on the ground, essentially on one skid.

"Over the intercom I told my crew I was ready to take the guy on. I've got a crew chief and medic in back. They waved the rescue team over. I was concentrating on keeping the helicopter stable, really just flying it while it was on the ground, but I listened in on the intercom. I could tell from all the shouting over the intercom that they were getting close. Once the guy was on board and the rescue team had backed away, my crew said we were secure. It was time to leave.

"At this point the problems were different. Now we've got additional weight and we've got the tail up slope. I've got to think about the fact that if the helicopter has settled in, a skid might get caught. I started pulling in power, feel it as it's coming up—caught skid? winds? circling gusts?—all that's critical. At that point things went as expected. We had a smooth lift up, and then I had to make a decision on my escape.

"I had already decided to go through the little pass between the outcrop and the face, because there was a steep drop that would give me a way to gain some forward speed fast—much faster than just trying to gain altitude from the hover. At that point, to deal with the added weight, I needed forward speed more than I needed altitude. By dropping quickly down the slope, I could do everything I needed to do.

"Once the aircraft transitioned through transitional lift, we went through the usual shudders and then fell away down into the clean air. I felt like we were home free, but I remained wary of a surprise downdraft. None came. It was dark by then so I wanted to make sure we didn't fly into one of those mountains. We were out of there, and flew right down the valley. Then it was off to Harborview. We flew a compass heading to Seattle until we were picked up by air traffic control. Since we were on an emergency flight, we had priority."

Steve May, exhausted and drained, stood on the slope watching the helicopter drop down into the valley. "We watched you fly off. I usually go with the injured party, and I didn't really like letting you go off by yourself like that. But there was no choice. We had to throw you on board; there was not much chance of my going with you. Then there we were, high on the mountain, full dark, no place to go. We were really beat, and kind of bummed that we had to walk out. Everybody was hoping for a ride off the mountain. We started deciding if we should try to walk out in the dark or bivvy there until morning."

McBride and Christensen, with the primary objective of their carefully choreographed thirty-six-hour operation already met, weren't done yet. They felt an obligation to the climbers who had been working nonstop for almost twenty-four hours. McBride wanted very much to get those guys off the mountain *that night*. He knew they had to be exhausted and hungry.

"How do you get the MAST people to fly the climbers off the mountain in full dark with the injured party already evacuated?" remembered

McBride. "We call it sweet talkin 'em. 'Gosh darn, what would I have to do to talk you people into going up to get those guys?' We work with the people at MAST a lot, so they know when we ask for something it's important." McBride's country charm worked.

"We were all up there on the glacier, said Ed Boulton, "trying to decide if we could climb down the icefall in the dark. It was risky, but possible. But then there were those rocky slopes and gullies below that, and we were thinking *that* was too dangerous. No one wanted to start a descent that would take all night and half the next day. Then we heard over the radio the sheriff had got another helicopter to come get us off the glacier. We were skeptical, but hopeful."

Incredibly, as Greg Krueger's crew dropped me off at Harborview, another MAST pilot named Malcolm Wiggins had agreed to try to evacuate the rescue climbers. As aircraft commander, when the call came in, he could make the decision whether to try or not. Wiggins decided to try, and flew from his base at Fort Lewis to the mountain that night in total darkness. The distinctive slap of the Huey's heavy rotors as he approached the mountain was music to the ears of the climbers still on Chimney Rock. But they really didn't believe the helicopter could land that high, in the dark, much less multiple times.

"As we shivered in the dark," said Ed Boulton, "the MAST bird approached and began circling the mountain, then our location. He flew around for a long time, checking things out, and we were pretty sure the guy would end up deciding it was too dangerous. We signaled our location with flashlights. To our relief, the pilot slowly approached and let down with his halogen lights flooding the surface of the glacier. As he touched the snow, one crewman jumped out and beckoned for two of us to get in. Everyone wanted to go home badly but we didn't want to quarrel about it. Finally the people who said they *had* to be back at work the next day climbed on board. We watched the bird fly the seven or eight miles or so back to base, where the Seattle radio truck had its flashers on to show the way.

"Back the bird came, landing this time without hesitation. Two more loaded, and it rose a couple of feet then settled down again. In dismay I watched the door open, thinking the pilot was going to off-load a climber. Instead, the crewman leaped out and waved for a *third* passenger. I handed the guy next to me a big hunk of cheddar cheese and bread, and leaped aboard like a gazelle."

"Those of us who were last off the face," said Mike Eberle, "were getting a little worried. By the time we hit the glacier, you were history. You were gone. Then we saw the chopper come and pick up some of the glacier team. But we still had about a half mile to go to reach the landing zone and were afraid that by the time we got there, the helicoper would be out of gas and have to go home."

"We were glad to see that second helicopter," remembered Denny Fenstermaker. "It could only take two or three people at a time, and we weren't sure how much gas he had. After a couple of trips there were just two of us left, me and Fred Stanley. We stayed until last to make sure everybody else got down safely. We figured we'd have to walk out the next day, but then to our great surprise the guy came back for a third run and lifted us off, too. It was totally dark. They had a big spotlight, and the pilot kept flying all around, really cautious, but he eventually got in and took us off."

"Those guys had been working their butts off all day," remembered the helicopter pilot, Malcolm Wiggins. "They weren't really prepared for a night out, so I figured I'd try to get them off. My previous experience allowed me to be fairly comfortable flying in the mountains at night. I was able to manage by using my searchlights and landing lights. Tricky part was all I had to go on terrainwise was the silhouette of the mountains. Once you get close enough the searchlight shows you the way, but it can screw up your night vision. Then when you land you've got only a little bit of time to darken down. Each trip got more routine. It took three or four loads to get everybody down."

"I was very surprised the helicopters were up there that late making the pick ups," remembered Fred Stanley. "The flight before the one that picked up Denny and me, I figured that was it, so the two of us were prepared to stay. I felt like I could sit the night out there without any problems. I was very surprised when the helicopter came back a third time. I have been in more difficult situations, helicopterwise—such as bad weather—but I had *never* had an army helicopter come up to pick us up at night. That was a welcome sight, completely unexpected. It was a fitting conclusion to a very special deal."

After being airlifted off the glacier, the rescue volunteers were deposited at base camp. McBride and Christensen were still there. So was Doug. Dozens of rescue volunteers were waiting in the event a litter-carry down the mountain had been necessary. The Red Cross had set up a field kitchen to feed the forty or more volunteers at the site. It had been a long day for everyone.

"We all realized that we'd been part of one of the more memorable rescues," said Steve May. "We were quite proud and pretty tired. Nobody wanted to sleep. Everybody had a lot of adrenaline running, we just kept chattering away."

"They had some hot food down at base camp," remembered Denny Fenstermaker. "Everybody was feeling pretty good about getting you off alive. That's what it's all about, especially when you get 'em out alive. Your particular case is very rare. It seems to always be at two extremes. Most people are just mildly hurt, broken ankle and such, or they're dead big time. The fact is, most people with your injuries just don't make it. So it felt good to get you out. That was definitely more of technical rescue than we usually get. Only a handful are like that, it's the kind of situation that comes around only every four or five years. I have to admit it was one of the most frightening I've ever been on—steep, loose, dark, bad rock. Very hairy. But unforgettable."

"Was it a hard rescue?" McBride reflected. "I tell you what the rescue people told me after they got out of the chopper. We were all gathered around eating a bowl of chili. These guys are all technical climbers, Fred Stanley being one of the best. They told me that technically, that was the most demanding rescue we've ever been on. I was just glad to get you down safely, and get everybody else off safely."

"Once we touched down," said Ed Boulton, "I immediately drank about a gallon of Red Cross orange Kool-Aid. I was gobbling beef stew and sandwiches when the helicopter landed with the last load.

"At that moment, I don't think I ever felt more contentment and satisfaction in my life. It was real euphoria. We got the guy off alive, and we didn't have to walk out!"

"I really felt good after that operation," said Fred Stanley, "because we had at least three different mountain-rescue groups from all over the state and everybody did a good job. It helped foster communication for the future, helped bring the rescue community together. Chimney Rock was a situation where people worked very well together to pull off something that was amazing. I think it will be remembered a long time."

"Bruce and Freeman and I have talked it about it since, many times," said Steve May. "And when we do, we all three feel lucky to have participated in the greatest rescue ever done around there. It may sound strange to you, I mean you had to get hurt for this to happen, but it was a special thing. All of us felt proud to have been a part of it."

The official Kittitas County Sheriff's Department report noted the outcome: "The subject was airlifted by MAST helicopter after 8:00 P.M. to Harborview Medical Center with fractures to the left arm and shoulder, pelvis, and left knee. He was severely dehydrated from his time on the ledge. The thirteen mountain climbers were airlifted by another MAST helicopter to base camp. The search number was cancelled at 5:00 A.M."

INDEX

ABOUT THE AUTHOR

Peter Potterfield is a career journalist and author who for more than a decade served as editor-in-chief of the award-winning *Pacific Northwest* magazine in Seattle. He has written for *Outside, Reader's Digest, Summit, Backpacker, Condé Nast Traveler, Travel & Leisure, Smithsonian Air & Space,* and other publications. He wrote the climbing sections for *Fodor's* adventure guide and is the coauthor of the best-selling *Selected Climbs in the Cascades* (The Mountaineers, 1993).

THE MOUNTAINEERS, founded in 1906, is a nonprofit outdoor activity and conservation club, whose mission is "to explore, study, preserve, and enjoy the natural beauty of the outdoors. . . . " Based in Seattle, Washington, the club is now the third-largest such organization in the United States, with 15,000 members and five branches throughout Washington State.

The Mountaineers sponsors both classes and year-round outdoor activities in the Pacific Northwest, which include hiking, mountain climbing, ski-touring, snowshoeing, bicycling, camping, kayaking and canoeing, nature study, sailing, and adventure travel. The club's conservation division supports environmental causes through educational activities, sponsoring legislation, and presenting informational programs. All club activities are led by skilled, experienced volunteers, who are dedicated to promoting safe and responsible enjoyment and preservation of the outdoors.

If you would like to participate in these organized outdoor activities or the club's programs, consider a membership in The Mountaineers. For information and an application, write or call The Mountaineers, Club Headquarters, 300 Third Avenue West, Seattle, WA 98119; (206) 284-6310; clubmail@mountaineers.org

The Mountaineers Books, an active, nonprofit publishing program of the club, produces guidebooks, instructional texts, historical works, natural history guides, and works on environmental conservation. All books produced by The Mountaineers are aimed at fulfilling the club's mission.

Send or call for our catalog of more than 300 outdoor titles:

 The Mountaineers Books
1001 SW Klickitat Way, Suite 201
Seattle, WA 98134
1-800-553-4453; e-mail: mbooks@mountaineers.org